Footprint

Alan Murphy

Glasgow

Contents

4 About the author
4 Acknowledgements

5 Introducing Glasgow
6 Introduction
8 At a glance
10 Trip planner
14 Contemporary Glasgow

17 Travel essentials
19 Getting there
25 Getting around
28 Tours
31 Tourist information

Guide

5 Glasgow
35 George Square and the Merchant City
42 Trongate to the East End
52 Buchanan Street to Charing Cross
66 West End
78 Along the Clyde
88 South of the Clyde
97 Museums and galleries

99 Around Glasgow
101 Firth of Clyde
106 Isle of Bute
109 The Clyde Valley
114 Loch Lomond and the Campsies

Listings

119 Sleeping
137 Eating and drinking
163 Bars and clubs
179 Arts and entertainment
181 Cinema
182 Comedy
182 Music
188 Theatre
191 Festivals and events
195 Shopping
205 Sports
215 Gay and lesbian
223 Kids
229 Directory

233 Background
234 A sprint through history
237 Art and architecture
239 Books
241 Glasgow on screen

243 Index
247 Publishing stuff

250 Maps (see inside back cover for Around Glasgow map)
250 Map 1 Glasgow
252 Map 2 City centre
254 Map 3 West End
256 Map 4 Cathedral and East End

About the author

Born and raised in Fife, **Alan Murphy** then moved to Dundee to begin a career in journalism. Ten years later he swapped shorthand notebook for rucksack and escaped to Bolivia, where he wrote for an English language newspaper, taught English and helped out in a home for orphaned street children. Many months later, Alan turned up in London, where fate played her propitious hand and introduced him to the editor of the legendary *South American Handbook*. The rest, as they say, is history. Alan now lives in the southwest of England with his wife and family. As well as co-writing the Glasgow guide, he has written Footprint guides to Scotland, Edinburgh, Highlands and Islands, Bolivia, Ecuador, Peru and Venezuela.

A graduate of St Andrews University, **Rebecca Ford** worked in public relations and advertising for several years, before becoming a full-time travel writer and photographer. Her travels now take her all over the world, although she specializes in writing about the British Isles and Italy. Her work has appeared in newspapers such as *The Guardian*, the *Daily Express* and *Scotland on Sunday*. She also writes and contributes to many other guidebooks.

Acknowledgements

Alan and Rebecca would like to thank the Greater Glasgow & Clyde Valley Tourist Board for their help and support throughout the entire project. Thanks to Jane Hamilton and John Binney for their knowledge, advice and contributions to the Bars and clubs and Gay and lesbian sections. Thanks also to the National Trust for Scotland, the Charles Rennie Mackintosh Society and Debbie Brown at Caledonian MacBrayne. A big thank you to all the friends who chipped in with information on their favourite restaurants, bars and shops.

Finally a big shout to all those at Footprint, especially wee Dav.

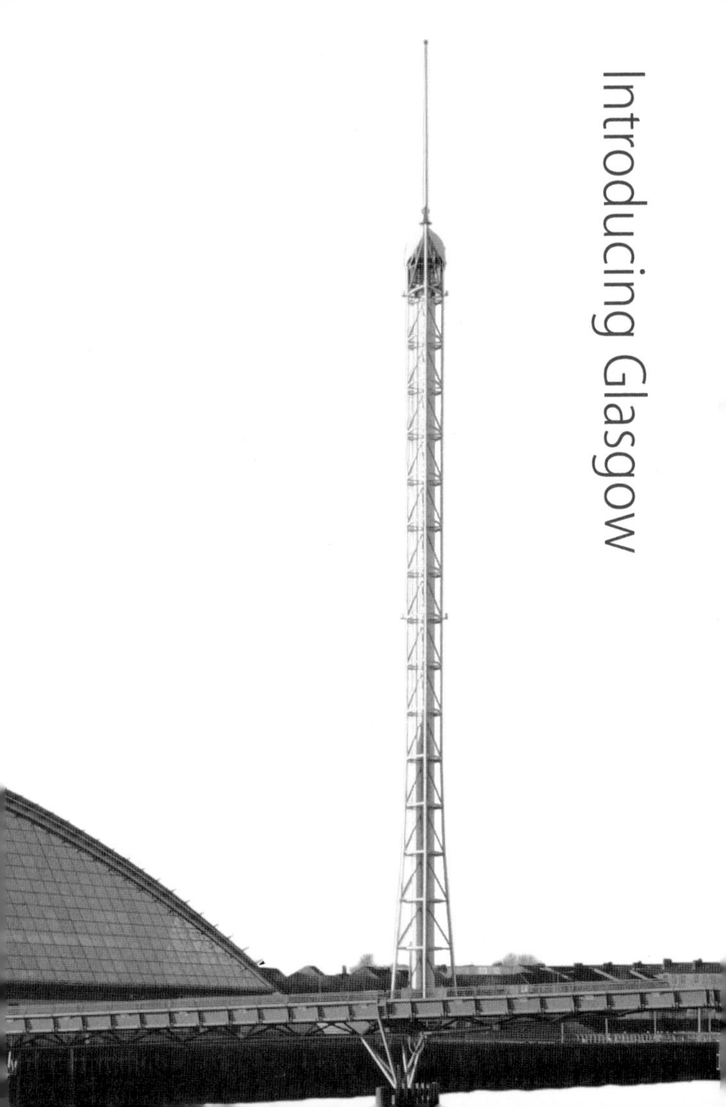

Introducing Glasgow

Glasgow is hard to define. This spontaneous free-spirit has cast off its industrial past to become a modern, design-conscious city with none of the sober grey stone that gives other Scottish cities a restrained, slightly austere appearance. Glasgow is a beguiling blend of old red sandstone and quirky ironwork, laced with glinting contemporary glass and steel. It is often described as Scotland's most European city, but it could also be compared to Manhattan, with its grid of streets, its tall, narrow buildings, and its wisecracking citizens. And then it has an air of Celtic edginess like Liverpool, a distinctive swagger like London, and a lingering sense of Victorian civic pride like Manchester. Just take a stroll round the Merchant City or along Byres Road in the West End and sit in one of the many stylish bars and cafés and you'll witness a degree of posing that is almost continental in its fervency. The country's caffeine capital is really more Barcelona or Greenwich Village than west coast of Scotland. Definitely a different place.

Second City of the Empire

There's an old saying that Edinburgh is the capital but Glasgow has the capital. This dates back to the late 19th century, when Glasgow proclaimed itself the 'Second City of the Empire'. It was a thriving, cultivated city, grown rich on the profits from its cotton mills, coal mines and shipyards, and a city that knew how to flaunt its wealth. The legacy of Glasgow's prosperous past is all around: in the City Chambers in George Square; the neoclassical architecture of the Merchant City; the sweeping terraces of the West End and honey-coloured villas of South Side; and its galleries full to bursting with priceless art treasures, from Rodin to Rembrandt.

Better by design

Glasgow is unusual among great cities in that it has no single defining monument: no Eiffel Tower; no Trafalgar Square; no Empire State Building; or Edinburgh Castle. Ironically though, this, the world's first successful post-industrial city, has picked itself up from the near terminal trauma of economic wipe-out and re-invented itself as a major European tourist attraction, thanks mainly to its buildings. Glasgow's great architects have risen from the grave to breathe new life back into the city; their monuments standing as testimony to the city's former glories.

Glasgow smiles better

It may be a cliché to say that Glasgow people are friendly, but it's true. Writer William McIlvanney once said that Glasgow wasn't a city, it was a twenty-four hour cabaret, and this sums up perfectly one of the city's greatest attractions – its sense of humour. The city that gave us Billy Connolly, Jerry Sadowitz and Rab C Nesbit does not take itself too seriously – and cannot be serious for very long. Humour is integral to life here and Glaswegians find it in everything – particularly people from Edinburgh, who they traditionally see as humourless.

At a glance

City centre

Glasgow city centre is built on a grid system across some steep hills on the north side of the River Clyde and covers the large area from Charing Cross train station and the M8 in the west to Glasgow Green in the east, near the cathedral. The heart of the city is George Square. Here you'll find the Tourist Information Centre (TIC), and the two main train stations (Central station and Queen Street station), as well as the Buchanan bus station; all are within a couple of blocks.

To the east of George Square is the Merchant City, where the elegant warehouses of the 18th century tobacco and sugar merchants have been cleaned up and reclaimed by the professional classes, not only as the latest des res, but also as a fashionable place to eat, drink, shop and play. Further east is Glasgow's East End, a traditional working-class stronghold which is gradually giving way to the relentless drive of urban gentrification. Here chic café-bars and art galleries rub shoulders with no-nonsense pubs, artery-hardening greasy spoons and sprawling markets selling everything from dodgy video games to second-hand clothes.

The finest examples of Glasgow's rich Victorian architectural legacy can be found in the commercial centre, stretching from George Square west to the M8. Here, in the streets around Blytheswood Hill, great canyons of stone were constructed, transforming the city into a Scottish equivalent of New York or Chicago – a city of high testosterone architecture. While George Square is the heart of modern Glasgow, the area around the medieval cathedral was the heart of the old city. In fact, until the 18th century Glasgow consisted only of a narrow ribbon of streets running north from the river past the Glasgow Cross and up the High Street to the cathedral. Then came the city's rapid expansion west and the High Street became a dilapidated backwater.

West End

On the other side of the M8 is the West End, an area which contains many of the city's major museums, as well some of its finest examples of Victorian architecture. During the course of the 19th century the West End grew in importance as wealthy merchants moved there, away from the dirt and grime of the industrial city. In 1870, the university moved to its present site overlooking Kelvingrove Park, and in 1896 the Glasgow District Subway was extended west. Now, Glasgow's West End is a mix of youthful hedonism and suburban calm. The streets between Kelvingrove Park and the Great Western Road, around Hillhead Underground and Byres Road, are alive with students, shoppers and revellers. Nearby are the Hunterian Museum and Transport Museum, as well as Kelvingrove Park and the Botanic Garden. Head further along the Great Western Road, however, and the wild west becomes the mild west as you enter the residential districts of Kelvinside, Anniesland and Knightswood, all bywords for genteel respectability.

South of the Clyde

South of the River Clyde is a part of Glasgow largely unknown to most tourists, except perhaps for the Gorbals, a name once synonymous with urban violence, but now more likely to inspire ennui rather than fear. Venture further south and you enter a different world, of sedate suburbs known as South Side. Here you'll find two of the city's most notable attractions, the Burrell Collection and Pollok House, both set in the sylvan surrounds of Pollok Country Park, and which can easily be reached from the city centre by train or bus. There are other reasons to venture south of the river, not least of these being to see Charles Rennie Mackintosh's House for an Art Lover in nearby Bellahouston Park. Further east is another stop on the Mackintosh trail, the Scotland Street School Museum, and to the south, in Cathcart, is Holmwood House, Alexander 'Greek' Thomson's great architectural masterpiece.

Trip planner

To get the most out of Glasgow bring a sense of humour and a rainproof jacket. You could spend a great few days simply wandering round soaking up the atmosphere and the renowned Glasgow 'patter' of the locals or you could visit the world-class museums and galleries, many of which are free.

Glasgow is one of the wettest cities in the UK. There's a saying in Scotland that if you don't like the weather, then wait 20 minutes. Generally speaking, May to September are the warmest months, with an average summer high of around 18-19°C, and though they are often the driest months, you can expect rain at any time of the year, even in high summer. The high season is from May to September and this is when the city receives the vast majority of visitors. Prices at this time of year will also be higher. Another busy time is Hogmanay, or New Year.

A day

Twenty-four hours is just not enough to do the city justice, but the following itinerary will give an indication of why Glasgow is becoming one of Britain's most interesting and exciting cities. Start the day at the **People's Palace** on **Glasgow Green** for an introduction to the city's history. Head across to **Sauchiehall Street** for elevenses in the **Willow Tea Rooms** and admire the interior design of **Charles Rennie Mackintosh**. Then it's down to **Princes Square** for shopping, followed by a walk around the **Merchant City** and lunch at **Café Gandolfi**. After lunch, head up to the **School of Art**, and take a guided tour. Then head across the M8 to **St George's Cross Underground** and take the subway to **Hillhead** for a browse round the shops of **Byres Road**. Stop for an aperitif in one of the many bars and cafes then it's off for dinner to the one-and-only **Ubiquitous Chip**. Take a cab back to the city centre for a cruise round some of the pre-club bars before hitting one of the city's clubs.

A weekend

The best place to head after the **School of Art** is the **Lighthouse**, Glasgow's centre for architecture and design, which was designed by the Charles Rennie Mackintosh and features the 'Mack Room'. Next, head west to the **Mackintosh House** at the **Hunterian Art Gallery**, opposite **Glasgow University**, before stopping off at **Queen's Cross Church**, CRM's only ecclesiastical building. Now the trail heads south of the river to the **Scotland Street School Museum**, opposite **Shields Road Underground**, and the **House for an Art Lover**, in **Bellahouston Park**. While you're on the south side of the city, check out the work of Glasgow's other great architect, **Alexander 'Greek' Thomson**, at **Holmwood House**, in **Cathcart**. Not forgetting Thomson's greatest achievement, his **St Vincent Street Church**.

Glasgow boasts more than 70 parks in all, from **Glasgow Green** in the **East End** to **Kelvingrove Park** in the **West End**, but it is **Pollok Country Park** in the **South Side** which exerts the greatest pull as this is home to the **Burrell Collection**, Glasgow's most visited sight and one of the largest art collections in the UK outside London.

A long weekend

Aside from London, Glasgow is probably the best city in the UK for shopping. **Buchanan Street** is the main shopping street and is lined with good clothes shops as well as some of the city's best malls. East of Buchanan Street, the **Merchant City** is home to many expensive designer shops, bars and cafés and a trip here could inflict some serious damage on your bank account.

At the other end of the scale, **The Barras** market, the city's largest, in the East End, may not be the best place for souvenirs, but is guaranteed to offer a big, thick slice of authentic working class Glasgow and a chance to hear the legendary 'patter'. Close by, on Glasgow Green, the **People's Palace** offers an interesting insight into this city's fascinating history.

There are several walkways and cycle paths in and around the city, and several long-distance ones which start there too. One of these long-distance paths is the **West Highland Way**, which starts in the northern suburb of **Milngavie** (pronounced *mull-guy*), runs up the east bank of **Loch Lomond** (see below) and through **Glen Coe** before ending near **Fort William**, some 95 miles later. The **tourist office** has maps and leaflets detailing these routes.

The **River Clyde** itself has been added to the list of visitor attractions in recent years. The **Clydeside Walkway**, which runs all the way from the **Scottish Exhibition and Conference Centre** (SECC) beyond the city limits to **Bothwell Castle** in **Uddingston** (see p111), is an attempt to direct Glasgow's river towards a future of leisure and tourism. There are also trips up and down the river in a variety of craft. Also worth visiting is the **Tall Ship** at **Glasgow Harbour** and state-of-the-art **Science Centre**.

A week

One of the most surprising pleasures of this great city is its proximity to some genuinely wild and woolly scenery. The city's northern suburbs tickle the edge of the Highland Boundary Fault Line, with **Loch Lomond**'s shores within easy reach (many would say too easy). Though the loch's western side is awash with day trippers, the quiet east bank offers more gentle pleasures. The new **Loch Lomond & the Trossachs National Park** is so close as to almost function as the city's back garden, a vast adventure playground of lochs and mountains, where you can sail, waterski, walk, cycle and climb to your heart's content, or go off in search of ospreys, pine martens, deer, wildcats, ptarmigan and red squirrels. To the west of the city lies the **Firth of Clyde**. A day trip could be to take the train to **Largs** and a ferry across to **Great Cumbrae** for a complete circuit of the island by bike. Alternatively, take a ferry across to **Bute** and spend a few days exploring this relatively little-known island, or hire a car for the trip down through **Cowal** to **Tighnabruaich**, one of the most scenic drives in Scotland.

Best

Ten of the best

1. **Burrell Collection** Top of everyone's list, and the city's most popular visitor attraction, is this state-of-the-art building stuffed with priceless antiquities from around the world, p91.
2. **Science Centre** Kids of all ages will love the whizz-bang technology of Glasgow's shiny new Millennium attraction, p79.
3. **Glasgow School of Art** Charles Rennie Mackintosh's majestic masterpiece shows why he is so revered as an architect and designer, p62.
4. **People's Palace** This treasure trove of local artefacts lets you get under the skin of this great city, p48.
5. **Tenement House** Indulge in a little voyeurism at this strangely beguiling time capsule of life in pre-war Glasgow, p64.
6. **Holmwood House** Designed by Alexander 'Greek' Thomson, Glasgow's other great architect, this has been described as a 'sonnet in stone', p94.
7. **Mount Stuart** The grandest Gothic pile in Britain, on the beautiful Isle of Bute, is a dazzling fantasy of sheer excess, p107.
8. **Byres Road** The heart of the West End with its little cobbled lanes chock full of lively bars, restaurants and quirky, bohemian shops, p72.
9. **Merchant City** Elegant 18th-century mansions and warehouses restored and converted into designer shops and trendy bars, cafés and restaurants, p35.
10. **Old Firm Derby** Anyone who thought football is 'only a game' should attend a Celtic v Rangers fixture, the most passionate and bitterly-contested football match on the planet, p209.

The ★ symbol in this guide is used to indicate recommended sights.

Contemporary Glasgow

Glasgow has been many things to many people over the years. It has variously been named 'Dear Green Place', 'Second City of the Empire', 'Workshop of the World' and 'No Mean City'. Today, it is simply one of the most interesting cities to visit in Britain. Yet for most of the 20th-century people would have laughed if anyone had suggested visiting it for pleasure. The city had a reputation for both violence and poverty and the conditions in its sprawling slums (ironically a legacy of the very industries that had made the city wealthy) were amongst the worst in Britain. It is a reputation that has been slow to shift. As late as 1996, a survey by *The Scotsman* newspaper asking residents of Edinburgh (only 40 miles away) what they associated with Glasgow, came up with: deep-fried pizzas, rickets, Rangers and Celtic, Irn Bru and Billy Connolly. Hardly a ringing endorsement.

In the face of such entrenched attitudes other, less gutsy cities might have given up and spiralled further into decline, but Glasgow refused to accept the seemingly inevitable. Under the banner of its 'Glasgow's Miles Better' campaign, the city began to reinvent itself.

Someone once said that all Glasgow needed was a good bath, and they were right. Buildings, blackened by years of pollution, were scrubbed clean, creative talent was nurtured, smart shops and restaurants encouraged to open up in the city. Designers, realising that Glaswegians loved clothes and were prepared to pay for good ones, opened outlets here and soon the city's Italian Centre was the home of both *Armani* and *Versace*. The campaign was so successful that in 1990 the city was nominated European City of Culture, a success it followed by becoming European City of Architecture and Design in 1999. Not only were these triumphs, to the delight of many Glaswegians, the nominations also put Edinburgh's nose severely out of joint. A few rough edges remain, of course, to provide the essential urban grit and the backdrop for the occasional TV detective.

A tale of two cities

With the coming of the industrial age, Glasgow had grown rapidly from a small, provincial town into a large city. This sudden growth in size and wealth led to the beginnings of the famous and long-standing rivalry between Glasgow and Edinburgh. While this rivalry is never far from the surface it's mostly good-humoured.

For example, Edinburgh's residents joke that in the capital tables and chairs on the pavement signals an open-air café while in Glasgow it means the bailiffs are calling, while Glaswegians claim that Edinburgh folk have double glazing to prevent their kids from hearing the ice-cream van.

It's true that the city's renaissance suffered a few blows in the late 1990s when its great rival Edinburgh was announced as the permanent home of the Royal Yacht Britannia – a ship that had been built on the Clyde and that would have provided a welcome boost to the city's tourist industry. This was followed by the announcement that Edinburgh would also be the site of the new Scottish parliament and – even worse for Glasgow's fashionistas – would be the location for Scotland's first branch of Harvey Nichols. It would be much harder now for Glasgow cabbies to happily dismiss Edinburgh as 'one street and a castle'.

But Glasgow has been fighting back. An enormous shopping centre, the Buchanan Galleries, recently opened in the city centre, and a gleaming, futuristic Science Centre has been built on the banks of the Clyde. New homes, offices and hotels are being built on derelict land along the river. Of course the city still has its social problems and areas of deprivation – what city doesn't – and now signs of racial tension are beginning to show as more and more asylum seekers are housed in the city. But the

Everyday people

Glasgow has more than its fair share of top-class tourist sights – from the palatial 18th century mansions of the Merchant City to the genius of Charles Rennie Mackintosh – but the driving force of the city is its people, with their distinctive mix of guts, determination, energy and humour.

city no longer has to prove itself, it knows that it can now compete with the best in Europe, and while it has gained a new confidence in recent years, it hasn't lost its irreverent sense of humour along the way. Glaswegians might drink cappuccino now – but they'll soon spot if it's got too much froth on top.

Travel essentials

Generally speaking, the cheapest and quickest way to travel to Glasgow from outside the UK is by air. There are daily direct flights to Glasgow from airports in London, as well as from provincial UK airports, Ireland, Europe and North America. Road links to Scotland are excellent, and a number of companies offer express coach services day and night. This is the cheapest form of travel to Glasgow from other parts of the UK. There are fast and frequent rail services to and from London Euston (5 hours). There are also daily services to Birmingham (4 hours) and Manchester (3½ hours) and other main towns and cities in England. The best way to explore the city centre sights is by walking, although some of the hills are very steep. If you want to explore the West End or South Side, you'll need to use the public transport system, which is generally good and efficient. It tends to be reasonably priced and there are a number of discount passes you can buy that can save you money.

Getting there

Air

There are direct flights to **Glasgow International Airport** almost hourly from **London Heathrow**, **Gatwick**, **Stansted** and **Luton** airports. There are also daily flights from provincial UK airports and from **Dublin**. There are a number of low cost airlines which regularly offer cheap flights if you book online, but check for hidden surcharges. You'll often have to travel at inconvenient times and the flights are subject to restrictions. They are non-refundable, or only partly refundable, and non-transferable. A flexible and refundable fare from London to Glasgow or Edinburgh will cost at least £150-200 return.

Fares are highest from around early June to mid-September, which is the tourist high season, and drop mid-September to early November and mid-April to early June. They are cheapest in the low season, from November to April. The exception is during Christmas and New Year when prices rise sharply. Flying at the weekend is normally more expensive. During the peak season charter flights link Glasgow to many popular holiday destinations. *Emirates Airlines* are also starting a daily service to Dubai in spring 2004.

From UK and Ireland **To Glasgow International Airport**: *British Airways* fly from Gatwick, Heathrow, Bristol, Southampton, Birmingham, Manchester, Cork, Isle of Man, Stornoway, Cambeltown and Inverness; *bmi* from Manchester, Heathrow, Leeds/Bradford. *easyJet* from Bristol, Belfast, Luton, Stansted. *bmi baby* from East Midlands. **To Prestwick Airport**: *Ryanair* fly from Stansted and Bournemouth, *bmi* from Cardiff.

From continental Europe **To Glasgow International Airport**: *bmi* fly from Copenhagen, *easyJet* from Amsterdam and *KLM* from Amsterdam. **To Glasgow Prestwick Airport**: *Ryanair* fly from Paris Beauvais, Dublin, Franfurt Hahn, Stockholm, Brussels, Milan, Oslo, Barcelona.

Airlines and travel agents

Aer Lingus, T 0845-084 4777, www.aerlingus.com.
bmi, T 0870-607 0555, www.flybmi.com.
British Airways, T 0870-850 9850, www.britishairways.com.
easyJet, T 0870-600 0000, www.easyjet.com.
Emirates, T 0870-243 2222, www.emirates.com/uk.
Icelandair, T 0845 -7581111, www.icelandair.com.
KLM, T 0870-507 4047, www.klm.com.
Ryanair, T 0871-246 0016, www.ryanair.com.

Other websites
www.expedia.com
www.travelocity.com
www.lastminute.com
www.ebookers.com
www.opodo.com
www.cheapflights.com

From rest of the world *Continental Airlines* fly from New York, *Icelandair* fly from Reykjavik, *Emirates* fly from Dubai.

Airport information **Glasgow International Airport** (**T** 0141-887 1111, www.baa.co.uk/glasgow), is 8 miles west of the city, at junction 28 on the M8. It handles domestic and international flights. Terminal facilities include car hire, bank ATMs, currency exchange, left luggage, tourist information (**T** 0141-848 4440) and shops, restaurants and bars. There's also a **Travel Centre** (**T** 0141-848 4330, *daily 0800-2200 in summer and till 1800 in winter*) in the UK arrivals concourse, and a **First Options Hotel** (**T** 0141-848 4731) and travel reservations desk in the international arrivals concourse. To get into town take a **Glasgow Airport Link**

bus from outside the arrivals area. They leave every 15 minutes to Buchanan bus station, with drop-off points at Central and Queen Street train stations (*25-30 mins, £3.30 single, £5 return*). Tickets can be bought from the driver. Buses to the airport leave from Buchanan Street bus station and stop outside the main TIC (see below). A taxi from the airport to the city centre costs around £17.

Glasgow Prestwick (**T** 01292-511000, www.gpia.co.uk), is 30 miles southwest of the city. Trains to and from Central Station leave every 30 minutes (*45 mins; £5, £2.50 single if you show your Ryanair ticket*).

Bus

A number of companies offer express coach services day and night around the country and to most English cities; these include **Citylink Coaches** (**T** 08705-505050, www.citylink.co.uk) and **National Express** (**T** 08705-808080, www.nationalexpress.com). Tickets can be bought at bus stations or from a huge number of agents throughout the country. Fares from London with *National Express* are between £28 and £36 return. The journey takes around 8 hours. There are several services daily, with links to other major English cities, including: Manchester (4 hours); Birmingham (5½ hours); Newcastle (4 hours) and York (6½ hours).

All long-distance buses to and from Glasgow arrive and depart from **Buchanan bus station** (Killermont St, **T** 0141-332 7133), three blocks north of George Square. There's a left-luggage office at Buchanan bus station, open daily 0630-2230.

There are discounts available for full-time students or those aged under 25 or over 50, and also a family card which allows two children to travel free with two adults, though children normally travel for half price. Passes can be bought at travel agents and at the booking office at Buchanan bus station (**T** 0121-423 8499 for details). In **North America** these passes are available from **British Travel International** (**T** 1-800-327 6097, www.britishtravel.com) or from **US National Express** (**T** 502-298 1395).

Car

The main route if driving to Glasgow from the south is the M6, which becomes the A74 in Scotland and is dual carriageway all the way from the border. The journey north from London takes around 8-10 hours. There's an **Autoshuttle Express** (**T** 08705-133714; reservations **T** 08705-502309) service to transport your car overnight between England and Scotland and vice versa while you travel by rail or air.

Car hire is expensive and you may be better off making arrangements in your home country for a fly/drive deal through one of the main multi-national companies. The minimum you can expect to pay is around £150-180 per week for a small car. Small, local hire companies often offer better deals than the larger multinationals. Most companies prefer payment with a credit card, otherwise you'll have to leave a large deposit. You'll need to have your driver's licence and be aged between 21 and 70. **Motorcycle** hire is very expensive, ranging from around £200 up to £350 per week.

Ferry

There are ferry services to the west coast of Scotland from Northern Ireland. **P&O Irish Sea** (**T** 0870-2424777, www.poirishsea.com), has several crossings daily to Cairnryan from Larne. The journey takes 1 hour. **Stena Line** (T 0870-707070, www.stenaline.co.uk), run numerous ferries (3 hours) and high-speed catamarans (1½ hours) from Belfast to Stranraer. **Seacat Scotland** (**T** 08705-523523, www.seacat.co.uk) run daily services from Belfast to Troon (2½ hours). There are several trains daily from Stranraer to Glasgow Central (2¼ hours) and regular services from Troon (45 minutes).

Train

Glasgow has two main train stations: **Central station** is the terminus for all trains to southern Scotland, England and Wales; and **Queen Street** serves the north and east of Scotland. A shuttle

Station to station

One of the city's main landmarks is the massive bulk of Central Station, where rail travellers from the south are debouched and from where holidaying Glaswegians begin their journey to the west coast for ferries across the Firth of Clyde.

bus runs every 10 minutes between Central station (Gordon Street entrance) and Queen Street, at the corner of George Square. It takes 10 minutes to walk between the two.

Two companies operate direct services from London to Scotland: **GNER** trains leave from Kings' Cross and run up the east coast to Edinburgh, Aberdeen and Inverness; and **Virgin** trains leave from Euston and run up the west coast to Glasgow. **Scotrail** operate the **Caledonian Sleeper** service if you wish to travel overnight from London Euston to Glasgow. This runs nightly from Sunday to Friday. There are left-luggage lockers at Glasgow Central and Queen Street train stations (£2 per day).

Eurostar (**T** 08705-186186, www.eurostar.com) operates high-speed trains through the Channel Tunnel to London Waterloo from Paris (3 hours), Brussels (2 hours 40 minutes) and Lille (2 hours).

Travel extras

Money Glasgow needn't be an expensive city to visit. Cheap accommodation is available in hostels or B&Bs, transport is relatively cheap and you can get by on £20-25 per day if you eat in cafés and pubs or cheap restaurants. Also, most of the museums and galleries are free. If you want to enjoy the city's better restaurants and go out at night, then you'll need at least £50-60 per day. Single travellers will have to pay more than half the cost of a double room in most places and should budget on spending around 60% of what a couple would spend.

Safety Glasgow is, in general, a reasonably safe and civilized place, and the vast majority of people are friendly. Aside from the ubiquitous nuisance of drunks on public transport and around the city centre at the weekend, most visitors should encounter few problems. In saying that, however, some precautions should be taken. As in all large cities, you should avoid walking alone at night in quiet unlit streets and parks.

Telephone code Dial 0141 for Glasgow from outside the city.

Time Greenwich Mean Time (GMT) is used from late October to late March, after which the clocks go forward an hour to British Summer Time (BST). GMT is 5 hours ahead of US Eastern Standard Time.

Tipping Tipping is at your discretion. In a restaurant you should leave a tip of 10-15% if you are satisfied with the service. If the bill already includes a service charge, you needn't add a further tip. Tipping is not normal in pubs or bars. Taxi drivers will expect a tip for longer journeys, usually of around 10%, and most hairdressers will also expect a tip. Porters, bellboys and waiters in more upmarket hotels rely on tips to supplement their meagre wages.

You then have to change trains, and stations, for the onward journey north to Scotland. If you're driving from continental Europe you could take **Le Shuttle** (**T** 08705-353535 for bookings), which runs 24 hours a day, 365 days a year, and takes you and your car from Calais to Folkestone in 35-45 minutes.

Contact **National Rail Enquiries** (**T** 08457-484950, www.thetrainline.co.uk) for information on all rail services and fares. They also do advance credit/debit card bookings (**T** 08457-550033). Alternatively, you can contact the following train companies individually: **GNER**, T08457-225225, www.gner.co.uk; **Virgin**, T08457-222333; **ScotRail**, T08457-550033, www.scotrail.co.uk.

Getting around

Bus

Buses in the city are run by **First Glasgow** and use white buses with a pink stripe. **Arriva** operate buses linking the city centre to Paisley and Braehead and use white and green buses. Tickets are bought from the driver and you'll need to provide the exact fare, as no change is given. For short trips in the city fares are 80p and all-day tickets £2.50. After 2400, till 0400, there's a limited night bus service (more frequent at weekends). The frequency of bus services depends on the route, but generally speaking buses run every 10-15 minutes on most main routes Monday to Friday 0700-1900. Outside these peak times services vary so it's best to check timetables with **Traveline Scotland** (**T** 0870-608 2608). The areas around Queen Street and Central stations are the city's main transport hubs. Among the saver tickets on offer is a FirstDay Tourist Ticket which allows visitors to hop on and off any First bus in Glasgow all day. It's £2.50, before 1000 and £2.20 after. There's a useful bus map of the city, *Mapmate*, produced by First Glasgow available from SPT travel outlets, the TIC and various shops in the city, price £1. See also Transport enquiries on p232.

Transport discount tickets

There are some useful saver tickets available that can save you money and are very flexible. **Roundabout Glasgow ticket** covers all Underground and train transport in the city for one day (*£4, valid Mon-Fri after 0900 and weekends*). A **Discovery ticket** (*£1.70*) gives unlimited travel on the Underground for 1 day (*valid after 0930 Mon-Fri and weekends*). There's also a **Daytripper ticket** (*valid for 1 day and costs £8 for 1 adult and 2 children, or £14 for 2 adults and up to 4 children*) which gives unlimited travel on all transport networks throughout Glasgow, the Clyde coast and Clyde valley.

Car

It is relatively easy to get around Glasgow by car, especially as the M8 runs right through the heart of the city. The city is laid out on a grid system, which makes the numerous one way streets relatively easy to negotiate – though try and get hold of a map before you arrive. Parking is not too much of a problem either, particularly when compared to car-hating Edinburgh, although it is expensive and parking wardens operate widely. There are sufficient street meters and 24-hour multi-storey car parks dotted around the centre, at the St Enoch Centre, Mitchell Street, Oswald Street, Waterloo Street and Cambridge Street. For car hire companies, see p230.

Ferry

The majority of ferry services on the west coast are operated by **Caledonian MacBrayne** (CalMac). They run services on the Firth of Clyde, sailing from Gourock to Dunoon, Wemyss Bay to Rothesay and Largs to Great Cumbrae. Fares are expensive, especially with a car, but if you're planning on using ferries a lot, you can save a lot of money with an **Island Hopscotch** ticket, which offers reduced fares on 17 set routes. The ticket is valid for one month and you need to follow your set itinerary, though this can be changed en route without too much fuss. For more details contact Calmac (**T** 01475-650100, **T** 08705-650000 for reservations, www.calmac.co.uk, The Ferry Terminal, Gourock, PA19 1QP).

Taxi

Taxis are plentiful and reasonably priced and can be hailed from anywhere in the city. There are taxi ranks at Central and Queen Street train stations and Buchanan bus station. To call a cab, try **Glasgow Taxis** (**T** 0141-429 2900), who also run city tours. Minimum fare around the city centre is £2. To the Burrell collection from the city centre (about 3 miles) should cost around £8-9.

Train

Trains leave from **Glasgow Central** mainline station to all destinations south of the Clyde, including to Greenock (for ferries to Dunoon), Wemyss Bay (for ferries to Rothesay), Ardrossan (for ferries to Arran) and to Prestwick airport. There's a low-level station below Central station which connects the southeast of the city with the northwest. This cross-city line serves the SECC and a branch runs north to Milngavie, at the start of the West Highland Way. There's a line from **Queen Street station** which runs west all the way to Helensburgh, via Partick and Dumbarton. Branches of this line run to Balloch, at the south end of Loch Lomond, and to Milngavie. There's also a suburban train network run by **SPT** (www.spt.co.uk), which is a fast way to reach the suburbs south of the Clyde.

Underground

The best way to get from the city centre to the West End is to use the city's Underground, or subway as it's also known. The stations are marked with a huge orange 'U' sign. This is less effective for the

! Locals affectionately refer to the Underground as the 'Clockwork Orange', as there's only one circular route serving 15 stops and the trains are bright orange.

South Side but there's a vast range of buses from the city centre. There's also an extensive suburban train network which is a fast and efficient way to reach the suburbs south of the Clyde. It's easy to use and there's a flat-rate fare of 90p per journey. Trains run roughly every 4 minutes during peak times and every 6-8 minutes at other times. Trains run from 0635 till 2310 Monday-Saturday and from 1100 till 1750 on Sunday. See also Transport enquiries, p232.

Tours

Glasgow's a large city and it's well worth taking one of the many tours on offer to help you get your bearings. Several firms offer guided bus tours on open-topped double-decker buses, which might sound cheesy but are a good value option as you can hop on and off as you choose. They'll take you right out to the West End and will also go to the main sights along the Clyde. They depart regularly from George Square from 0930, and have wheelchair access. If you don't fancy the bus, there are always boat trips along the Clyde – the river that was once the focus of city life. You can choose from short trips in the heart of the city, or do as generations of Glaswegians have and take a day trip along the river to one of the Clyde's coastal resorts – known locally as going 'doon the watter'. Among the walking tours on offer are the enjoyably creepy ghoulies and ghosties ones, ideal if you like a supernatural thrill, while those who prefer to kick up their heels and try a highland fling can take a pub tour that includes entry to a ceilidh club.

Boat tours

The Waverley, T 0141-221 8152, www.waverleyexcusions.co.uk. *Sailings take place from Easter-mid May and from Jun-late Aug. Office open summer Mon-Fri 0900-1700, Sat 0900-1300, winter Mon-Fri 0900-1700. Trips range from £10-30.* At Anderston Quay, east of the Science Centre is the world's last ocean-going paddle-steamer and one of a former fleet of pleasure boats that used to take

Glaswegians on trips 'doon the watter' to Clyde coast resorts. She has now completed a £7 million refit and has been restored to her original glory. You can take still take day trips on the Waverley along the Clyde to destinations like Dunoon, Largs, the Kyles of Bute and Arran.

Seaforce, T 0141-221 1070, www.seaforce.co.uk. *£50, with lunch, £25 concessions, open all year, trips must be booked. Office open 0800-2200.* Situated next to the Tall Ship, this company offers high speed powerboat trips along the Clyde. Trips range from a 15-minute 'taster' (*£3*) to a 4-hour trip to the village of Kilcreggan (*£35, £15 concession*). There's also a mystery tour which goes to, well, it's a surprise.

The Clyde Waterbus, T 0771-125 0969, www.clydewaterbusservices.co.uk. *Trips go about every 1½ hrs and include a commentary on the history of the river. Services run Mon-Fri from 1045-1815, Sat from 1115, Sun from 1145. £3, £5 return; concessions £2, £3.50 return*. Pride of the Clyde is a riverbus that runs along the Clyde between Broomielaw and Braehead (where there is the large Braehead shopping centre and Clydebuilt maritime museum).

Bus tours

One of the best ways to see the city sights is to take a guided bus tour on board an open-top, double-decker bus with a multilingual guide.

City Sightseeing Glasgow, T 0141-204 0444, www.citysightseeingglasgow.co.uk. *£8, £6 seniors/students, £3 children, £19.50 family (2 adults, up to 4 children). Tours leave from George Sq and run every 15 mins (from 0930 in summer)*. The complete tour takes in Glasgow Cathedral, the Merchant City, the People's Palace, the Tall Ship and the Transport museum. It lasts for 1 hour 20 minutes, although you can hop on and off as you please.

Glasgow Corporation Transport, T 0845-120 8091. *£6, £3.50 concessions/children, tickets valid for 2 days.* Open-top bus tour that runs from George Square every 30 minutess. The tour last 1 hour 20 minutes and again covers all the main sights like the Cathedral and the Tall ship. You can hop on and off all day.

Charles Rennie Mackintosh tours
For information and dates contact the Mackintosh Society (see p74). The Charles Rennie Mackintosh Society run 'Mackintosh in Style Weekends'. They visit the main sights around the city, and Hill House in Helensburgh, and the tour includes two nights dinner, bed and breakfast, plus lunch in the Willow Tea Rooms.

Taxi tours
Glasgow Taxis, T 0141-429 7070, www.glasgowtaxisltd.co.uk., *£25 per taxi for a 1 hr tour, £45 per taxi for a 2 hr tour (maximum 5 passengers), available 24 hrs.* "Guess who I had in the back of my cab!" Glasgow taxi drivers are known for their patter and knowledge of the city, so a taxi tour is an option worth considering: think about it, history, culture – and an opinion on everything. City tours last 1 hour and take you round all the main places of interest. There's also a 2-hour tour, which also takes you past South Side attractions like Scotland Street School Museum, House for an Art Lover and the Burrell Collection (where you can finish the tour if you choose). Pick-ups can be at any point on the route.

Walking tours
Journeyman Tours, **T** 0800-093 9984, www.journeymantours.co.uk. *Starts from the war memorial in George Sq at 1900 on Fri, Sat and ends around 2400. Price of £15 per adult includes some drinks and entry to ceilidh club. They also do a history tour – 'Secrets of the Merchant City' – that leaves George Square at 1930 Thu-Sun. £5 adults, £4 concessions, £2.50 children, under-12s free.* If you fancy a night out as well as a tour, try Journeyman's Glasgow Fling. It's a night-time tour that takes

Glasgow

George Square and the Merchant City 35
The heart of present-day Glasgow is flanked by rejuvenated streets lined with handsome 18th century mansions and warehouses.

Trongate to the East End 42 The shabbier end of the city centre is slowly catching up with its chic counterparts on the west side.

Buchanan Street to Charing Cross 52
Glasgow's high testosterone architecture shown off at its confident best amidst high canyons of brick, steel and glass.

West End 66 Palatial residential homes and offices mix with trendy bars, clubs and restaurants in the city's student quarter.

Along the Clyde 78 Life is returning to Glasgow's river after years of neglect, as shiny new developments replace the rusting remnants of docks and shipyards.

South of the Clyde 88 The sedate suburbs of Glasgow's south side are home to several of the city's top attractions, including the magnificent Burrell Collection.

George Square and the Merchant City

The heart of modern Glasgow is George Square – which makes it the obvious starting point for a tour of the city centre. The tourist information centre is also located here, on the south side of the square. The grid of streets to the east of George Square, stretching as far as the High Street, form the Merchant City, where the Tobacco Lords built their magnificent Palladian mansions. They made Glasgow the most important tobacco trading city in Europe and can also take the credit for it being one of the lung cancer capitals of the world by the mid-20th century. The Tobacco Lords, however, gave way to King Cotton, and by 1820, the area between ***Candleriggs*** *and Miller Street was largely taken up by the textile industry.*

The Merchant City's days as a desirable residential district were numbered when fashionable merchants were lured west by the fine new houses being built on Blytheswood Hill. Banks, markets and warehouses all followed and by the mid-19th century the city's financial heart had been transplanted into the West End. The Merchant City became a wholesale area, largely neglected and under threat of postwar high-rise housing development. Luckily, it escaped, and the return of Glasgow's concert hall to Candleriggs saw the beginning of the regeneration of this area.

Money has been poured into the restoration of its 18th century warehouses and homes in an attempt to revitalize and regenerate the city's old historic core. Though many of the buildings are little more than façades, the investment has succeeded in attracting expensive designer clothes shops and a plethora of stylish bistros, cafés and bars, which are packed with the city's young professionals and media types. It's a very pleasant and interesting area to explore, with the advantage that when all that neoclassical architecture gets too much, you can pop into one of the trendy café-bars for some light relief.

⏩ *See Sleeping p122, Eating and drinking p140, Bars and clubs p165*

Sights

George Square

There are free guided tours of the City Chambers, **T** 0141-287 2000, Mon-Fri at 1030 and 1430. Entry to Merchant's House by appointment only, **T** 0141-221 8272. *Free. Map 2, D/E8, p253*

George Square was named after George III and laid out in 1781. For several years it was not much more than a watery patch of ground where horses were taken to be slaughtered and puppies to be drowned. The plan was to make it an upmarket, elegant square with private gardens at its centre. However, many of the buildings (designed by the Adam brothers) were never built, while the gardens didn't last long as Glaswegians objected to such an obvious display of privilege and ripped the railings down in disgust. The square only became the heart of the city when the council decided to make it the location for the City Chambers – the most visible symbol of Glasgow's position as Second City of the Empire.

Although there's a statue of Burns in the square, the poet did not have very strong links with Glasgow. On the few times he did come to the city he seemed to have gone shopping – buying, on various visits, some books, some cocoa, and some black silk for his wife. Other statues which adorn the square are those of Queen Victoria, Prince Albert, Sir Walter Scott, Sir Robert Peel and James Watt, while the Greek Doric column is dedicated to Walter Scott (1837).

The Square is surrounded by fine civic buildings, most notable of which is the grandiose **City Chambers**, which fills the east side, a wonderful testament to the optimism and aspiration of Victorian Glasgow. It was designed in the Italian Renaissance style by William Young and the interior is even more impressive than its façade. The imposing arcaded marble entrance hall is decorated with elaborate mosaics and a marble staircase leads up to a great banqueting hall with a wonderful arched ceiling, leaded glass windows and paintings depicting scenes from the city's history.

One wall is covered by a series of murals by the Glasgow Boys. On the northwest corner of George Square, opposite Queen Street Station, is another fine building, the **Merchants' House**, now home to Glasgow Chamber of Commerce. The interior is worth a look as it boasts some beautiful stained-glass windows and chocolate-brown wood panelling.

The Gallery of Modern Art

Queen St, **T** 0141-229 1996, www.glasgowmuseums.com. *Mon-Thu and Sat 1000-1700, Fri and Sun 1100-1700. Free.* *Map 2, E7, p253*

Just to the south of George Square, facing the west end of Ingram Street, is **Royal Exchange Square**, which is almost completely filled by the Gallery of Modern Art (GOMA) – yet another example of the city's penchant for setting major public buildings within built-up squares. The building dates from 1778, when it was built as the Cunninghame Mansion, home to one of Glasgow's wealthy Tobacco Lords. It passed to the Royal Bank of Scotland in 1817 and 10 years later the magnificent portico was added to the front and the building then became the Royal Exchange, the city's main business centre. Following a stint as a telephone exchange in the 1920s, it latterly became the local public library, until 1996 when the magnificent barrel-vaulted interior was converted to house one of the city's newest, and most controversial art venues, drawing the ire of many a critic for its unashamed eclecticism and populism.

The gallery features contemporary works by artists from around the world, displayed on three themed levels: the Earth Gallery on the ground floor; the Water Gallery; and the Air Gallery. It's a bold, innovative art space, making excellent use of the original interior. The works you can see are varied and include paintings by Peter Howson, the Imperial War Museum's war artist in Bosnia, photographs by Henri Cartier-Bresson, and Beryl Cook's jolly work *By the Clyde*. There's also a top-floor café, with great views. In front of the gallery is an equestrian statue of the Duke of Wellington. The

Arriverderci Barga

A wet winter's day in Glasgow feels like a world away from sunny Rome or Florence, yet the city has very strong links with Italy and the 'Glasgow Italians' have made a huge contribution to the life of the city. The majority of the Italian community in Glasgow originate from the beautiful hilltop town of Barga, not far from Lucca in Tuscany. The Italians migrated to Glasgow for a variety of reasons. Some came to the city while selling plaster religious statues, others were said to have arrived by ship - apparently mistaking Glasgow for New York. Still more came seeking work in the mines and shipyards. Whatever the reason, the Barghigiani who settled in Glasgow liked it and told their families and friends, many of whom came to the city in their turn. To make a living, many of the Italians began to make ice cream and to fry fish and chips - and with their entrepreneurial skills they were soon able to open cafés throughout Glasgow and down the Clyde coast. Today you can still find many of these original cafés (like Nardini's in Largs) as well as many excellent Italian-run restaurants and fish and chip shops. Other notable west coast 'Italians' include the actors Peter Capaldi ('It's a Wonderful Life'), Daniella Nardini ('This Life') and Tom Conti. And if you go to Barga in August you will find it full of Glasgow-Italians visiting friends and family. In fact, links with Glasgow are so close that Barga even has an annual fish and chip festival.

Duke can often be seen wearing a traffic cone on his head at a jaunty angle, placed there by over refreshed locals or by students (what is it with undergraduates and traffic cones?). The cone is there so often – and has featured in so many photographs – that the Duke now looks undressed without it.

Hutcheson's Hall

158 Ingram St, **T** 0141-552 8391, www.nts.org.uk. *Mon-Sat 1000-1700. Free. Map 2, E9, p253*

This is a distinguished Georgian building which is now the National Trust for Scotland's regional headquarters. It was built by David Hamilton in 1805 in neoclassical style with a traditional Scottish 'townhouse' steeple. It was once home to the Scottish Educational Trust, a charitable institution founded by the 17th century lawyer brothers George and Thomas Hutcheson, which provided almshouses and schools for the city. Their statues gaze down towards the site of the original almshouse in Trongate. Upstairs is the ornate hall where you can see a film on Glasgow Style, the distinctive style of art that evolved from the works of artists such as Charles Rennie Mackintosh. Downstairs there's an exhibition, also on Glasgow Style, featuring jewellery, textiles, furniture and prints by contemporary Glasgow artists and crafts people. All the works are for sale – for anything from a few pounds to several hundred pounds.

● *Hutcheson's Hall faces down the street, closing the vista. This is a feature of many of the Merchant City's civic buildings.*

The Italian Centre and The Corinthian

The Italian Centre: John St/Ingram St, **T** 0141-552 6099. The Corinthian: 191 Ingram St, T 0141-552 1101, www.g1group.co.uk. *Map 2, E8/9, p253* *See also p199*

Further west, between South Frederick Street and John Street, is the **Italian Centre**, restored by Page & Park from the former Bank of Scotland building, designed by William Burn in 1828. Famous for its designer-label shopping and the fact that it houses the first *Versace* store in the UK. Further west on Ingram Street is the Edwardian former **Lanarkshire House**, designed by John Burnet in 1876-79 as a refacing of David Hamilton's former Union Bank (1841) which itself replaced Virginia Mansion. Its interior riches

What's in a name?

The roots of the city's name are difficult to pin down and have become enmeshed in the city's folklore. The earliest records state that St Kentigern, or Mungo, set up his church in a place called deschu (later changed to glaschu), which translates as 'dear place'.

Another theory is that the name is derived from two gaelic words, glas meaning 'green' and cau meaning 'hollow' or 'valley'. Over the years these explanations have been amalgamated to from 'Dear Green Place'.

have been lovingly restored as **The Corinthian**, a stunning combination of bars, restaurants and meeting rooms. It is particularly impressive at night when floodlit.

Trades Hall and around

85 Glassford St, **T** 0141-552 2418, www.bbnet.demon.co.uk/ thall. *Free. Guided tours by appointment only. Map 2, F8, p253*

The Trades Hall, designed by Robert Adam and built in 1794 as the headquarters of the city's trade guilds, is Glasgow's oldest secular building, and it still serves its original purpose. The **Grand Hall** is an impressive sight, lined with a Belgian silk tapestry depicting the work of a range of former city trades such as bonnetmakers (not much call for them nowadays) and cordiners (bootmakers).

Running south off Ingram Street is **Virginia Street**, whose name recalls Glasgow's trading links with America. About halfway down, on the right heading towards Argyle Street, is the **Virginia Galleries**, the three-tiered arcade of the original Tobacco Exchange. Parallel to Virginia Street is Miller Street, originally a street of villas which was redeveloped as very grand textile and clothing factories and warehouses. Here you'll find the Merchant City's oldest surviving house (No 42), the **Tobacco Merchant's House**. Designed by John Craig and dating from 1775, it was restored by Glasgow Building Preservation Trust in 1995.

St David's (Ramshorn) Church

98 Ingram St. *Map 2, F10, p253*

East of Hutcheson's Hall is Ramshorn Church, designed by Thomas Rickman in 1826 and one of the earliest examples of Gothic revival ecclesiastical architecture in Scotland. A plaque on the west side of the tower testifies to the church's association with John MacDonald who became the first Prime Minister of Canada. The real delight here lies in the church graveyard, which is well worth a stroll around and offers a quiet picnic refuge in summer. Among the local worthies buried here are David Dale, the pioneering industrialist who helped build **New Lanark** (see p112) and John Anderson, founder of Strathclyde University. Also here is the grave of Pierre Emile L'Angelier (his name is not on the tombstone), whose mysterious death led to one of Glasgow's most famous trials.

Candleriggs

City Hall, **T** 0141-287 5024. *Map 2, F/G10, p253*

Head down Candleriggs, and you'll pass the **City Hall**, dating from 1817. This was the first concert hall in the city built for public gatherings and musical performances, and was converted back to a concert hall following the destruction of St Andrew's Hall, which once stood on the site of the present-day Mitchell Library (see p67). The auditorium, designed by George Murray in 1840 (who also designed the Egyptian entrance on Albion Street), was built over the bazaar, itself designed by James Cleland in 1817. The Candleriggs frontage, with its Corinthian pillars, was designed by James Carrick in 1885. This block, bordered by Ingram Street, Bell Street, Candleriggs and Albion Street, was the site of many of the city's markets, including the fresh fruit and flower market, the cheese market and the charmingly-titled dead-meat market. The Bell Street entrance has been completely restored and revamped as a stylish new shopping and restaurant complex called **Merchant Square**.

At the foot of Candleriggs, look to the right across the Trongate to see the rather shabby exterior of the former **Britannia Music Hall** (1857). Originally the Panopticon, the music hall still survives on the upper floors of this faded Italianate beauty. It has been described by the UK Theatres Trust as the finest surviving early music hall theatre in the UK. It closed its doors in 1938, but during its lifespan has played host to the likes of Stan Laurel, Cary Grant and Harry Lauder.

Trongate to the East End

East of the Merchant City, the Trongate leads towards the High Street, once the heart of Glasgow but now the shabby poor relation to the shiny, rejuvenated city centre. Beyond the High Street lies the city's East End, a staunch working class area and centre of the large Irish immigrant population in the late 19th century. Even here, though, the seemingly inevitable reach of gentrification is evident, especially around the Saltmarket and St Andrew's Square.

▸▸ *See Sleeping p124, Eating and drinking p145, Bars and clubs p167*

 Sights

Glasgow Cross

Trongate and High St Map 2, H10, p253

The Merchant City is bound to the east by the High Street and to the south by Trongate. These two streets meet at Glasgow Cross, once the centre of trade and administration and regarded as the city centre, until the coming of the railway in the mid-19th century. It is now little more than a traffic junction, in the centre of which stands the 38 m-high **Tolbooth Steeple**, one of only three crowned steeples in the country, and the only remnant of the original tolbooth built in 1626, which housed the courthouse and prison (described by Sir Walter Scott in his novel Rob Roy).

● *The nearby Mercat Cross is a 1929 replica of the medieval original, and is notable as the work of Edith Burnet, Britain's first registered female architect. It stands in front of the impressive, though isolated, Mercat Building, designed in 1922 by Graham Henderson.*

Tron Steeple

Trongate *Map 2, G10, p253*

Only a few yards west of the Tolbooth Steeple is the Tron Steeple, the only surviving part of St Mary's Collegiate Church, dating from 1485 and converted to a civic church in 1586. The original old kirk was accidentally burnt to the ground by members of the aptly named Glasgow Hellfire Club in 1793. After a meeting, they went to the church to warm themselves by a fire, which got out of control. It was replaced a year later by a James Adam design. The steeple has been incorporated into the modern frontage of the **Tron Theatre** (see p146), and the interior of the replacement church forms the theatre auditorium. The name comes from the public weighing machine – or tron – which was located just outside the church

---

Sharmanka Kinetic Gallery and Theatre

14 King St **T** 0141-552 7080, www.sharmanka.com. *Performances on Sun at 1500,short programme for children, and 1900, Tue 1900, Thu 1900, £4, children free Map 2, H9, p253*

Just south of Trongate, is **King Street** – a lively area crammed with contemporary art galleries and studios, and laid-back bars and cafés. The Sharmanka at number 14, puts on performances by mechanical sculptures made from carved wooden figures and old bits of junk. A great place to take the kids.

The Briggait

141 Bridgegate *Map 2, I8, p253*

On Bridgegate (or Briggait), is the **Merchants' Steeple** (1665), 164 feet-high with details in Gothic and Renaissance style. It is all that's left of the old Merchants' House, built in 1659. The Merchants left this part of the city in the early 19th century to escape the growing squalor, and moved several times before finally settling in George Square in 1877. The old steeple was eventually incorporated into the Briggait, built originally as the Fishmarket in 1872-73. The huge hall, with its cast-iron galleries, has been beautifully restored and now houses production and events facilities for artists' studios.

The area between the Briggait and the **Sheriff Court** (see below) is the site of **Paddy's Market** (every weekend 1000-1700), so named because in the mid-19th century this was where famine-stricken Irish immigrants sold their clothes for money to feed their families. It's a great place for bargain hunters and thrift store aficionados to rummage around to their heart's content.

Saltmarket and St Andrew's Square

10 mins' walk from St Enoch centre. Map 4, E1, p256

Sweeping down from Glasgow Cross to the river is the Saltmarket, the city's most 'des res' district in the early 18th century, with its peaceful and secluded riverside location. The arrival of slaughterhouses, bleachfields, the Sheriff Court House and, in 1829, the construction of Hutcheson's Bridge, put an end to its secluded status. The late 19th century sandstone tenements which line the street have recently been cleaned up and represent a fine example of the East End's ongoing gentrification. At the bottom of the Saltmarket is the original court house, whose delicate neoclassical symmetry was, in effect, destroyed by the building of Hutcheson's Bridge. The new courthouse building is tucked in behind.

Heading back north along the Saltmarket towards Glasgow Cross, St Andrew's Street turns right into St Andrew's Square, which is filled by the magnificent **St Andrew's Church**, one of the finest classical churches in Britain. Sadly neglected for many years, it has now been restored to its Georgian splendour. It no longer functions as a church but has been cleverly converted to house a sleek café (see p147) downstairs and a Scottish music venue upstairs, where you can see the stunning original stained-glass windows and intricate plaster work. Concerts and ceilidhs are staged throughout the year (tickets are available from Café Source, **T** 0141-5486020).

Nearby, on the corner of Turnbull Street and Greendyke Strret, is the Episcopalian kirk, **St Andrew's-by-the-Green**, which aroused the anger of the city's staunch Presbyterians with its sinfully ornate decoration, cushioned seats, and the positively debauched notion of introducing an organ, which earned it the name 'the Whistlin' Kirkie'. The innocent-looking church is a startling example of 18th century Glasgow amidst much 21st century development.

The Barras

The market is held every weekend, 1000-1700. Main entrance on Gallowgate. Map 4, E2/3, p256

East of Glasgow Cross, Gallowgate and London Road lead into the city's East End, only a stone's throw from the Merchant City. It may look shabby and run-down by comparison, but this is where you can sample a slice of pure Glasgow, especially in The Barras, the famous market which occupies almost the entire area between Gallowgate and London Road, and from Ross Street to Bain Street. Its main entrances are marked by distinctive red, cast-iron

! The name Barras is presumed to be a corruption of 'the barrows' named after the flea market, but this area was once known as Barrowflats, a name which dates back to the 16th century.

Best Buildings

- Trades Hall, p40
- St Vincent St Church, p59
- St Andrew's Church, p45
- Bridgegate (Briggait), p44
- Gardner's Warehouse, p53

gateways which lead you in to a scruffy jumble of tenements, warehouses, sheds and pavements. You could spend days rummaging around through acres of cheap, new and second-hand goods. A lot of it's junk (dodgy computer games, pirate videos etc) but there are plenty of bargains to be found. The real attraction though, is the atmosphere of the place and wit and repartee of the market traders. This is also the site of the famed Barrowlands dance hall, one of Glasgow's great music venues (see p184).

Glasgow Green

Main entrance on Saltmarket. Map 4, F1/2-G2, p256

South of The Barras is the wide expanse of Glasgow Green, said to be the oldest public park in Britain. It has been common land since at least medieval times and Glaswegians still have the right to dry their washing here. Bonnie Prince Charlie reviewed his troops here in 1745 before they were hung out to dry by the English at Culloden. The Green has always been dear to the people of Glasgow and is a vital part of the city's folklore. It served as the first home of the **Glasgow Golf Club**, established in the 18th century and was also where the two Old Firm clubs were founded, in the 19th century. Throughout its history, the Green has been the scene of mills, washing houses and abattoirs and the **Glasgow Fair** was held here for years. Some of the city's political demonstrators have held meetings here, including the Chartists in the 1830s and Scottish

It's no fair

Glasgow Green will always be associated with the city's annual fair. Initially established as a trade fair in the 12th century, by the early 19th century it had evolved into a giant carnival, held in mid-July when most of the working population was on holiday.

It soon earned something of a reputation for excessive drinking and such offensive activities as spontaneous dancing, and was frowned upon by the more temperate sectors of society. There were also professional entertainers, mostly of the freak-show variety, and what were known as 'penny theatres', which many considered lewd and subversive.

Basically, the Glasgow Fair was an opportunity for the low-paid and oppressed Glasgow working-class to let off steam, and this worried the authorities who saw it as a threat to the city's moral welfare. The arrival of cheap holiday excursions resulting from the expansion of the rail and steamship network brought a collective sigh of relief from the city's moral guardians.

republican campaigners in the 1920s. There are various monuments dotted around, including a 44 m-high monument to Lord Nelson, erected in 1806, one to James Watt, and the 14 m-high Doulton Fountain, first seen at the 1888 International Exhibition in Kelvingrove and later moved to its present site.

On the edge of the green, opposite the People's Palace, is **Templeton's Carpet Factory**, or Doge's Palace as it is nicknamed. This bizarre but beautiful structure was designed in 1889 by William Leiper in Venetain style and is surely one of the most extravagantly incongruous buildings in the world. Once described as 'the world's finest example of decorative brickwork', it's Britain's best example of polychromatic decoration. The building was converted to the Templeton Business Centre in 1984.

★ People's Palace

Glasgow Green, **T** 0141-554 0223, www.glasgowmuseums.com.
Mon-Thu and Sat 1000-1700, Fri and Sun 1100-1700. Free. Bus 16, 18, 43, 64, 203, 263. *Map 4, F2, p256* *See also Kids, p226*

On the northern end of the green, approached from London Road, is the People's Palace, opened in 1898 as a folk museum for the East End. The recently refurbished museum is a genuinely fascinating place to visit and gives a real insight into life of this great city and its people from the mid-18th century to the present day. This is very much a social history, told from the perspective of so-called 'ordinary folk', though their ability to survive in often desperate conditions proves just how extraordinary they often were.

How they survived was through their famous gritty humour which has been exported worldwide thanks to comic genius, Billy Connolly, the 'Big Yin'. You can hear him on the audio phones scattered throughout the galleries. These also feature other Glasgow comedians such as Stanley Baxter and Ricki Fulton. The Big Yin's famous banana boots are on display – part of the wealth of artefacts, photographs, cartoons and drawings, in addition to a series of films, music and people's anecdotes. There's a reconstructed 'steamie' (communal laundry) from nearby Ingram Street, brochures extolling the delights of a trip 'doon the watter' on the Clyde, and video displays on 'the patter' – Glaswegian à la Rab C Nesbitt.

The museum doesn't shrink from covering the less salubrious aspects of city history either. There's a display on 'the bevvy' (drink) which includes a barrow once used regularly by the police to wheel drunks home. There's also a small display on the sectarian divide in city football – evidenced by a t-shirt protesting at Rangers' signing of Mo Johnston (their first Catholic player). A visit to the People's Palace should be on everyone's itinerary, particularly if you're interested in scratching beneath the city's surface and getting to know it better. Allow at least an hour, preferably two, to take it all in.

Best

Things to do in Central Glasgow

- Find out all about the city's fascinating history through the eyes of its people at the **People's Palace**, p48.
- Take a tour round the **School of Art**, Charles Rennie Mackintosh's art nouveau masterpiece, p62.
- Wander round the **Barras** market listening to the famous Glasgow East End patter and maybe you'll unearth a hidden treasure, p202.
- Take in the latest arthouse movie at the wonderful **GFT** and while you're there enjoy a cheap lunch at Café Cosmo, p151.
- Party 'til you drop at the **Arches**, home to some of Glasgow's best club nights, p168.

When you start to suffer from information overload, take a break in the café in the very wonderful **Winter Gardens**, a gigantic conservatory at the rear of the museum, full of exotic plants and without doubt the most relaxing cup of coffee in the entire city.

Glasgow Cathedral

High St, **T** 0141-552 6891, www.historic-scotland.gov.uk. *Apr-Sep Mon-Sat 0930-1800, Sun 1400-1700, Oct-Mar Mon-Sat 0930-1600, Sun 1400-1600. Free. Map 4, B3, p256*

A 15-minute walk from George Square is Glasgow Cathedral. The early Gothic structure is the only complete medieval cathedral on the Scottish mainland. It was built on the site of St Mungo's original church, established in AD 543, though this has been a place of Christian worship since it was blessed for burial in AD 397. Most of the building was completed in the 13th century though parts were built a century earlier by Bishop Jocelyn. The choir and crypt were added a century later and the building was completed at the end of the 15th century by Robert Blacader, the first Bishop of Glasgow.

During the Reformation, the city's last Roman Catholic Archbishop, James Beaton, took off for France with most of the cathedral treasures, just ahead of the townsfolk who proceeded to rid the building of all traces of 'idolatry' by destroying altars, statues, vestments and the valuable library. The present furnishings mostly date from the 19th century and many of the windows have been renewed with modern stained-glass. The most outstanding feature in the cathedral is the fan vaulting around St Mungo's tomb in the crypt. There's also fine work in the choir, including a 15th century stone screen, the only one of its kind left in any pre-Reformation secular (non-monastic) church in Scotland.

Behind the cathedral looms the Western Necropolis, a vast burial ground overlooking the city from the top of a high ridge. It was modelled on the Père Lachaise cemetery in Paris. Around 3,500 tombs have been built here and around 50,000 burials have taken place. Most of the burials took place in the 19th century and the ornate nature of many of the tombs makes it appear as if the city worthies buried here really were trying to take their money with them when they died. It's the ideal vantage point from which to appreciate the cathedral in all its Gothic splendour and many of the tombs are well worth a look. The graveyard is overseen by a statue of John Knox, the 16th century firebrand reformer. There's also a monument to William Miller who penned the nursery rhyme *Wee Willie Winkie*. Look out for a monument to Alexander McCall; a Celtic Cross as it's the first solo work by Charles Rennie Mackintosh.

St Mungo Museum of Religious Life and Art

2 Castle St, **T** 0141-553 2557, www.glasgow.gov.uk *Mon-Thu and Sat 1000-1700, Fri and Sun 1100-1700. Free.* Provand's Lorship*: same phone number and opening hours.* *Map 4, B3, p256*

In front of the cathedral is the weetabix-coloured St Mungo Museum of Religious Life and Art, which features a series of displays of arts and artefacts representing the six major world religions, as well as a

What they said about Mackintosh

- "The North façade is one of the greatest achievements of all time, compared in scale and majesty to Michelangelo". Robert Venturi, architect, on Glasgow School of Art,1985.
- "Why is it all white, Dad?" "Because the man was a genius". Wee boy to his father in Mackintosh House.
- "Building in his hands becomes an abstract art, both musical and mathematical". Nikolaus Pevsner, Art Historian, 1935.

Japanese Zen garden in the courtyard outside – great for a few moments of quiet contemplation. Highlights include Salvador Dalí's astounding *Christ of St John of the Cross*, purchased by the city from the artist in 1951. You can also see a Native American ceremonial blanket depicting sacred animals, masks used in African initiation rites, and an Islamic prayer rug. Displays on religion in the west of Scotland cover everything from the Temperance Movement of the late 19th century, to the religious life of the modern city's vibrant ethnic communities. Don't miss the extremely interesting comments on the visitors' board. There's also a bookshop and a café serving hot meals, snacks and drinks.

Across the street is the **Provand's Lorship**, the oldest remaining house in Glasgow, built in 1471 as part of a refuge for the city's poor and extended in 1670. It has also served as an inn of rather dubious repute in its time. Now it's a museum devoted mainly to medieval furniture and various domestic items. In the grounds is a specially created medieval garden.

● *Close to the cathedral, at Parson Street, just off the High Street and M8, is one of Charles Rennie Mackintosh's lesser-known works, the Martyrs' Public School (T287 8955, daily 1300-1600, free). Built in 1895, on the very street where CRM was born, this solid red sandstone building is clearly visible from the top of the High Street.*

Buchanan Street to Charing Cross

Glasgow's commercial heart is the area between Buchanan Street and the M8 to the west. This vast grid-plan – which inspired town planners in the USA – is home to the city's main shopping streets and arcades, as well as its businesses and financial institutions. It is also where you'll find many of its architectural treasures.

▸▸ *See Sleeping p124, Eating and drinking p147, Bars and clubs p168*

Sights

St Enoch Square

Nearest Underground is St Enoch. Map 2, G6/7, p252

At the bottom (south) end of Buchanan Street is St Enoch Square, dominated by the **St Enoch Centre**, a gigantic glass-covered complex of shops, fast-food outlets and an ice rink. Opposite the shopping complex are some notable buildings, such as the Royal Bank of Scotland and the Teacher building, headquarters of the whisky maker until 1991. In the centre of the square is the St Enoch subway station, and an attractive little Jacobean pavilion which now houses the **SPT Travel Centre**.

Argyle Street

Nearest Underground is St Enoch. Map 2, E1-G8, p252/3

St Enoch Square looks onto Argyle Street, one of Glasgow's most famous shopping streets. Though its status has been usurped in recent decades by the more fashionable streets to the north, it does boast the **Argyle Arcade**, Scotland's first ever indoor shopping mall, built in 1827 in the Parisian style, at the junction with Buchanan Street. Argyle Street runs west from here under the railway bridge at Central Station.

Jamaica Street

Nearest Underground is St Enoch.   Map 2, F/G5, p252

Just before Central Station, turn left into Jamaica Street and on the corner with Midland Street is one of the city's most stunning buildings, the former **Gardner's Warehouse**, which was modelled on the Crystal Palace in London and is now a vast pub of the same name. Known as 'The Iron Building' it has variously been described by architectural experts as "one of the great landmarks of Western architectural history" and "one of the most remarkable cast-iron warehouses of its date anywhere in Britain". It certainly matches anything in the Cast Iron district of New York's Soho.

● *Opposite the Crystal Palace pub is MacSorley's Bar, named after the famous Phillip MacSorley's bar in New York that was owned by the man himself. He imported one of his barmen to run the Glasgow version.*

Union Street

Nearest Underground is St Enoch.   Map 2, E/F5, p252

Head back up Jamaica Street, cross Argyle Street into Union Street and on the right you'll see the magnificent **Egyptian Halls** (1871-73), a stunning piece of architectural brilliance from Glasgow's somewhat overlooked genius, Alexander "Greek" Thomson. The fact that this masterpiece lies empty and unused is surely bordering on criminal negligence.

At the top of Union Street, on the corner with Gordon Street, is another of the city centre's great cast-iron buildings the **Ca d'Oro**, designed by James Honeyman in 1872 and modelled on the famous Golden House in Venice. It was originally built as a

! The bridge at Central Station has always been known as the 'Heilanman's Umbrella', owing to the local joke that Highlanders would stand under it rather than buy an umbrella.

furniture warehouse and the unusual name comes from a restaurant once housed inside. The building was badly damaged by fire in 1987 but has since been reconstructed in its original form.

● *Only a few yards away, at 20-26 Renfield La, is one of Charles Rennie Mackintosh's lesser-known designs, the former Daily Record building (1901), which can only be viewed from outside.*

The Lighthouse

11 Mitchell La, **T** 0141-221 6362, www.thelighthouse.co.uk. *Mon, Wed, Fri and Sat 1030-1700, Tues 1100-1700, Thu 1030-1700, Sun 1200-1700. £3. £1.50 concession. Map 2, E6, p252*

If you head east on Gordon Street and turn into Mitchell Lane you will find The Lighthouse – another of Glasgow's architectural beauties. It was designed by the ubiquitous Charles Rennie Mackintosh in 1893 to house the offices of the Glasgow Herald. The Herald vacated the premises in 1980 and it lay empty, until its recent transformation into Scotland's Centre for Architecture, Design and the City, a permanent legacy of the Glasgow's role as UK City of Architecture and Design in 1999.

The Lighthouse offers a programme of lively temporary exhibitions associated with architecture and design. Situated in the original part of the building is The **Mack Room**, or **Mackintosh Interpretation Centre**, on the third floor, which features original designs and information on the life and work of the great architect. There are interactive displays telling the story of his life and scale models of his works. From this gallery you can ascend the **Mackintosh Viewing Tower**. Reached by a 135-step spiral staircase, it was part of the original building and offers unbeatable, panoramic views of the city. There are workshops, seminars and events, including a number of activities based on Mackintosh and the Glasgow Style, and specialized tours of the building. There's also a shop and café on the fifth floor (see p151) and another café on the ground floor.

Recommended retail place

If there's one thing Glaswegians like to do, it's spend money on looking good; Glasgow is second only to London in the UK for shopping.

Buchanan Street and around

Nearest Underground is Buchanan St. Map 2, C7-F6, p252/3

Running north from Argyle Street to Sauchiehall Street is Buchanan Street, perhaps Glasgow's finest street, as much for its variety of retail outlets as for its architectural importance. A short walk north on Buchanan Street is **Princes Square**, one of the most stylish and imaginative shopping malls in Britain. Even if you're not buying or looking, it's worth going in to admire this beautifully ornate art nouveau creation, or to sit in the Zinc bar (see p171) and watch others spend their hard-earned cash in the designer clothes shops below. A little further north, on the opposite side of the street, is a branch of the famous **Willow Tea Rooms** (see p152) with replicas of Mackintosh designs. Almost opposite is a Borders bookshop, housed in the huge and impressive former Royal Bank of Scotland, which backs onto Royal Exchange Square.

Mack, the life
The Lighthouse, once the home of the Glasgow Herald newspaper, has been transformed into a major sight, with a room devoted to Charles Rennie Mackintosh, a fine café and great views from the Viewing Tower.

"Edinburgh is, if not quite a spinster lady, at least a respectable one. Glasgow is no lady."

Jack McLean, The Scotsman, 1997.

Buchanan Street continues north, crossing St Vincent Street, to reach **Nelson Mandela place** which is completely filled by the baroque splendour of **St George's Tron Church**, the oldest church in the city centre, designed in 1808 by William Stark. Opposite is the **Stock Exchange**, designed in French Gothic style by John Burnet Senior in 1875. A short walk further north, close to Buchanan Street Underground station, is the **Athenaeum**, designed in 1886 by JJ Burnet and showing early signs of his later modernism.

St Vincent Street

Nearest Underground is Buchanan St. Map 2, C1-E8, p252/3

Running west from George Square, between Argyle Street and Sauchiehall Street, is St Vincent Street, where at No 142, you'll find one of the city's most unusual buildings – **The Hatrack**. Designed in 1902 by James Salmon II, it's 10 storeys high but only 9 m wide. It gets its name from the series of projecting finials which once surmounted it and made the building look like an old hatstand.

Further along St Vincent Street, near the intersection with Pitt Street, is one of the jewels in Glasgow's architectural crown, the **St Vincent Street Church**, designed in 1859 by Alexander 'Greek' Thomson, the city's "unknown genius" of architecture. It is described by many architectural commentators as one of the most important 19th century buildings in Europe. The Presbyterian church is fronted by Ionic columns like those of a Greek temple and the church also shows Egyptian and Assyrian decoration. The main tower is Grecian in style, while the dome could have come straight out of India during the Raj. Thomson's other ecclesiastical designs were destroyed by German bombs and local vandals. This, his only church that still remains intact, is now on the World Monument Fund's list of the 100 most endangered sites, for the second time. Its owners, the city council, have come under withering criticism for their apparent inaction in the face of the building's continuing deterioration. The church is not open to the public other than during services (*Sun at 1100 and 1830*). For more details, try writing to the **Alexander Thomson Society**, 1 Moray Pl, Glasgow G41 2AQ or phone on **T** 0141-221 1937.

Around Blythswood Square

10 mins' walk from Blythswood Sq. Map 2, C3, p252

Climbing north from St Vincent Street, heading towards Sauchiehall Street, is the grid pattern of streets which composed Glasgow's second New Town (the first being the Merchant City). Built in the first decades of the 19th century, the plan was drawn up by James Craig, coincidentally the name of the architect of Edinburgh's New Town. But though there are similarities between the two designs, there is no conclusive proof that it was the same person. The plan was modified by architect James Gillespie Graham and followed the principles of the simplicity of the late Georgian period. Over the years the requirements of first Victorian commerce and then 20th century development have intruded on the original look, though Blythswood Square still hints at the area's original classical beauty.

● *Worth noting is the door at 5 Blythswood Sq, designed by Charles Rennie Mackintosh for the former Glasgow Society of Lady Artists' Club in 1908.*

Sauchiehall Street

Buchanan St Underground for East end, St George's Cross for West end. Map 2, A1-B7, p252/3

Further north is Sauchiehall Street, another of the city's main shopping thoroughfares. If there's one thing Glaswegians like to do it's spend money and Glasgow is second only to London in the UK in terms of retail spending. The newest of the city's shopping centres is the upmarket **Buchanan Galleries** (see p203), next door to the Royal Concert Hall, at the east end of Sauchiehall Street, where it meets the north end of Buchanan Street.

There are a few notable places of interest on Sauchiehall Street, including Charles Rennie Mackintosh's **Willow Tea Rooms** (see p152), at No 217, above Henderson's the Jewellers. This is a faithful reconstruction on the site of the original 1903 tearoom, designed by Mackintosh for his patron Miss Kate Cranston, who already ran three fashionable tearooms, in Argyle Street, Buchanan Street and Ingram Street. The tearoom was very much peculiar to Glasgow, promoted by the Temperance Movement as a healthy alternative to the gin palaces, popular throughout the country in the late 19th century, and Miss Cranston's were the crème de la crème of tearooms. They offered ladies-only rooms, rooms for gentlemen and rooms where both sexes could dine together.

Mackintosh had already worked with Miss Cranston on her other tearooms, but Sauchiehall Street was their tour de force. Sauchiehall means 'alley of the willows' and this theme was reflected not only in the name, but throughout the interior. Mackintosh was allowed free rein to design the fixtures and fittings; everything, in fact, right down to the teaspoons. The exclusive Salon de Luxe, on the first floor, was the crowning glory, and the most exotic and ambitious part of the tea rooms, decorated in purple, silver and white, with silk and velvet upholstery. Visitors today can relive the splendour of the original tea rooms as they relax in the high-backed chairs with a cup of tea.

A few yards west, on the opposite side of the street, are the **McLellan Galleries** (**T** 565 4137, www.glasgowmuseums.com, *Mon-Thu and Sat 1000-17000, Fri and Sun 1100-1700, free*), another fine example of classical architecture. While **Kelvingrove Art Gallery and Museum** (see p68) is closed for refurbishment (until early 2006) these galleries are hosting a display of the most important artworks from the collection. These include Botticelli's *Annunciation*, Giorgione's *The Adultress Brought Before Christ* and Rembrandt's *Man in Armour*. There are also outstanding examples of French Impressionism, Post-Impressionism and Dutch schools, including works by Degas, Monet, Turner, Bonnard, Pissaro, Vuillard, Braque and Derain. There are also excellent works by many of Scotland's finest artists, including, Sir Henry Raeburn, Horatio McCulloch and Alexander Naysmith. The Glasgow Boys are also well represented, with works by George Henry, Joseph Crawhall, Sir James Guthrie and Sir John Lavery.

Further west on Sauchiehall Street, on the north side, is the **Centre for Contemporary Arts** (CCA) (**T** 332 7521, www.cca-glasgow.com, *centre open Mon-Sat 0900-2400, Sun 1200-1900, galleries Mon-Sat 1100-1800, Sun 1200-1700, free*), housed in the Grecian Buildings, a former commercial warehouse designed by Alexander 'Greek' Thomson in 1867-68. The centre presents a changing programme of contemporary theatre, dance and other cultural events. On the ground floor is the excellent Tempus at the CCA café-bar and upstairs is the CCA Bar (see p150). There's also a shop on the ground floor.

A block further west is **Baird Hall**, built in 1938 as the Beresford Hotel for the Empire Exhibition, now part of Strathclyde University and the city's finest example of 1930s architecture. A short distance west, at 518 Sauchiehall Street, is the **Royal Highland Fusiliers Museum** (**T** 332 0961, *Mon-Fri 0830-1600, free*), which details the history of the three regiments from 1678 to the present day. There are medals, uniforms, weapons and musical instruments as well as a wealth of other artefacts on show.

★ Glasgow School of Art

167 Renfrew St, **T** 0141-353 4526, www.gsa.ac.uk. *Tour times Oct-Jun Mon-Fri at 1100 and 1400, Sat 1030 and 1130; Jul-Sep Mon-Fri 1100 and 1400, Sat/Sun 1030, 1130 and 1300. Closed late Jun for graduation and from Christmas through to New Year. £5, £4 students. Booking is advised. For more information on Charles Rennie Mackintosh and his work, contact the CRM Society, at Queen's Cross Church (see p74). Map 2, A3, p252 See also p172*

A very steep walk up from Sauchiehall Street is the Glasgow School of Art, the city's seminal architectural masterpiece and one of the

Art class

Glasgow School of Art, one of Glasgow's biggest attractions, has been the inspiration for many artists, including the 'new Glasgow Boys', as well as writers Alasdair Gray and Liz Lochead and actor Robbie Coltrane.

most prestigious art schools in the country. The building was designed by Charles Rennie Mackintosh, after his proposal won a competition set in 1896 to find a design for the school. It was built in two stages from 1897-1899 and completed in 1907. The school is now regarded as Mackintosh's architectural masterpiece and gives full expression to his architectural ideals: the brilliant use of Scottish vernacular forms and the imaginative and minute interior details which are subtly mirrored in the exterior of the building. Much of the inspiration for his design came from nature and from his drawings of traditional Scottish buildings. He was also influenced by the art nouveau style, particularly the illustrations of Aubrey Beardsley.

The building is rooted in tradition with medieval, castle-like features such as turrets and curving stairwells, but it also has a thoroughly modern-looking exterior of austerity. The interior is spacious and utilitarian and shows his desire to create a unified and harmonious working environment for both students and teachers. The studio walls and high ceilings are painted white, with huge windows allowing light to pour into the spaces. The corridors and staircases are decorated with glazed, coloured tiles to help guide students and staff around the massive building. The overall effect is part Gothic castle, part museum and part modern functional space, reflecting his blending of creative genius and Scots pragmatist.

The spectacular two-tier library is the pièce de résistance. Mackintosh designed everything, down to the light fittings, bookcases and the oak furniture, to create a sense of light filtering through the trees in a forest clearing. There are symbols of nature everywhere throughout the building, used to inspire the students to produce their own works of art. And who could fail to be inspired in such a stunning environment? Several of the city's distinguished writers studied here, including Alasdair Gray and Liz Lochead, as well as dramatist John Byrne and actor Robbie Coltrane, who plays Hagrid in the Harry Potter films.

As it is still a working art school, entry is by student-led guided tour only. The tour visits the main rooms containing many of the well-known pieces of furniture and includes the famous library. The shop on the ground floor, where you collect your tour tickets, has a wide range of Mackintosh paraphenalia.

★ The Tenement House

145 Buccleuch St, **T** 0141-333 0183, www.nts.org.uk. *1 Mar-31 Oct, daily 1300-1700. £4, £3 concessions.* *Map 2, above A2, p252*

A few hundred yards northwest of the School of Art, down the other side of the hill is the Tenement House, a typical late-Victorian tenement flat. In 1911, 25-year old Miss Agnes Toward and her mother moved into the flat. Agnes, a shorthand typist and spinster, was to live here for most of her life, until she moved out in 1965. During that time, Agnes changed absolutely nothing in her home and it is now a fascinating time-capsule of life in the first half of the

The Sarry Story

Few pubs can have had such an eventful past as the legendary Saracen's Head – or Sarry Heid as it is know in these parts – in the Gallowgate . The present watering hole stands on the site of the original inn, which was Glasgow's first hotel, established in 1755. A sign on the side of the present building tells the story, how it was built from the ruins of the Bishop's Palace on the site of Little St Mungo's Church. Legend has it that St Mungo (officially known as Kentigern) met St Columba here. You can just imagine them discussing matters spiritual while enjoying a 'hauf and hauf'.

Robert Burns stayed here, as did Johnson and Boswell in 1773 on their grand tour. During their stay Dr Johnson managed to upset political economist Adam Smith, who was thrown out after calling Johnson a "son of a bitch". It is presumed that William and Dorothy Wordsworth didn't resort to such foul language during their visit in 1803.

20th century, retaining most of the original features such as the bed recesses, kitchen range and coal bunker. The whole experience is a little voyeuristic, as the flat includes many of Agnes' personal possessions, and in the parlour the table is set for afternoon tea, lending a spooky atmosphere redolent of the Marie Celeste. On the ground floor is an exhibition on tenement life.

The Piping Centre

30-34 McPhater St, **T** 0141-353 0220, www.thepiping centre.co.uk. *May-Sep daily 1000-1630, Oct-Apr Mon-Sat 1000-1630. £3, £2 concession. Map 2, A6, p252*

On the other side of Cowcaddens Road, behind the Royal Scottish Academy for Music and Drama, is the Piping Centre. It's a place for the promotion of bagpipes and contains rehearsal rooms, performance spaces and accommodation for aficionados of the instrument which divides opinion so sharply. There's a café and a museum which features a collection of antique pipes. The museum also has audiovisual displays and gives you personal headsets so you can listen to samples of bagpipe music as you go round.

West End

On the other side of the M8 to the city centre is the West End, an area which contains many of the city's major museums, as well as some of its finest examples of Victorian architecture. During the course of the 19th century the West End grew in importance as wealthy merchants moved there, away from the industrial city. Soon after, in 1870, the university also moved west, to its present site overlooking Kelvingrove Park, and in 1896 the Glasgow District Subway was extended west.

Now, Glasgow's West End is mix of youthful hedonsim and suburban calm. The streets between Kelvingrove Park and the Great Western Road, especially around Hillhead Underground and ***Byres Road****, are alive to the sound of students, shoppers and late-night revellers. Here you'll find some the city's most interesting independent shops, as well as many of the best bars and restaurants. Within a stone's throw is a triptych of great attractions – the* ***Hunterian Museum****, Kelvingrove Art Gallery and Museum and* ***Transport Museum*** *– as well as some dear green spaces, namely* ***Kelvingrove Park*** *and the* ***Botanic Gardens****. Head further along the Great Western Road, however, and the wild west becomes the mild west as you enter the residential districts of Kelvinside, Anniesland and Knightswood, all bywords for genteel respectability.*

▸▸ *See Sleeping p129, Eating and drinking p152, Bars and clubs p175*

Sights

Mitchell Library

201 North St, **T** 0141-287 2999, www.mitchelllibrary.org.
Mon-Thu 0900-2000, Fri and Sat 0900-1700. Nearest Underground St George's Cross. *Map 3, J8, p255*

Overlooking the motorway, a short distance west of Charing Cross, is the edifice of the Mitchell Library, which is impressive when floodlit at night. Founded in 1874, it is the largest public reference library in Europe, with over 1½ million volumes. The **Glasgow Room**, on the fifth floor, entered via the south entrance, is a veritable treasure trove of information on the city. The western façade of the building is all that remains of **St Andrew's Hall**, the city's former concert hall, which was all but destroyed in a terrible conflagration in 1962. It must have been an awesome sight, judging by what's left of it.

The Park Conservation Area

Nearest Underground Kelvinbridge; from there head down South Woodside Rd into Woodlands Rd. *Map 3, G/H6/7, p255*

Heading north from the library, or west from St George's Cross Underground station, across Woodlands Road, you enter another world, where elegant classical terraces sweep around the contours of Woodlands Hill, punctuated by the magnificent Romanesque towers of Trinity College. If the sun is shining (yes, it happens occasionally) it is very difficult not to believe you haven't been magically transported from the west coast of Scotland to the Italian region of Umbria. By the middle of the 19th century the Park Conservation Area had been established and was described as one of the finest pieces of architectural planning of the century. The most impressive of all the terraces in the conservation area are Park Quadrant and Park Terrace, with views across Kelvingrove Park and beyond.

Kelvingrove Museum and Art Gallery

Argyle St, **T** 0141-287 2699, www.glasgowmuseums.com. *Nearest Underground Kelvinhall. Map 3, H4, p255*

Glasgow's Kelvingrove Art Gallery and Museum stands below the university, on the other side of the River Kelvin, at the most westerly end of Argyle and Sauchiehall Streets, near Kelvingrove Park. This massive sandstone Victorian building, when open, houses one of the finest municipal collections of Scottish and European paintings in the country. The art gallery and museum were built in 1901 with the proceeds from the hugely successful Glasgow Exhibition of 1888.

The museum is closed for refurbishment until early 2006. Artworks from the collection are temporarily on display at the McLellan Galleries (see p61).

Transport Museum

1 Bunhouse Rd, **T** 0141-287 2720, clyde-valley.com/glasgow/index.htm. *Mon-Thu and Sat 1000-1700, Fri and Sun 1100-1700. Free. Buses 9, 16, 18, 42 and 63. Nearest Underground Kelvinhall. Map 3, I3, p255, see also Kids, p227*

Opposite the Kelvingrove Museum and Art Gallery, just off Argyle Street, is the huge Kelvin Hall, which houses the national indoor running track and sports complex, as well as the Transport Museum. The name may lack appeal but this is one of the city's most fascinating museums. There are collections of trams, trains, motor cars, horsedrawn vehicles, bicycles, motorbikes, as well as a whole

! Visitors can access Kelvingrove museum and gallery from the back as well as the front, lending weight to one of Glasgow's most popular urban myths, that it was mistakenly built back to front and when the architect found out he was so distraught he actually jumped from one of the towers.

Best

Things to do in the West End

- Sing a few tunes from 'Meet me in St Louis' as you play on the trams in the **Transport Museum**, p68.
- Immerse yourself in history at **Glasgow University** and the **Hunterian Museum**, p69.
- Browse around the quirky, bohemian shops in **Byres Road**, p72.
- If the weather's fine, take a stroll along the **Forth and Clyde Canal** towpath, or the **Kelvin Walkway**, p75.
- Sample a blast of hot, spicy cooking and jangly music at **Mother India**, one of a clutch of great Indian restaurants at the west end of Sauchiehall Street, p156.

room dedicated to models of Clyde-built ships. Everything you ever wanted to know about the history of transport but were too uninterested to ask? Well, this place will change all that. There's also a reconstruction of a 1938 cobbled street, an old Underground station and a cinema showing old films of Glaswegians heading 'doon the watter'. Something for everyone, as they say in the tourist brochures, and a great place for kids, large and small.

Glasgow University and the Hunterian Museum

University: University Av, **T** 0141-330 5511, www.gla.ac.uk. *Mon-Sat 0930-1700; Sun 1400-1700 May-Sep only. Free.* Hunterian Museum: University Av, **T** 0141-330 4221, www.hunterian.gla.ac.uk. *Mon-Sat 0930-1700. Free. Map 3, G4/5, p255*

The university's roots date back to 1451, when Pope Nicholas V authorized William Turnbull, Bishop of Glasgow, to found a seat of learning in the city. At first there was just an arts faculty, and lectures were held in the cathedral crypt and neighbouring monastery. In 1660 the university moved to new premises, the 'Old

University challenge

Sir George Gilbert Scott's Gothic university building is one of the West End's most defining features. The large student population lends this part of the city its vitality and energy.

College', in the High Street. This complex of fine buildings, quadrangles and gardens, was sadly demolished in 1870 when the University moved west to its present site, on Gilmorehill, overlooking Kelvingrove Park.

The university building designed by Sir George Gilbert Scott in 1866-86 represents one of his finest achievements, a supremely coherent Gothic structure loosely based on the layout of the Old College and retaining a few fragments from the original, namely the Lion and Unicorn balustrade on the stone staircase opposite the Principal's Lodging and part of the gatehouse, which forms the façade of the Pearce Lodge. Soaring over all this Gothic glory is the Flemish tower, the university's defining feature, which seems almost omnipresent in the West End. Other features worth seeking out are the university chapel, the Randolph Hall and the Bute Hall, added in 1878, which is now used for graduation and other ceremonies.

Beneath the Hunterian Museum is the **University Visitor Centre**, which features interactive displays on the university and a coffee bar. Historical tours are also available.

Contained within the university buildings is the Hunterian Museum, named after William Hunter (1718-83), a student at the university in the 1730s. His bequest to the university of his substantial collections led to the establishment of the Hunterian Museum in 1807, Scotland's oldest public museum. It has displays of social history, archaeology and geology and includes Roman relics from the Antonine Wall and one of the largest coin collections in Britain. There's also a **Zoology Museum**, housed in the Graham Kerr Building, a few minutes' walk from the main museum.

Hunterian Art Gallery

82 Hillhead St, **T** 0141-330 5431, www.hunterian.gla.ac.uk.
Mon-Sat 0930-1700. Mackintosh House closed daily 1230-1330. Free. To get there take buses 44 or 59 from the city centre (Hope St), or the Underground to Hillhead and walk. Opposite the entrance is the student refectory. ***Map 3, F4, p254***

This gallery is in a modern building containing the more interesting part of Hunter's bequest, the fabulous art collection. The gallery holds an important collection of European paintings including works by **Rembrandt**, **Koninck**, **Rubens**, **Pissaro** and **Rodin**, as well as 18th century British portraits by **Ramsay** and **Reynolds**. There is also a fine collection of Scottish 19th and 20th century paintings, including major displays of paintings by the Scottish Colourists, **Fergusson**, **Peploe**, **Cadell** and **Hunter**. The pièce de résistance is the huge collection of works by the American painter, **James McNeill Whistler**. There are some 70 paintings and a selection of his personal possessions (including his specially made long-handled paintbrushes) on show, making it the largest display of his work outside the USA. Among the works are many of his distinctive full-length portraits and some moody depictions of the River Thames. The gallery's graphics collection, one of the most important in Scotland, holds 30,000 prints, which can be seen by prior appointment in the Print Room.

Attached to the gallery is the **Mackintosh House**, a stunning reconstruction of the main interiors from 78 Southpark Avenue, the Glasgow home of Charles Rennie Mackintosh and his wife, Margaret MacDonald, from 1906 to 1914. A stairway leads to an introductory display containing drawings and designs, including those for his major buildings, furniture and interiors. From there you are led into cool rooms, lovingly reconstructed and furnished with some 80 original pieces of his furniture. These give the perfect example of just why this innovative designer and architect is so revered. Among the highlights are the studio drawing room, decorated in white and flooded with natural light, and the guest bedroom, a later commission, with its bold and dazzling geometric designs. When guest George Bernard Shaw was asked if the décor would disturb his sleep, he replied, 'No, I always sleep with my eyes closed.'

★ Byres Road and around

Hillhead Underground. Map 3, D4-F3, p254

Heading west, University Avenue meets Byres Road, the bustling hub of the West End, running south from the Great Western Road past Hillhead Underground. It's an area populated mostly by students and is full of fashionable shops, bars, cafés and restaurants. It's a great place to go shopping on a weekend and ideal for a night out, when it is positively buzzing with energy. Many of the best places are listed on p175. Just off Byres Road, and very close to Hillhead Underground is the **Western Baths Club** (**T** 0141-576 0294). It was founded in 1876 and is an original Victorian bath house. The pool still has a trapeze and exercise rings hanging above it, and there is also a gym, sauna, turkish bath and steam room. Temporary membership is available (for £15 for a week) and they are also happy to let you have a look around if you just want to see the interior.

Botanic Gardens

730 Great Western Rd, **T** 0141-334 2422. *Daily 0700 till dusk. Kibble Palace and all glasshouses open daily 1000-1645 in summer, 1000-1615 in winter. Free. No 89/90 Inner Circle bus or catch the Underground to Hillhead. Map 3, C/D4, p254*

At the top of Byres Road, where it meets the Great Western Road, is the entrance to the Botanic Gardens, a smallish but perfectly formed park where you can lose yourself along the remote paths that follow the wooded banks of the River Kelvin (see p75). The gardens were created to provide medical and botanical students at the university with fresh plant material, but soon became a fashionable place to promenade. There are two large hothouses in the park, one of which is the **Kibble Palace**, built as a conservatory for the Clyde Coast home of Glasgow businessman, John Kibble, and then shipped to its present site in 1873. It was once used for public meetings and British Prime Ministers William Gladstone and Benjamin Disraeli both gave their rectorial addresses here when they became Rectors of the university. The domed glasshouse contains the national collection of tree ferns and temperate plants from around the world. The main glasshouse is more attractive and has 11 sections featuring plants such as cacti, palms, insectivorous plants and palms. The collections of orchids and begonias are outstanding. There is also a herb garden with five beds growing medicinal, culinary, dye and scented plants. The central bed has plants that have historically been used in Scotland. Look out for meadowsweet, used for headaches; coltsfoot used for coughs and chest complaints; and yellow flag iris – the leaves of which give a bright green dye and the rhizomes a black dye which were traditionally used in the Harris tweed industry. In the Outer Hebrides the black dye was used for the cloth from which suits worn on Sundays were made.

West of Byres Road

Fossil Grove, **T** 9592391, www.glasgow.gov.uk, Apr-Sep, Mon-Sat 1000-1700, Sun 1100-1700. Free. *Buses 44, 44C and 44D from city centre to park entrance. Map 1, D2/3, p250*

The Great Western Road continues west, straight as a pool cue, until it finally relents and takes a turn around the salubrious district of **Knightswood**, turning northwest then west to meet the **Dumbarton Road**, east of Dumbarton (see p101). The Dumbarton Road, meanwhile, follows the course of the Clyde. On its way, by the junction with Balshagray Avenue (A739), near the north mouth of the Clyde Tunnel, it skirts **Victoria Park**, home of the **Fossil Grove**, which has a glasshouse containing a grove of fossil tree stumps dating back some 350 million years. Information boards provide explanations of the scientific importance of the site.

Queen's Cross Church

Mackintosh Society: at the junction of Garscube Rd and Maryhill Rd, **T** 0141-946 6600, www.crmsociety.com. *Mon-Fri 1000-1700, Sun 1400-1700. £2, £1 concession. Buses 21, 61 and 91 from Hope St (west side of Central Station), or Underground to St George's Cross and 10 mins walk along Maryhill Rd. Entrance on Springbank Rd. Map 3, C8, p254*

The Queen's Cross Church was the only church Mackintosh designed and it opened for worship in 1899. It's a little bit out of the way but well worth the effort as it is a fascinating piece of architecture. Those who have recently plighted their troth will come away thinking "we want to get married there", and possibly even up sticks and move here just for the privilege of doing so.

The distinctive shape of the church and its dark orangey-brown hue can be appreciated all the way from the foot of Maryhill Road, and as you draw nearer you can also see the style reflected in the immediate surroundings. The interior is beautifully simple, with echoes of the symbolism of his other buildings and the characteristically dramatic interplay of light and space. The highlights are the stained-glass and relief-carving on wood and stonework. The overall effect is impressive yet humble in scale, and the dark wood gives the place a warm feel, unlike many other ecclesiastical buildings.

The church now functions as the headquarters of the **Charles Rennie Mackintosh Society**. There's an information centre, a small display and a gift shop. The church also plays host to regular jazz concerts. Programme details are available from the website or by calling the society.

Ruchill Church

15-17 Shakespeare St, **T** 0141-946 0466. *Mon-Fri 1100-1500, closed Jul/Aug. Free. To get there head northwest from Queen's Cross Church along Maryhill Rd until you reach the turning for Shakespeare St (10-15 mins walk).* *Map 3, A5, p254*

Follow Firhill Road north, across the Forth and Clyde Canal, and you'll reach Ruchill Park, from where you get fantastic views across the whole city and surrounding hills. West of Ruchill Park, and northwest of Queen's Cross Church, is one of Mackintosh's minor treasures, Ruchill Church Hall. It was originally built as a church mission and consists of two halls and two committee rooms, which are still in use.

Kelvin Walkway

There are frequent train services to and from Queen St, also bus 119 from Hope St to Milngavie. *Starting point: map 3, H4, p255*

The Kelvin Walkway follows the **River Kelvin** from Kelvingrove Park through the northwest of the city all the way to **Milngavie** (pronounced *Mull-guy*), a distance of eight miles. Along the way, it crosses underneath the **Forth and Clyde Canal** (see p78) and, with the appropriate maps, you could follow one waterway out and return along the other. The route is flat and fairly easy, though muddy and overgrown in places, so you'll need sturdy footwear.

The route starts on Bunhouse Road, outside the Kelvin Hall, by the bridge on the Old Dumbarton Road, close to Kelvin Hall Underground. Follow the right bank of the river, passing the Hunterian Art Gallery and Museum on the right and the university towering over the scene on the left.

Cross the Kelvin Way, the road which runs through Kelvingrove park, and you enter the park by crossing the footbridge over the river. The path passes under Kelvin Bridge. About 400 yards further on the path re-crosses the river to the left bank and goes under the Great Western Road bridge, by Kelvinbridge Underground, then a few hundred yards further on under Belmont Bridge. The path recrosses the river again, where the remains of an old mill can be seen, with the BBC's Queen Margaret Drive studios on the opposite bank. This is the entrance to the **Botanic Gardens** (see p73).

The walkway continues northwest towards Maryhill, passing under the red sandstone Kirklee Bridge and past blocks of high-rise flats on the right. About 500 yards further on it crosses Kelvindale Road and, in another 500 yards, passes beneath the aqueduct that carries the Forth and Clyde Canal above the Kelvin River. You can join the canal towpath here by a path that heads off to the right.

To continue along the walkway, walk through the arch and under the small bridge (do not follow the track that heads left towards the river). You pass under another bridge at Skaethorn Road, and follow the river as it curves to the right. Up ahead, on the opposite bank, you'll see a low cliff, and soon after you enter a small wood.

The Kelvin Walkway leaves the riverbank at Dalsholm Road. From the bridge, head up Dalsholm Road, cross Maryhill Road and enter Maryhill Park. From the top of the park there are views across the entire city and east to the Campsie Hills. On the other side of the park, follow Caldercuilt Road back towards the river.

The path then follows the river as it meanders through open countryside. After passing through a wooded area, the path enters an open stretch and heads along the top of an earth flood-dyke, passing a very smelly rubbish tip in the process. Keep going until you reach Balmore Road. Cross the road and continue along the dyke till it reaches the point where the Allander Water flows into the Kelvin.

Here the path leaves the Kelvin and turns northwards to follow the right bank of the Allander back towards Balmore Road. Cross Balmore Road and the B8049 into Bearsden, and rejoin the Allander Water. The path then gently descends towards Milngavie, crossing a footbridge and then joining the Glasgow Road in town. Head up the hill and turn left into Station Road to reach the train station.

Mugdock Country Park

Craigallian Rd, 2 miles north of Mingavie, **T** 0141-956 6100, www.mugdock-country-park.org.uk. *Dawn to dusk every day. Trains from Glasgow Central then bus 69 from Milngavie station to park.*

Eight miles north of Glasgow city centre, near the select suburb of Milngavie, is Mugdock Country Park. The park is well worth a visit. Here, you can pretend that you're in the country as there are 750 acres of unspoilt grounds and ancient woodlands to explore. As well as some good walking, there are a few sites of historic interest in the park. Near Mugdock Loch is the 13th century **Mugdock Castle**, which was once home to the Graham family, supporters of the king. In 1644 the castle was badly damaged by Covenanter troops sent by the Duke of Argyll and in 1649 James Graham was tried as a traitor and hanged. The castle was in the hands of Argyll, till he himself was executed by Charles II in 1660.

Also in the park is **Craigend Castle**, designed by James Smith in 1818 for the Smith family, lairds of Craigend. Ownership of the estate passed on to Sir Andrew Buchanan, ambassador to the Viennese court. Subsequently, it was owned by Sir Harold Yarrow, the Clyde shipbuilder, and George Outram, one of the former owners of the Glasgow Herald.

The **West Highland Way**, which runs for 92 miles to Fort William, begins in Milngavie, only a few hundred yards from the train station, by Allander Water. You can follow the route as far as Craigallian Road and then enter Mugdock park via the Kyber car park, from where there are great views of the city.

Forth and Clyde Canal

T 0141-332 6936, www.wwww.scottishcanals.co.uk. *A series of 'Walk Cards' are available from British Waterways.*
Starting point: map 1, E6, p250

The Forth and Clyde Canal was opened in 1790 and provided a convenient short-cut for trading ships between Northern Europe and North America, linking both coasts of Scotland. The canal became Glasgow's main trading link until the Clyde was dredged. In 1962 it was closed, but was recently granted £32 million of lottery funding for a major regeneration programme and now offers a pleasant and easy walk through a little-known part of the city. The tow-path starts at Port Dundas, just north of the M8 by Craighall Road, and runs to the main canal at the end of Lochburn Road, off Maryhill Road. It then runs east all the way to Kirkintilloch and Falkirk, and west, through Maryhill and Drumchapel to Bowling and the River Clyde. It passes through sections of bleak industrial wasteland, but there are many interesting sights and open, rural stretches along the way.

● *For those who wish to combine their walk with lunch, or a drink, the Lock 27 pub is recommended (see p176).*

Along the Clyde

This chilly grey river has, for centuries, played a vital role in the life of the city, providing employment and entertainment for generations of Glaswegians. It was on the Clyde that Glasgow's famous shipyards grew and flourished; on the Clyde that goods were transported and unloaded to be traded by the city's merchants; and on the Clyde that poor people escaped from the grime of the industrial city. The Clyde has also always been an important link to the wider world and has helped to give Glasgow its cosmopolitan appeal and restless energy. It was the route taken by thousands of Glaswegians seeking a new life in other parts of the world, and also brought migrants to the city.

▸▸ *See Sleeping p78, Bars and clubs p178*

Sights

★ Glasgow Science Centre

50 Pacific Quay, **T** 0141-420 5000, www.gsc.org.uk. *Science Mall daily 1000-1800. IMAX Theatre Sun-Wed 1100-1700, Thu-Sat 1000-2030 (hours subject to change). Science Mall £6.95, £4.95 concession. IMAX or Glasgow Tower £5.95, £4.45 concession. Discounts available if purchasing tickets to more than 1 attraction. Arriva buses 23 and 24 go to the Science Centre from Jamaica St, or simply walk across the footbridge from the SECC and Armadillo.* *Map 1, F4, p250 See also Kids, p225*

After all the years of neglect, it is good to see that Glasgow's newest, most dazzling development is to be found on the Clyde. The £75 million Glasgow Science Centre, opened in late 2001 on the south side of the Clyde on the former garden festival site. This complex aims to demystify science, bringing it to life with imaginative displays and interactive exhibits covering everything from the human body to the internet. Kids love it – as do their parents.

The heart of the Centre is the **Science Mall**, with its three floors of themed exhibits. The first floor looks at how we experience the world, the second floor looks at science in action and the third floor looks at how science affects us daily. You can find anything here from laboratories where you can study your own skin or hair through a microscope, to an infrared harp which you play with a beam of light. The **Glasgow Tower**, the tallest free standing building in Scotland at 300ft, has experienced some engineering problems and at the time of writing it's shut. Check the website for when it is due to reopen as it's worth a look at each of its floors that have different themes and take a serious look at aspects of science, from the basic rules of nature to cloning and genetic modification. At the top there's a viewing cabin and great views over Glasgow and the Clyde. The Centre also contains an **IMAX** theatre.

SECC and Clyde Auditorium

T 0141-248 3000, **F** 0141-226 3423, www.secc.co.uk.
To get there, take a train from Central Station to the Exhibition Centre Station (5 mins), otherwise it's a long walk from the city centre.
Map 3, L4, p255

Opposite the Science Centre is the Scottish Exhibition and Conference Centre (SECC), built in 1987 on the site of the former Queen's Dock. It is now the country's top rock and pop venue. Next door is the controversial Clyde Auditorium, known locally as the 'Armadillo', which was designed by Sir Norman Foster and built in 1997. It also hosts pop and rock concerts as well as business conferences.

Tall Ship at Glasgow Harbour

100 Stobcross Rd, **T** 0800-328 1373, www.thetallship.com. *Mar-Oct daily 1000-1700, Nov-Feb daily 1100-1600 £4.50, £3.95 concession. Trains from Central Station to Finnieston/SECC. Map 3, K2, p255*

Further west, also on the north bank of the Clyde, is a romantic-looking sailing ship, the *SS Glenlee* – otherwise known as the Tall Ship at Glasgow Harbour. Launched in 1896, this three-masted ship was built on the Clyde and is one of only five Clydebuilt sailing ships that remain afloat in the world. She circumnavigated the globe four times and carried cargo as varied as coal, grain and even guano – which was transported from Chile to the European ports of Antwerp and Rotterdam to be used as fertiliser. The ammonia fumes from the guano were so pungent they

A bit of fun
Norman Foster's controversial Clyde Auditorium, or 'Armadillo' as it's better known, brings some welcome humour and inventiveness, standing next to the concrete bulk of the SECC.

corroded the lining of sailors' noses and even killed the ship's cat occasionally. The Glenlee was saved from the scrapyard in 1992 and has now been restored. Exhibitions on board provide a vivid insight into the daily lives of the sailors and the conditions on-board ship in 1896 (not fragrant – especially when carrying all that guano).

Clydebuilt

King's Inch Rd, Braehead, **T** 0141-886 1013, www.scottishmaritime museum.org. *Mon-Thu and Sat 1000-1800, Sun 1100-1700. £3.50, £1.75 concession. Clydebuilt is at junction 25a (westbound) off the M8 or can be reached on the Clyde waterbus (see p29). Map 1, D1, p250*

Further west still, at **Braehead**, is Clydebuilt, a museum charting the close relationship between Glasgow and the Clyde. There's an audiovisual presentation on the history of shipbuilding and

A fishy tale

It's not every day you hear about a saint colluding in an act of adultery, but trust Glasgow to come up with an example of such an unsaintly act.

Though it's many years since salmon were caught in the Clyde, two appear in the city's coat of arms. Each fish has a ring in its mouth, recalling an old local legend. Queen Languoreth of Strathclyde was given a ring by her husband, King Rydderch Hael, but then promptly gave it to her lover. The king found the lover wearing the ring as he slept beside the Clyde. He took the ring and threw it into the water, and then went to his wife and asked her to show it to him. The Queen prayed to St Mungo for help, and immediately one of her servants miraculously found the ring in the mouth of a salmon he had caught. The king then had to accept his wife's pleas of innocence, despite knowing something fishy was going on.

displays on a whole range of themes related to the river, from the cotton and tobacco trades, to emigration and immigration. There are also plenty of hands-on activities for kids and temporary exhibitions throughout the year. The museum is very close to **Braehead Shopping Centre** which has all the usual high street outlets as well as cafés, and skating and curling rinks.

Clyde Walkway

Starting point: map 1, F6, p250

The Clyde Walkway is a 40-mile walking route which is being developed to link the centre of Glasgow to the Falls of Clyde at Lanark, via the Clyde Valley (see p109). Sections of the waterfront walk are still rather empty and depressing but the central part, between Victoria Bridge and the SECC, is interesting and takes in some of the more distinguished bridges and much of Glasgow's proud maritime heritage.

Start the walk at **Victoria Bridge**, built in 1854 to replace the 14th-century Old Glasgow Bridge, and continue past the graceful Suspension Bridge, built in 1851 as a grand entrance to the 'new town' on the south bank. You can cross from here to Carlton Place, whose impressive Georgian façades have been restored and which were designed to front the never-completed 'new town'.

Back on the north bank is **Customs House Quay** and, further west beyond George V Bridge, **Broomielaw Quay**. From here, Henry Bell's Comet inaugurated the world's first commercial passenger steamboat service. This was also the departure point for many Scottish emigrants to North America, and later, for thousands of holidaying locals heading 'doon the watter' to the Firth of Clyde seaside resorts.

Further west, at **Anderston Quay**, is the **PS Waverley Terminal**. The *PS Waverley* is the world's last sea-going paddle steamer and still operates on the Clyde (see p28). Between here and the SECC is the huge 53 m-high **Finnieston Crane**, which was once used for lifting railway locomotives at a time when Glasgow was the largest builder of these in the world outside North America. Close by is the **Rotunda** (1890-96) which was once the northern terminal of the complex of tunnels which took horse-traffic and pedestrians under the river, until the building of a new road-tunnel in the 1960s. The Rotunda has been restored as a restaurant complex. Soon you come to the SECC and the Clyde Auditorium, or the 'Armadillo', p80, sitting opposite the silvery new Glasgow Science Centre. A short distance west is the Tall Ship at Glasgow Harbour (see p80).

Alternatively head east from Victoria Bridge along Bridgegate, or Briggait (see p44), then cut back on to Saltmarket and enter Glasgow Green via the huge arch opposite the old Sheriff Court. Head across the Green, under King's Bridge and alongside

Crane in vain

The Finnieston Crane stands on the banks of the Clyde, a legacy of Glasgow's proud shipbuilding tradition. The sun may have set on the city's heavy industries but the crane has re-invented herself as a major tourist destination.

Fletcher's Haugh, where Bonnie Prince Charlie reviewed his Jacobite troops in January 1746 after their long march north and only a few months before defeat at Culloden. The Walkway then goes under Shawfield Road at Rutherglen Bridge and follows the river. The path begins to narrow then passes under a railway bridge and a road bridge, before following the river in a U-turn, with Celtic Park football ground visible ahead. The path runs in a straight line between the river and the boundary fence of Belvedere Hospital, then reaches more attractive open countryside and runs along the top of a wooded embankment.

As you pass below some pylons, keep to the path as it curves away from the river. It rejoins the river and then crosses the Tollcross Burn before curving round to the right. It goes under a stone railway bridge, then a road bridge and then continues southwards and swings eastwards. The crossing point of the river is now **Cambuslang Bridge** following the closure of the disused Carmyle railway viaduct. Cross the bridge and turn left along Bridge Street till you reach a roundabout. Go straight across and follow Westburn Road, with the golf course on the right and factories on the left. After 500 yards, past the turning for Westburn Farm Road, Westburn Road branches left. Continue along it for a half a mile further then turn left along Newton Avenue. Follow this road as it crosses Newton Burn and about 400 yards on, where the road turns sharply to the right, you can rejoin the Walkway, which heads north towards the river.

The path shadows the river for about a mile, then you leave the Clyde where it joins a smaller river, the **Rotten Calder**. Here the path turns south and follows the Rotten Calder for some 400 yards to where a footbridge crosses it by a railway bridge. Cross a stile and turn right onto a farm road which goes under the railway line, before climbing steadily uphill to join the Blantyre Road (B758).

Turn right and head up this road for 50 yards till you see the path again on the other side of the road. From here the path is easy to follow. About half a mile further on the path rejoins the river. Cross the footbridge into **Uddingston** and then turn right and follow the path along the riverbank. It heads through a pleasant wooded area for about a mile. As it follows a bend in the river it then climbs to the top of a gorge to reach a gate. Go through the gate and you're at **Bothwell Castle**, which marks the the end of the walk. There are regular trains from Uddingston station to Glasgow Central station (see p22).

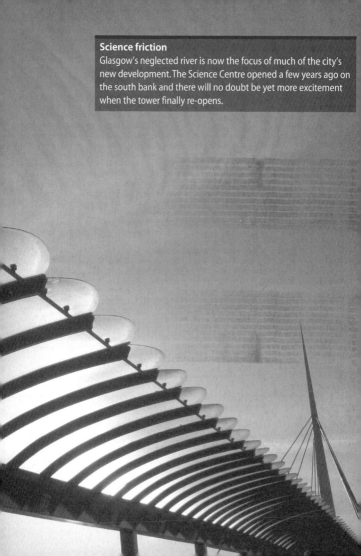

Science friction

Glasgow's neglected river is now the focus of much of the city's new development. The Science Centre opened a few years ago on the south bank and there will no doubt be yet more excitement when the tower finally re-opens.

South of the Clyde

First impressions can be misleading and most visitors' first sight of Glasgow's southern parts will be less than uplifting as they head in from the airport past a great swathe of industrial units and warehouses. South of the River Clyde is a part of Glasgow largely unknown to most tourists, except perhaps for the ***Gorbals****, a name once synonymous with urban violence, but now more likely to enervate rather than inspire fear.*

Venture further south and you enter a different world: the sedate suburbs and parks of ***South Side****. Here you'll find two of the city's most notable attractions, the Burrell Collection and Pollok House, both set in the sylvan surrounds of Pollok Country Park. There are other reasons to venture south of the river, not least of which is Charles Rennie Mackintosh's* ***House for an Art Lover*** *in Bellahouston Park. Further east is another stop on the Mackintosh trail, the* ***Scotland Street School Museum****, and to the south, in Cathcart, is* ***Holmwood House****, Alexander 'Greek' Thomson's architectural masterpiece, which stands overlooking the* ***White Cart****, another of the city's bucolic waterways.*

▸▸ *See Sleeping p135, Eating and drinking p160, Bars and clubs p178*

 Sights

Scotland Street School Museum

225 Scotland St, **T** 0141-287 0500, www.glasgowmuseums.com. *Mon-Thu 1000-1700, Fri-Sun 1100-1700. Free. Take the underground to Shields Rd, or buses 89, 90, 96 and 97 from the city centre.* *Map 1, F5, p250* *See also Kids, p226*

Directly opposite Shields Road Underground station is another of Charles Rennie Mackintosh's great works, the Scotland Street School, which opened in 1906 and closed in 1979. The entire school has been preserved as a museum of education and offers a wonderfully

Best

Things to do south of the Clyde

- Catch a show at the **Citizens' Theatre**, home to some of the UK's most exciting and innovative drama, p188.
- Relive your childhood at **Scotland Street School Museum**, another of Charles Rennie Mackintosh's class designs, p88.
- Marvel at the genius of Alexander 'Greek' Thomson in **Holmwood House**, an exquisite architectural gem, p94.
- Escape the city traffic with a stroll in **Pollok Park**, p92.
- It doesn't really need saying, but don't miss the outstanding **Burrell Collection**, p91.

evocative experience. There's a fascinating collection of school memorabilia and reconstructed classrooms dating from Victorian times up to the 1960s, as well as changing rooms, a science room and headmaster's office.

This is the most modern of Mackintosh's buildings and is notable for its semi-cylindrical glass stairtowers, the magnificent tiled entrance hall and its customary mastery of the interplay of light and space. The school was recently refurbished and new facilities have been introduced, including a lift, an audiovisual theatre and computer activities for children. There's also a café, but don't worry, they don't serve authentic school food.

Govan Old Parish Church

840 Govan Rd, **T** 0141-445 1941. *1st Wed in Jun to 3rd Sat in Sep, Wed 1030-1230, Wed, Thu, Sat 1300-1600, other times by appointment. Free. Take the Underground to Govan. Map 1, E3, p250*

On Govan Road, close to Govan Underground station, is one of Govan's forgotten sights. This old church is worth seeking out. Not only does it stand on an ancient Christian site, but it also has a unique collection of carved stones dating back to the 9th century.

There's also a sarcophagus which is covered in fine carvings, and a good collection of stained-glass windows.

● *Nearby is one of the city's other religious centres, Ibrox, home to the Glasgow Rangers.*

House for an Art Lover

Bellahouston Park, **T** 0141-353 4770, www.houseforanartlover.co.uk *Apr-Sep Mon-Wed 1000-1600, Thu-Sun 1000-1300; Oct-Mar Sat-Sun 1000-1300. Call for weekday access times. £3.50, £2.50 concession. Take the Underground to Ibrox station and walk (15 mins), or bus No 9 from Hope St or the No 57 bus from Union St or Jamaica St.* ***Map 1, F3, p250***

A short distance from Ibrox Stadium, across the M8 motorway, is **Bellahouston Park**, site of the most recent addition to the Charles Rennie Mackintosh trail, the House for an Art Lover. The building was designed in 1901 as an entry to a competition run by a German design magazine, the brief being to create a lavish country house for an art lover. The interior and exterior had to be a coherent work of art. Building never went ahead during Mackintosh's lifetime and it was not until 1989 that construction began, in accordance with his original drawings. The building was not completed until 1996, when it became a centre for Glasgow School of Art postgraduate students, though a number of rooms on the lower floor are open to the public.

Mackintosh worked closely with his wife on the design of the house and there is distinctive evidence of her influence, especially in the exquisite Music Room with its elaborate symbolism, particularly the rose motif, which is used throughout. But though the detail is, as ever, intense, the overall effect is one of space and light. The exterior of the house is equally impressive and totally original. On the ground floor is an excellent café, which is popular with locals.

★ The Burrell Collection

Pollok Country Park, **T** 0141-287 2550, www.glasgowmuseums.com. *Mon-Thu and Sat 1000-1700, Fri and Sun 1100-1700. Free. Buses 45, 48A and 57 from the city centre (Union St) pass the park gates on Pollokshaws Rd, also buses 34 and 34A from Govan Underground station. From the gates it's a 10-min walk to the gallery, or there's a twice-hourly bus. There are also trains from Central Station to Pollokshaws West station. A taxi from the city centre costs £6-7. Car parking at the Burrell Collection costs £1.50.* *Map 1, G3, p250*

Three miles southwest of the city centre this is Glasgow's top attraction and a must on any visit. It stands in the extensive wooded parklands of **Pollok Country Park**. The magnificent collection contains some 8,500 art treasures, donated to the city in 1944 by the shipping magnate William Burrell (1861-1958), who sold his shipping interests in order to devote the remainder of his life to collecting art. He began collecting in the 1880s, and in 1917 bought Hutton Castle near Berwick-on-Tweed to house his collection. There it stayed, even after his bequest to the city, as he stipulated that all the works in his collection be housed in one building in a rural setting – since he was concerned about the possible damage caused by the pollution that then blackened Glasgow. It wasn't until the Clean Air Act of the 1960s and the council's acquisition of Pollok Park, that a suitable site was found and the modern, award-winning gallery could be built – with £450,000 donated by Burrell. The building opened to the public in 1983.

The collection includes ancient Greek, Roman and Egyptian artefacts, a huge number of oriental art pieces, and numerous works of medieval and post-medieval European art, including tapestries, silverware, stained-glass, textiles, sculpture and exquisitely lit stained glass. The tapestries are particularly fine and date from the late 15th and 16th centuries. There's also an impressive array of paintings by **Rembrandt**, **Degas**, **Pissaro**, **Bellini** and **Manet** amongst many others. Look out too for **Rodin**'s famous sculpture *The Thinker*.

The gallery is a stunning work of simplicity and thoughtful design, which allows the visitor to enjoy this vast collection to the full. The large, floor-to-ceiling windows afford sweeping views over the surrounding woodland and allow a flood of natural light to enhance the treasures on view. Some sections of the gallery are reconstructions of rooms from Hutton Castle and incorporated into the structure are carved stone Romanesque doors. There's also a café and restaurant on the lower ground floor.

Pollok House and Country Park

T 0141-616 6410, www.nts.org.uk *Daily 1000-1700. £5, £3.75 child/concession. Nov-Mar free. Entry to the park is from Pollokshaws Rd, or Haggs Rd if you're on foot. Car parking is at the Burrell Collection and costs £1.50. T0141-632 9299.* *Map 1, G/H3, p250*

Also in Pollok Country Park, a 10-minute walk from the Burrell, is Pollok House, designed by William Adam and completed in 1752. This was once the home of the Maxwell family, who owned most of southern Glasgow until well into the last century. It contains one of the best collections of Spanish paintings in Britain, including works by Goya, El Greco and Murillo. There are also paintings by William Blake, as well as glass, silverware, porcelain and furniture. The most interesting part of the house, however, are the servants' quarters downstairs, which give you a real insight into life 'below stairs', with rows of bells waiting to summon servants to any part of the house. There's a good tearoom in the old kitchens.

If the weather's fine, the park is worth exploring. There are numerous trails throughout the woods and meadows and guided walks with the countryside rangers, who are located in the grounds. Most of the routes start from the free car park at Pollok House. You can wander to your heart's content and eventually you're bound to end up back where you started. There are two golf courses within the park grounds, as well as a herd of highland cattle.

Queen's Park

Take a train from Central Station to Queen's Park, then it's a 5-min walk down Victoria Rd to the gates on Queen's Dr. *Map 1, G5, p250*

To the east of Pollok Country Park, by Pollokshaws Road, is Queen's Park, named after Mary, Queen of Scots, whose reign ended after defeat here at the Battle of Langside, in 1568. A memorial outside the park marks the site of the battle. It's a pleasant place for a stroll and the views north across the city make it even more enjoyable.

Scottish Football Museum

Hampden Park, **T** 0141-616 6139, www.scottishfootballmuseum.com.
Mon-Sat 1000-1700, Sun 1100-1700. £5, £2.50 concession.
Tour of the stadium £2.50 (£5 if not visiting museum). Regular trains to Mount Florida station from Central station (turn left out of station and head straight downhill till you see the stadium; there are no signs. Buses 5, 7, 12, 31, 37, 75, 89, 90 or 44A.
Map 1, G/H3, p250 See also Kids, p225

South of Queen's Park, in Mount Florida, is Hampden Park, home of Scottish football and once the largest football ground in Britain, with a capacity of 135,000. When full, as was often the case, the famous 'Hampden roar' could be heard for miles around. Nowadays, the capacity is a mere 52,000. Hampden is also the home of the new Scottish Football Museum, which describes the history of the game in Scotland. This may strike some as a rather masochistic idea given some of the more infamous and embarrassing episodes, but there have been highs (Wembley '67 and Lisbon '69) as well as lows (Wembley '66 and Argentina '78). The museum is very large and includes a huge range of football memorabilia. It manages to avoid the obvious pitfall of overloading on Celtic and Rangers to the exclusion of all else and presents a very balanced view of Scottish football through the years. Most interesting are the more obscure details and the audio sets relating strories from players and fans (in particular the one about the Celtic supporters burning parts of their bus to keep warm on the long trip north to Aberdeen). It's all here, from the minutes of the very first meeting of Queen's Park, Scotland's first football club – dated 9th July 1867 – to advertising on team shirts. You can also get a guided tour of Hampden Park.

★ Holmwood House

61-63 Netherlee Rd, Cathcart, **T** 0141-637 2129, www.nts.org.uk. *Easter-31 Oct, daily 1330-1730, but access may be restricted at certain times; phone first. £3.50, £2.60 child/concession. Trains every ½ hr to Cathcart from Central Station, or take bus 44A or 44D from Sauchiehall St, or 66 from Argyle St opposite St Enoch Centre, to Cathcart Bridge, next to the train station. From the bridge turn onto Rhannon Rd and walk up it for 10 mins till you see the sign for Holmwood.*
Map 1, I5, p250

Holmwood House was designed by Alexander 'Greek' Thomson, Glasgow's greatest Victorian architect, who is now internationally recognised as one of Scotland's most original designers. Thomson was a brilliant exponent of the Greek Revival and his achievement at Holmwood was described as thus, by architect Thomas Gildard in 1888: "If architecture be poetry in stone and lime – a great temple an epic – this exquisite little gem, at once classic and picturesque, is as complete, self-contained and polished as a sonnet".

The building is a work of genuine originality and has become a monument of international importance, as Thomson was the first modern architect to apply a Greek style to a free, asymmetrical composition. The house also includes features reminiscent of Frank Lloyd Wright, which pre-date the great American architect by some 40 years. Thomson, like Robert Adam before him and Charles Rennie Mackintosh afterwards, exerted complete control over the interiors as well as the exterior. He designed everything in the house and conservation work is revealing very beautiful and elaborate stencilled decoration and friezes with Greek motifs.

The house was built for James Couper, a paper manufacturer, between 1857 and 1858, at a cost of £3,600. After Couper's death in 1877, Holmwood remained in possession of his trustees until 1909, when it was sold to a Mrs Anne Smith or Simpson. It has had several owners since, the most recent prior to the National Trust for Scotland (NTS) being The Sisters of Our Lady of the Missions, who acquired the house in 1858 and turned it into a primary school. In 1967, the local education authority took over the management of the school, until its eventual closure in 1992. The sisters moved to other premises and granted an option over the property to a developer, who proposed the construction of 93 flats and houses in the grounds. This caused concern and, thanks to the strong opposition of the newly formed Alexander Thomson Society, Glasgow City Council refused planning permission, to their eternal credit. The developer withdrew from their option, thus enabling the NTS to acquire the house in 1994. The Trust embarked on an extensive conservation project, with financial help from various sources, and Holmwood was opened to the public in 1998. Work is ongoing and it will take several years to fully restore Holmwood to its former glory.

The grounds of Holmwood slope gently down to the wooded valley of White Cart Water and are dominated by some magnificent sequoia trees. It's the perfect spot for a picnic. A lovely walk – described below – follows the river as it flows through Linn Park.

White Cart

Nearest train station Cathcart Map 1, I5, p250

The grounds of Holmwood look across the White Cart Water, one of the South Side's rural waterways, which flows through the middle of **Linn Park**. The park gets its name from the linn, or waterfall, over which the river cascades on its route through the lovely wooded glen towards **Snuff Mill Bridge**. A riverside walkway follows the White Cart through the park and can be joined at several points along its length.

A convenient starting point for those visiting Holmwood is Snuff Mill Bridge, on Snuff Mill Road, which is only a five-minute walk from Cathcart station and can be reached by turning off Rhannon Road.

Snuff Mill Bridge dates from the 18th century and at one time was the only crossing of White Cart Water, carrying the main road from Glasgow to Ayr. On the opposite bank is the grain mill, which was built in the 18th century, then switched production to cardboard in 1812, and two years later, to snuff milling. The original mill has long gone and some of the later buildings have been coverted into flats. From the bridge, a flight of steps leads into Linn Park. Follow the path, with the river on your left, then cross Millholm Road and the paths drops closer to the river. Wildlife is abundant here and you're likely to see kingfishers, wood pigeons, chaffinches, grey squirrels, wood mice, kestrels, dippers and rabbits, to name but a few.

The path passes the site of the old **Millholm Paper Mill**, which was owned by the Robert Couper and his brother James, who had Holmwood House designed for him by 'Greek' Thomson. The path continues through the wooded glen to reach Halfpenny Bridge, passing the linn which can be heard long before it's seen when the river is in spate. Cross the river by the pretty bridge, also called the White Bridge, which is said to get its name from the decorative circular holes in the spans.

Once across the river, head along an avenue of lime trees to reach Linn House, the mansion built as a summer home for the Campbell family. The park's countryside rangers are now based in the house. Head north from here along a tarmac road, with the golf course up on the right. After about 300 yards the road swings round to the right; here you should follow the tarmac path which leads down to the river. The path first runs downhill, then changes to a gravel surface past a grassy area. It then heads through woods before reaching Snuff Mill Road, which leads you back to Snuff Mill Bridge.

Museums and galleries

- **The Burrell Collection** Top dog amongst the city's art collections, featuring treasures such as Rodin's Thinker, p91.
- **Centre for Contemporary Arts (CCA)** Great space, shame about some of the exhibitions, p62.
- **Clydebuilt** Charts the history of shipbuilding in the city, p81.
- **The Gallery of Modern Art** Features contemporary artists from around the world, p37.
- **Heatherbank Museum of Social Work** Glasgow Caledonian University Campus, Cowcaddens Rd, **T** 0141-331 8637, *Mon-Fri 0900-1600, free.*
- **Hunterian Art Gallery** Fabulous art collection featuring a huge number of works by Whistler and the Mackintosh House, a reconstruction of CRM's former home, p71.
- **Hunterian Museum** Scotland's oldest public museum has displays of social history, archaeology and geology, p69.
- **The Lighthouse** This Charles Rennie Mackintosh building features a changing programme of temporary exhibitions associated with architecture and design, p54.
- **Marine Life Museum** Excellent aquarium sited on the little island of Great Cumbrae, p103.
- **McLellan Galleries** Temporary home to some of the major artworks from the Kelvingrove Art Gallery until its re-opening in 2005, p61.
- **Museum of Scottish Country Life** Little-known out-of-town attraction that puts the cult into agriculture, p110.
- **People's Palace** Superb introduction to the city's colourful past with the calming Winter Gardens at the rear, p48.
- **Pollok House** Contains one of the best collections of Spanish paintings in the UK, p92.

Listings

Museums and galleries

- **Royal Highland Fusiliers Military Museum** Military history with medals, uniforms and weapons, p62.
- **St Mungo Museum of Religious Life and Art** Displays on the world's six major religions, p50.
- **Science Centre** Huge new development that boldly aims to demystify science with lots of interactive exhibits and loud noises, p79.
- **Scotland Street School Museum** Dull-sounding museum of eduction but this Mackintosh building is worth admiring, p88.
- **Scottish Football Museum** Interesting, if painful (for Scots) trawl through the highs and lows of Scottish fitba, p225.
- **Scottish Maritime Museum** A must for shipbuilding enthusiasts, p102.
- **Sharmanka Kinetic Gallery and Theatre** Unusual but entertaining performances by sculptures made from old junk, p43.
- **Transport Museum** Sounds enervating but this is a genuinely fascinating museum with old trams to play on, p227.

- *For a full list of smaller private art galleries and details of forthcoming exhibitions pick up a copy of the of* ***The Glasgow Galleries Guide****, www.glasgowgalleries.co.uk, free from any of the featured venues.*

Around Glasgow

Firth of Clyde 101 The days of the Clyde steamers heading 'doon the watter' are long gone but the towns and islands of the Firth of Clyde have reinvented themselves as centres for outdoor activities.

Isle of Bute 106 The one-time favourite haunt of Glasgow grannies is now a major cycling destination as well as attaining a patina of cool with 2003's celebrity wedding.

The Clyde Valley 109 Glasgow's hinterland of former coal and steel towns is not the most obvious port of call but here lie some real treasures, such as the New Lanark World Heritage Site.

Loch Lomond and the Campsies 114
Glasgow's very own adventure playground has hills aplenty to climb and Britain's largest inland waterway to mess about on.

Firth of Clyde

West of Glasgow, the banks of the Clyde are still lined with the ghosts of this river's shipbuilding heritage. West of the ***Erskine Bridge****, which connects the north and south banks of the Clyde, is* ***Port Glasgow****, the first of a series of towns which sprawl along the southern coast of the Firth of Clyde. On the northern shores of the river, at* ***Helensburgh****, is the most far-flung outpost on the Mackintosh trail, and south of the Clyde ferry ports of* ***Gourock*** *and* ***Wemyss Bay****, is* ***Largs****, terminal for the short ferry trip to* ***Cumbrae Island****.*

▸▸ *See Sleeping p135, Eating and drinking p161*

Sights

Dumbarton Castle

T 01389-732167. *Apr-Sep daily 0930-1830, Oct-Mar Mon-Sat 0930-1630 Sun 1400-1630, £2.50, £1.90 concession. Trains to Dumbarton Central and Dumbarton East stations run regularly from Helensburgh and Balloch, and from Glasgow Queen St. Get off at Dumbarton East station for the castle.*

Once the capital of the ancient Britons of Strathclyde, **Dumbarton** dates back as far as the fifth century, when it was an important trading centre and of strategic importance. Today, though, it's a pretty awful place, and of little importance to tourists.

It's best to avoid the town and head straight for the spectacular Dumbarton Castle, perched on top of **Dumbarton Rock**, which is surrounded by water on three sides and commands excellent views over the Clyde estuary. This has been a strategic fortress for 2,000 years, though most of the current buildings date from the 18th century or later.

If you're interested in shipbuilding then you should visit the ***Scottish Maritime Museum*** *(Mon-Sat 1000-1600, £1.50), on Castle Street. It has a working ship-model experiment tank – the oldest one in the world, in fact.*

Hill House

Upper Colquhoun St, Helensburgh, **T** 01436-673900, www.nts.org.uk. *Daily 1330-1730. Apr-Oct. £7, concession £5.25. Helensburgh has 2 train stations. The Central station has a regular service (every 30 mins) to and from Glasgow (45 mins). From the station, walk about one and a half miles up Sinclair St, then turn left at Kennedy St and follow the signs.*

Twenty-three miles northwest of Glasgow on the A814, overlooking the Clyde, is the town of **Helensburgh**, best known for its connection with the great Glasgow architect, Charles Rennie Mackintosh. In the upper part of the town is Hill House, one of the best examples of Mackintosh's work. The house was designed for Glasgow publisher Walter Blackie in 1902-04, and is now owned by the National Trust for Scotland. The house is a masterpiece of balanced perfection and artistry and there's much to admire. The attention to detail, the use of natural light, the symbolism of the floral patterns and use of light and dark, hallmarks of Mackintosh's personal art nouveau style, are all very much in evidence. After exploring the house, you can visit the kitchen, which has been tastefully converted into a tearoom (*open 1330-1630*).

! Helensburgh boasts a few very notable connections; both Henry Bell, originator of the steamship, and John Logie Baird, who invented the television, were born here.

Gourock and Wemyss Bay

Regular trains from Glasgow Central.

Thirty miles west of Glasgow is the shabby old seaside resort of Gourock, the terminal for the CalMac ferry to **Dunoon**, on the **Cowal Peninsula** (see p104). Eight miles south of Gourock is Wemyss Bay, departure point for ferries to **Rothesay**, on the **Isle of Bute**. Every summer this place used to be packed full of holidaying Glaswegians heading "doon the watter" to Rothesay, and the magnificent Victorian train station is a proud legacy of those days. Briefly, in September 2003, the train station bar was one of the most fashionable places in the UK, when the likes of Madonna, Kate Moss and Chrissie Hynde stopped off for a drink before catching the ferry to Bute for Stella McCartney's wedding.

Great Cumbrae Island

Trains to Largs from Glasgow Central every hr (1 hr). Ferries leave Largs every 15 mins during the summer and every 30 mins in winter for the 10-min sailing to the slip on the northeast shore. Buses meet the ferry for the 4-mile trip to Millport. The return fare is £3.80 per person and £16.55 per car. Bikes cost £2 return. For more information, contact CalMac, T08705-650000, or at Largs pier, T01475-674134.

South of Wemyss Bay is the pleasant seaside resort of Largs, jumping-off point for the hilly island of Great Cumbrae. At only four miles long and a couple of miles wide, it's ideally suited for a day trip from Glasgow. The only settlement of any size is **Millport**, which is home to Europe's smallest cathedral, the beautiful **Cathedral of the Isles**, built in the mid-19th century (daily 1100-1600 except during services). About a mile east of town is the **Marine Life Museum**, part of Glasgow University Marine Biology department, which contains an excellent aquarium (**T** *01475-530581, Mon-Fri 0930-1215 and 1400-1645, Jul-Sep also Sat, £1.50, 75p children*).

The nicest parts of the island are away from Millport and are best explored by **bike**. The 14-mile main road runs right round the edge of the island, or there's a narrow Inner Circle Road which passes **The Glaidstone** (127 m), the highest point on the island. More information on these cycle routes is available from the Tourist Information Centre, housed in a caravan opposite the post office (*Easter-Sep*). For bike hire see p207. Great Cumbrae is also a major water sports centre and Millport beach is a popular place for windsurfing (see p214 for details).

Cowal Peninsula

Ferries from Gourock to Dunoon (see p26) or A82 to Tarbet and then A815.

The Cowal Peninsula, reaching out into the Firth of Clyde, framed by **Loch Fyne** and **Loch Long**, is a mere stone's throw from Glasgow. Most Glaswegians prefer the seaside resort of Dunoon, accessed by ferry from Gourock, leaving the best parts – namely the forests and mountains of Argyll Forest Park and the very lovely southwest coastline – relatively undisturbed.

Argyll Forest Park

Scottish Citylink buses between Glasgow and Oban stop off at Arrochar (1hr 10 mins to Glasgow), 3 daily in each direction (2 on Sun). Arrochar shares a train station with Tarbet, on the main west-coast line. Trains heading north to Oban (1¾ hrs) or Fort William (2½ hrs) or south to Glasgow (1¼ hrs) stop 3-4 times daily.

The northern part of the peninsula is largely covered by the sprawling Argyll Forest Park, which extends from **Loch Lomond** south to **Holy Loch**. This area contains the most stunning scenery in Cowal, and includes the **Arrochar Alps**, a range of rugged peaks north of Glen Croe which offer some of the best climbing in Argyll. The most famous of these peaks is **Ben Arthur** (881 m), better known as 'The Cobbler', but this, and the other 'Alps', are only for the more serious hill walker. Rather less imposing are the hills south of Glen Croe, between Loch Goil and Loch Long, in an area known as Argyll's Bowling Green (not because it's flat, but an English corruption of the Gaelic Baile na Greine, meaning 'Sunny Hamlet'). There are also numerous footpaths and cycle tracks threading their way through the park, and details of these can be found in the Forestry Commission leaflets available at the tourist office and visitor centre in **Ardgarten** (**T** 01301-702342, *daily Apr-Oct*) which provides useful advice and information on hillwalking and wildlife, as well as organizing various activities.

Southwest Cowal

There are buses from Tighnabruaich to Colintraive 1-2 times daily Mon-Thu (35 mins) for the ferry to Bute (see below), and to Rothesay (once or twice daily Mon-Thu; 1 hr).

One of the most beautiful parts of Argyll is the southwest of Cowal, particularly the route down to the little village of **Tighnabruaich**. The A8003 runs down the west side of Loch Riddon and there are few lovelier sights in the country than the view from this road across the Kyles of Bute, the narrow straits that separate Cowal from the island of Bute. Tighnabruaich gets busy in the summer with visitors who come here to enjoy some of the best sailing on the west coast. Much of the accommodation is booked up by those enrolled at the **Tighnabruaich Sailing School** (**T** 01700-811717), which offers dinghy sailing and windsurfing courses at all levels.

Isle of Bute

*Barely a stone's throw off the south coast of Cowal is the island of **Bute**, another favourite holiday destination for people from Glasgow and Ayrshire, who come here in droves during the busy summer months. But though the island is small (15 miles long by five miles wide), it's deceptively easy to escape the hordes, who tend to congregate around the east coast resort of **Rothesay**, leaving the delights of the sparsely populated **west coast** free for those who enjoy a bit of peace and quiet. Bute has been a popular place since late Victorian times, when a gaggle of Glasgow grannies were to be seen being pushed along the promenade in their bath-chairs under tartan blankets, taking in the invigorating sea air. Now, the island is successfully reinventing itself as a haven for walkers and cyclists, and in 2003 it hit the headlines when it hosted the celebrity-studded wedding of famous fashion designer Stella McCartney.*

▸▸ *See Sleeping p135, Eating and drinking p161*

Bute is easily accessible from Glasgow. Take a train from Glasgow Central to the ferry terminal at Wemyss Bay (1 hr 10 mins), and from there it's a 35-min crossing to Rothesay. There are also buses to Rothesay from Tighnabruaich in southwest Cowal (see above) once or twice a day Mon-Thu (1 hr). Ferries sail daily every 45 mins from 0715 till 1945 (later on Fri, Sat and Sun). For times, **T** 0141-502707. *The one-way trip costs £3.45 per passenger, £13.85 per car and £1 for bikes. Bute can also be reached from the Cowal Peninsula. The A8003 turns off the main A883, which runs right down the west of the peninsula and the east side of Loch Riddon to Colintraive, at the narrowest point in the Kyles, only a few hundred yds wide. A small car/passenger ferry makes the 5-min crossing from Colintraive to Rhubodach, at the northern end of Bute, daily every 30 mins or hr, from 0530-1955 Mon-Sat and 0900-1955 Sun in the summer. The one-way trip costs £1.10 per passenger and £7 per car.*

Sights

Rothesay

Tourist Information Centre: **T** 01700-502151, *daily Apr-Oct, Nov-Mar Mon-Fri.*

The sole town on Bute is Rothesay, a genteel and tasteful Victorian seaside resort, with handsome period mansions lining the broad sweep of bay, elegant promenade lined with palm trees and a distinctive 1920s **Winter Gardens**, now refurbished and housing a cinema, restaurant and Tourist Information Centre. A short walk from the ferry pier is **Rothesay Castle** (**T** 01700-502691.*Apr-Sep Mon-Sat 0930-1830, Sun 1400-1830, Oct-Mar Mon-Sat 0930-1630, Sun 1400-1630, closed Thu-Fri afternoon, £2.50, concession £1.90, children 75p*). Built around the 12th century, the castle was attacked by Vikings, before becoming a favourite with the Stewart kings. It fell into English hands during the Wars of Independence and was retaken by Robert the Bruce in 1311. It was also occupied by Cromwell's New Model Army after the Civil War and partly dismantled, but restoration work has preserved much of this circular, moated ruin.

★ Mount Stuart

3 miles south of Rothesay, **T** 01700-503877, www.mountstuart.com. *May-Sep daily except Tue and Thu. Gardens: 1000-1700; house 1100-1630. Also Sat and Sun in Apr. Closed in late Jul/early Aug for events, check in advance. House and gardens: £7, concession £5.50, children £3, family £17. Buses connect with the arriving ferries at Rothesay and run to Mount Stuart (15 mins).*

One of Bute's main attractions is Mount Stuart, a Victorian Gothic house set in 300 acres of lush woodland gardens. This magnificent architectural fantasy reflects the Third Marquess of Bute's passion for astrology, astronomy, mysticism and religion and the sheer scale and grandeur of the place almost defies the imagination. This is truly one of the great country houses of Scotland and displays breathtaking craftsmanship in marble and stained-glass, as well as a fine collection of family portraits and Italian antiques. Much of the existing house dates from 1877, and was built following a terrible fire which destroyed the original, built in 1719 by the Second Earl of Bute. Equally impressive are the landscaped gardens and woodlands, established by the Third Earl of Bute (1713-92), who advised on the foundation of Kew Gardens in London, and the contemporary visitor centre which houses a restaurant and shop. It's worth spending a whole day here in order to take in the amazing splendour of the house and to explore the beautiful gardens. And if the weather's fine, why not bring a picnic and enjoy the wonderful sea views.

Around Bute

An open-topped double decker bus circles the island. Buses leave from the stop opposite the ferry pier, details from the TIC.

South of Mount Stuart and the village of Kingarth is **Kilchattan Bay**, an attractive bay of pink sands and the start of a fine walk down to **Glencallum Bay**, in the southeastern corner of the island (details from TIC in Rothesay). Southwest of Kilchattan Bay is **St Blane's Chapel**, a 12th-century ruin in a beautifully peaceful spot near the southern tip of the island. The medieval church stands on the site of an earlier monastery, established in the 6th century by St Blane, nephew of St Catan, after whom Kilchattan is named. The ruin can be reached by road from Rothesay, or as part of the walk from Kilchattan Bay. Four miles north of St Blane's, on the west coast, is **Scalpsie Bay**, the nicest beach on the island and a good place for seal-spotting. A little further north is St Ninian's Point, looking across to the island of **Inchmarnock**. At the end of the beach are the ruins of a 6th-century chapel, dedicated to St Ninian.

The Highland-Lowland dividing line passes through the middle of Bute at **Loch Fad**, which separates the hilly and uninhabited northern half of the island and the rolling farmland of the south. The highest point on the island is **Windy Hill** (281 m) in the north, from where there are great views across the island. A less strenuous walk is up Canada Hill, a few miles southwest of Rothesay, above Loch Fad. Walk along Craigmore promenade and turn off at the old pier to **Ardencraig Gardens**. Then continue uphill along the golf course to the top of the hill for great views of the Firth of Clyde. One of the best ways to explore the island is by bike. For cycle hire see p207.

The Clyde Valley

The River Clyde undergoes a series of changes during the journey from its source, 80 miles southeast of Glasgow, through the orchards and market gardens of pretty ***Clydesdale*** *and the abandoned coal mines of North Lanarkshire on its way to the former shipyards of Glasgow. The M74 motorway follows the course of the river, straddled by the valley's two largest towns,* ***Hamilton*** *and* ***Motherwell****, the latter still reeling from the recent closure of its steelworks. Sandwiched between them is* ***Strathclyde Country Park*** *(see p), a huge recreational area which features a 200-acre man-made loch and is massively popular with watersports enthusiasts. The M74 then turns south towards the border with England, while the A72 takes up the task of shadowing the river to Lanark, the most interesting focus of this area, standing as it does beside the fascinating village of* ***New Lanark****.*

▸▸ *See Sleeping p135, Eating and drinking p161*

David Livingstone Centre

165 Station Rd, Blantyre, **T** 01698-823140. *Apr-Dec Mon-Sat 1000-1700, Sun 1230-1700, £3.50, £2.60 child/concession. Trains to Blantyre leave from Glasgow Central every half hour. It's a 20-min journey. Buses run regularly from Buchanan bus station; take bus 63 or 67 for Blantyre and bus 55 or 56 for Bothwell.*

Blantyre, now more of a suburb of Hamilton, is famous as the birthplace of **David Livingstone**, the notable Victorian missionary and explorer, who felt the white man's burden more than most and took off to Africa in 1840 to bring Christianity to the natives. He was born in the humble surroundings of a one-roomed tenement in 1813, and worked in the local cotton mill before educating himself and taking a medical degree. The entire tenement block, has been transformed into the David Livingstone Centre, which tells the story of his life, including his battle against slave traders and that famous meeting with Stanley. There's also an African-themed café, gift shop and garden. The centre is a short walk from the train station.

Museum of Scottish Country Life

Philipshill Rd, Wester Kittochside, East Kilbride, **T** 01355-224181, www.nms.ac.uk. *Daily 1000-1700, £3, £1.50 concession, children free. Take First Bus 31 from the St Enoch Centre in Glasgow to Stewartfield Way, or a train to East Kilbride.*

Located southwest of Blantyre, this museum gives an insight into the lives of people in rural Scotland. Situated on a 170-acre site complete with Georgian farmhouse, the land was gifted by the Reid family who farmed here for 400 years. The Reids resisted intensive farming methods, so the land is still rich with wild plants that have disappeared from much farming land in Britain. The exhibition building has galleries on the environment, rural technologies and people, and has thousands of exhibits, including the oldest threshing machine in the world, dating back to around 1805. The historic farm will be worked to demonstrate traditional agricultural methods of the 1950s, and will follow the seasons to show ploughing, seed time, haymaking and harvest. There is also an events area where there will be demonstrations of the working collection, plus a shop and café.

Bothwell Castle

Uddingston, **T** 01698-816894. *Apr-Sep daily 0930-1830, Oct-Mar Mon-Wed and Sat 0930-1630, Thu morning only, Sun 1400-1630, £2.20, £0.75 children.*

A 30-minute walk down the river towards Uddingston brings you to the substantial red-sandstone ruin of Bothwell Castle. This is commonly regarded as the finest 13th-century stronghold in the country and was fought over repeatedly by the Scots and English during the Wars of Independence. It has withstood the ravages of time well and is still hugely impressive. You can walk all the way to Bothwell Castle from the centre of Glasgow. For a detailed description, see p85.

Chatelherault

Ferniegair, near Hamilton, ***T** 01698-426213. Visitor centre Mon-Sat 1000-1700, Sun 1200-1700, free, house Mon-Thu and Sat 1030-1630, Sun 1230-1630, free.* Hamilton Mausoleum, *tours Apr-Sep on Wed, Sat and Sun at 1500, Oct-Mar Sat, Sun and Wed 1400, £1.15, 80p children.*

Hamilton has the longest history of any town in the area, with associations with Mary Queen of Scots, Cromwell and the Covenanters, who were defeated by Monmouth at nearby Bothwell Bridge in 1679. The town today is unremarkable, but a mile or so south are the gates to Chatelherault, an extensive country park and impressive hunting lodge and summer house, built in 1732 by William Adam for the Dukes of Hamilton. There are ornamental gardens and 10 miles of trails to explore along the deep wooded glen of the River Avon, past the 16th-century ruins of **Cadzow Castle** and into the surrounding countryside. The Ranger service offers guided walks around the park. Within the bounds of nearby Strathclyde Park is the **Hamilton Mausoleum**, a burial vault of the Hamilton family. It's an eerie place with an amazing 15-second echo: the longest in Europe, Europe, Europe…

New Lanark World Heritage Site

T 01555-661345, www.newlarnark.org. *Visitor centre daily 1100-1700. Passport tickets to all attractions £5.95, £3.95, concession/children. Access to the village at all times. Hourly trains from Glasgow Central station. Hourly bus service from Lanark train station to New Lanark, but the 20-min walk is recommended for the wonderful views. The last bus back uphill from the village leaves at 1700.* *See also Kids, p225*

Some 25 miles southeast of Glasgow is the little market town of **Lanark**. A mile below the town, beside the river, is the immaculately restored village of New Lanark, one of the region's most fascinating sights.

The community of New Lanark was founded in 1785 by David Dale and Richard Arkwright as a cotton-spinning centre, but it was Dale's son-in-law, Robert Owen, who took over the management in 1798 and who pioneered a revolutionary social experiment. He believed in a more humane form of capitalism and believed the welfare of his workers to be crucial to industrial success. He provided them with decent housing, a co-operative store, adult educational facilities, the world's first day nursery and the social centre of the community, the modestly-titled Institute for the Formation of Character. Here, in the visitor centre, you can see an introductory video about New Lanark and its founders, join the Millennium Ride (an atmospheric 'dark ride') and see original textile machinery. In

Robert Owen's School for Children, audio-visual technology allows you to see the 'ghost' of an imaginary mill girl. There is also a reconstruction of an early classroom. You can wander through the village and see the 1920s shop, a restored mill-worker's house and even Robert Owen's House. There's also a tearoom and gift shop.

Falls of Clyde Nature Reserve

SWT Wildlife Centre, **T** 01555-665262, www.swt.org.uk. *Daily 1100-1700, Jan and Feb 1200-1600, free.*

Just beyond the village lies the wooded Falls of Clyde Nature Reserve, managed by the **Scottish Wildlife Trust** (SWT). You can visit the **SWT Wildlife Centre**, housed in the old dyeworks, which provides information about the history and wildlife of the area. You can walk to the Falls of Clyde and beyond from the SWT centre. Head up the steps into the nature reserve above Dundaff Linn, the smallest of the three waterfalls on the walk. A boardwalk takes you past an old weir, and just beyond the end of the boardwalk go right at the junction to pass the power station.

Steps then lead up to a viewing platform above the **Corra Linn**, the highest falls on the Clyde, where the river plunges 27 m in three stages. Continue up the steps and follow the path through woodlands to reach another set of falls at **Bonnington Linn**.

You can retrace your steps back to the village, or extend the walk by crossing the weir at Bonnington Linn and turning right, down the track on the opposite bank, taking a narrow path on the right after a few hundred yards. Take care here as the path is very close to the lip of the gorge! After about a mile, the path leads you to the crumbling ruin of **Corra Castle**. To return to Bonnington Linn, retrace your steps for about 100 yds and then follow the vehicle track on the right. The total distance, including the extension, is about 5½ miles. Allow three to four hours there and back and wear boots or strong shoes as some parts can be muddy.

Craignethan Castle
Lesmahagow**T** 01555-860 364. *Apr-Sep daily 0930-1830; Oct-Mar Sat 0930-1630, Sun 1400-1630, Sun 1400-1600 £2.20, children 75p. To get there, take a bus from Lanark to Crossford, then it's a 15-min walk.*

Five miles northwest of Lanark is the village of **Crossford**, from where you can visit Craignethan Castle, an ornate tower-house standing over the **River Nethan**. It was built by Sir James Hamilton for James V, in 1530, and was the last major castle to be built in Scotland. Mary, Queen of Scots left from here to do battle at Langside (at Queen's Park in Glasgow), where she was defeated and fled to France before her eventual imprisonment. The castle, like so many others in Scotland, is said to be haunted by her ghost.

Loch Lomond and the Campsies

Britain's largest inland waterway, measuring 22 miles in length and at certain points up to five miles wide, is one of Scotland's most famous lochs, thanks to the Jacobite ballad about its "bonnie banks". These same banks are now one of the busiest parts of the Highlands, due to their proximity to Glasgow (only 20 miles south along the congested A82). During the summer the loch becomes a playground for day-trippers who tear up and down the loch in speedboats and on jet skis, obliterating any notion visitors may have of a little peace and quiet. The loch, along with a large chunk of the ***Cowal peninsula****, the* ***Campsies*** *(see p117) and the* ***Trossachs****, are all part of the Loch Lomond and the* ***Trossachs National Park*** *– which became Scotland's first National Park, in 2002. Running southeast from Loch Lomond, and bordered by the broad farmlands of the* ***Carse of Stirling*** *to the north and the northern suburbs of Glasgow to the south, are the Campsies. This is an area of gently rolling hills and fertile farmland, comprising the Fintry, Gargunnock, Strathblane and Kilsyth Hills and the Campsie Fells. Other than weekend hikers from Glasgow, the Campsies attract few visitors and their unspoiled peace* *and beauty is their main attraction. There's a string of picturesque villages nestled in the hills, amongst them Killearn, Kippen, Gargunnock and Balfron, birthplace of Alexander 'Greek' Thomson, Glasgow's great Victorian architect. There's also plenty of good walking to be done here.*

» *See Sleeping p135, Eating and drinking p161*

Sights

Loch Lomond

www.loch-lomond.net. *Scottish Citylink, buses run regularly from Glasgow to Balloch (45 mins), and on to Luss and Tarbet (1 hr 10 mins). Some buses go to Ardlui (1 hr 20 mins) and on to Crianlarich. There are 2 rail lines from Glasgow to Loch Lomond. One runs to Balloch every 30 mins (35 mins) the other is the West Highland line to Fort William and Mallaig, with a branch line to Oban. It reaches Loch Lomond at Tarbet and there's another station further north at Ardlui.*

At the southern end of the loch is the resort town of **Balloch**, packed full of hotels, B&Bs, caravan parks and any number of operators offering boat trips around the loch's overcrowded waters. At the northern end of the town is **Loch Lomond Shores**, (www.lomondshores.com), a huge visitor centre/shopping mall, which includes the **Tourist Information Centre** and **National Park Gateway Centre** (**T** 01389-722199, *daily year round*), as well as shops, restaurants, bars and cafés. Here you can pick up all the information you need on the National Park, as well as book a loch cruise with **Sweeney Cruises** (**T** 01389-722406, www.sweeney.uk.com). You can also hire bikes, kayaks or sailing dinghies (see p207) or simply enjoy the views from the **Drumkinnon Tower**.

Loch, stock and barrel

The bonny banks of Loch Lomond are a magnet for day trippers, caravanners, golfers and watersports enthusiasts, though the east side offers some welcome peace and quiet.

The west bank of the loch, from Balloch north to **Tarbet**, is one long, almost uninterrupted development of marinas, holiday homes, caravan parks and exclusive golf clubs. **Luss**, the most picturesque village on the west bank is, however, more of theme park than a real village. It is to the genuine Highland experience what Ozzy Osbourne is to philosophical debate. Boat trips leave from Luss pier (1 ½ hrs, £4). Further north, things begin to quieten down a bit. At **Inverbeg**, you can take a **pedestrian ferry** across the loch to **Rowardennan** (see below, **T** 01360-870273 for times). North of Tarbet, at the narrow northern end of the loch, things quieten down a great deal more and the road to **Ardlui**, at the loch's northern tip, is very beautiful and peaceful. The A82 continues north of Ardlui, past Inverarnan, to join the A85 at **Crianlarich**.

The tranquil east bank of Loch Lomond is a great place for walking. The **West Highland Way** follows the east bank all the way from Drymen, through Balmaha, Rowardennan and Inversnaid. Beyond Rowardennan, this is the only access to the loch's east bank, except for the road to Inversnaid from the Trossachs. From Rowardennan you can climb **Ben Lomond** (974 m), the most southerly of the Munros. It's not too difficult and the views from the top (in good weather) are astounding. There are two routes: the easier one starts from the car park at the end of the road just beyond the Rowardennan Hotel; the other route, known as the 'Ptarmigan Route', starts from beyond the youth hostel. You can also go up by one route and return by the other. Allow about five to six hours there and back. An easier climb is **Conic Hill**, on the Highland fault-line and very close to Glasgow. The route starts from the Balmaha car park. It takes about 1½ hours to reach the top, from where the views of the loch are stunning.

The Campsies

There are several buses daily to Drymen from Glasgow, via Queen's View. There are also buses through the region from Stirling. A postbus service, **T** *01752-494527, www.royalmail.com/postbus leaves from Denny, 5 miles south of Stirling, to Fintry (Mon-Sat at 0955), from where 2 buses (Mon-Sat) run to Balfron. There are regular buses to Denny from Stirling bus station.*

Lying at the heart of the Campsies is the attractive little village of **Fintry**, at the head of the Strathendrick valley, and regular winner of the 'Scotland in Bloom' competition. Two miles east of the village is the 90-ft-high Loup of Fintry waterfall. At the western end of the Campsie Fells is the village of **Drymen**, the busiest of the Campsie villages due to its proximity to the eastern shores of Loch Lomond. Drymen also lies on the West Highland Way. There's a seasonal **tourist office** in the library on The Square (**T** 01360-660068) and bike hire (see p207).

South of Killearn on the A81 is the excellent **Glengoyne Distillery** (**T** 01360-550254, *tours hourly on the hour Mon-Sat 1000-1600, Sun 1200-1600, £3.95*). Glengoyne is the starting point for two excellent walks in the Strathblane Hills, to the top of both **Dumgoyne Hill** (427 m), and **Earl's Seat** (578 m), the highest point in the Campsies. Further west, on the other side of Strathblane, is **Queen's View** on **Auchineden Hill**, from where there are wonderful views up Loch Lomond as far as Ben Ledi. Queen Victoria was particularly impressed with the view – hence its name. The path to the top starts from the busy car park on the A809 Bearsden to Drymen road. It takes about 45-50 minutes each way. From the car park a path also leads up to **The Whangie**, a deep cleft in the rock face with sheer walls rising over 9 m on either side. A path runs for 100 yds through the narrow gap.

Queen Elizabeth Forest Park

Regular buses to Aberfoyle from Glasgow, via Balfron. Postbus service, **T** *01752-494527, www.royalmail.com/postbus from Aberfoyle to Inversnaid on Loch Lomond (see above).*

North of the Campsies, bordered by Loch Lomond to the west and the Trossachs to the east, is Queen Elizabeth Forest Park, a vast and spectacular wilderness covering 75,000 acres. The park is run by the Forestry Commission and is criss-crossed by a network of less difficult, waymarked trails and paths which start from the **Queen Elizabeth Park Visitor Centre** (*Mar-Oct daily 1000-1800, Oct-Dec 1100-1600, parking £1*), about half a mile north of Aberfoyle on the A821. Available at the centre are audiovisual displays on the park's flora and fauna and information on the numerous walks and cycle routes around the park. Full details of the park are available from the **Forest Enterprise** in Aberfoyle (**T** 01877-382258). The **Tourist Information Centre** is on the main street (**T** 01877-382352, *Apr-Oct daily, weekends only Nov-Mar*).

Sleeping

Glasgow has a good range of accommodation. Most of the hotels, guesthouses, B&Bs and hostels are in the city centre or south of the river, around Queen's Park. The best area to stay in however, is the West End, around Kelvingrove Park and the university. Here you get good value mid-range accommodation and a convenient base for several of the city's major sights as well as many of the best bars and restaurants. Glasgow has undergone something of a revolution on the hotel front in recent years and the market is highly competitive. A large number of big chains have opened up in the city, offering everything from deluxe accommodation to simple low-cost lodging – meaning that there are often good deals available for those prepared to shop around. There's now a bewildering number of large, no frills, chain hotels in the city centre, all doing just what it says on the tin. They're ideal for those on a budget who want to spend their time out and about in the city centre, stay out late and then crash somewhere clean.

£ Price

Sleeping codes

L	£80 and over	D	£26-35
A	£66-80	E	£16-25
B	£46-65	F	£15 and under
C	£36-45		

Prices are per person for two people sharing a double room in high season.

The city also has several boutique hotels, offering stylish accommodation with more character than the international chains. Finding a decent room for the night can be difficult during the major festivals (see p191) and in July and August so it's best to book ahead at these times. The **Tourist Information Centre** can help you find somewhere to stay and also publishes a free accommodation guide.

There is plenty of **Scottish Tourist Board** (STB) approved self-catering accommodation available. The minimum stay is usually one week in the summer peak season, or three days or less at other times of the year. Expect to pay from around £300 to over £1000 per week in the city. Much of this self-catering and serviced accommodation in the city is quite upmarket.

Glasgow's universities open their halls of residence to visitors during the summer vacation (late June to September), and some also during the Easter and Christmas breaks, (see p129 and 134). Many rooms are basic and small, with shared bathrooms, but there are also comfortable rooms with private bathrooms, twin and family units and self-contained apartments and shared houses. Full-board, half-board, B&B and self-catering options are also available. Prices for bed and breakfast tend to be roughly the same as for most B&Bs, but self-catering can cost as little as £50 per person per week. Local tourist offices have information, or contact the British Universities Accommodation Consortium, **T** 0115-9504571 for a brochure.

Best Hostels run several hostels in the city. There are three in Berkeley St, Charing Cross (take a 57 bus from the city centre and get off near the Mitchell Library): **Berkeley Globetrotters**, at number 56, a 60 bed hostel with 2- and 4- and 6-bedded rooms; **Rucksacks**, at number 60, 40 beds all in 8-bedded dorms (book ahead for both) and **International Hostel**, at number 62, with 60 beds all 4- and 6-bedded. In summer 2004 two more hostels will open.

George Square and the Merchant City

Hotels

A The Brunswick Merchant City Hotel, 106-108 Brunswick St, **T** 0141-552 0001, **F** 0141-552 1551, www.scotland2000.com/brunswick. *Map 2, F9, p253* 18 rooms. Chic minimalism in the heart of the Merchant City. Ideal for cool dudes wishing to sample the delights of Glasgow nightlife. Their excellent bar-restaurant, *Brutti ma Buoni* (that's 'ugly but good' in Italian), is stylish and relaxed – and does a particularly good line in ice cream.

A Millennium Hotel, George Sq, **T** 0141-332 6711, **F** 0141-332 4264, www.millennium-hotels.com. *Map 2, D8, p253* 117 rooms. Huge 18th century hotel in the heart of the city, right next to Queen St station – you can't miss it. It's an ideal location for those wanting to explore both the Merchant City and the shops in Buchanan Street, while the conservatory bar on the ground floor provides great people-watching potential.

B The Carlton George Hotel, 44 West George St, **T** 0141-353 6373, **F** 0141-353 6263, www.carltonhotels.co.uk. *Map 2, D8, p253* Established chain with 65 rooms and a rooftop restaurant. No surprises, just a traditional, plush hotel very close to George Square and the shops.

B-C Ramada Jarvis, 201 Ingram St, **T** 0141-248 4401, **F** 0141-226 5149, www.ramadajarvis.co.uk. *Map 2, E8, p253* 91 rooms. Conveniently placed for shopaholics as it's just opposite Ralph Lauren and Escada. Often do special deals such as weekend shopping breaks, which can make it a more affordable option.

C City Travel Inn Metro, 187 George St, **T** 0141-238 3320, **F** 0141-553 2719, www.travelinn.co.uk. *Map 2, E10, p253* Has 254 rooms and is close to Glasgow Cathedral and the Merchant City.

C Rab Ha's, 83 Hutcheson St, **T** 0141-572 0400, **F** 0141-572 0402, www.rabhas.com. *Map 2, F9, p253. See also P166* Just 4 rooms available at this central Merchant City institution best known for its food. Stylish décor with bright contemporary rooms, crisp sheets and white bathrobes. It's above the pub so it could be noisy at night.

C-D Babbity Bowster, 16-18 Blackfriars St, **T** 0141-552 5055, **F** 0141-552 7774. *Map 2, F11, p253. See also p144 and p165* 6 rooms. A local institution and one of the first of the Merchant City townhouses to be renovated. Typical Glaswegian hospitality, a cosy pub downstairs (see p165) and an excellent restaurant.

D The Merchant Lodge, 52 Virginia St, **T** 0141-552 2424, **F** 0141-552 4747, www.themerchantlodge.sagenet.co.uk. *Map 2, F8, p253* 40 rooms. Renovated old building that's tucked away in quiet side-street close to the Merchant City's bars and restaurants.

Self-catering and serviced accommodation

The Serviced Apartment Company, SACO Ho, 53 Cochrane St, **T** 0845 1220405, **F** 0117-923 7571, www.sacoapartments.co.uk. *Map 2, E9, p253* 12 1-bedroom apartments in heart of the Merchant City. Weekly rates from £560.

Trongate to the East End

Hotels

B **Cathedral House**, 28-32 Cathedral Sq, **T** 0141-552 3519, **F** 0141-552 2444, www.cathedralhouse.com. *Map 4, B3, p256* 8 rooms. This hotel overlooks Glasgow's ancient cathedral, one of the city's finest attractions. It's an atmospheric old building with comfortable rooms and a very good moderately priced restaurant.

C **The Inn on the Green**, 25 Greenhead St, **T** 0141-554 0165, **F** 0141-556 4678, www.theinnonthegreen.co.uk. *Map 4, G3, p256* Well-established small hotel in the East End featuring hand-crafted furniture quirky rooms. It's by the striking Templeton buildings (modelled on the Doges' Palace) and very convenient for visiting the family friendly People's Palace.

Self-catering and serviced accommodation

Number 52 Charlotte St, 52 Charlotte St, **T** 01436-810264, www.52charlottestreet.co.uk. *Map 4, E2, p256* A former tobacco merchant's mansion now converted into 6 1- and 2-bedroom apartments. Weekly rates start at £415.

Buchanan Street to Charing Cross

Hotels

L-A **Glasgow Hilton**, 1 William St, **T** 0141-204 5555, **F** 0141-204 5044, www.hilton.co.uk. *Map 2, D1, p252* 319 rooms. This gigantic, futuristic-looking luxury hotel is regarded as one of the city's best and most reliable places to stay. Full facilities include the Living

Well leisure centre and shopping mall. Their restaurant, Cameron's, is also widely held to be one of the finest around (see p147).

L-A Radisson SAS, 301 Argyle St, **T** 0141-204 3333, **F** 0141-204 3344, www.radisson.com/glasgowuk. *Map 2, F3, p252* Shiny glass branch of this reliable chain with 247 rooms. It's handily placed for the shops and other city centre sights and also has a health club with a 20m swimming pool.

L-B Langs Hotel, 2 Port Dundas Pl, **T** 0141-333 1500, **F** 0141-333 5700, www.langshotel.co.uk. *Map 2, B7, p253* This ultra cool, stylish hotel has 110 contemporary bedrooms, which have CD players and power showers. There's also a trendy bar and Californian-inspired restaurant. Sex and the City comes to Glasgow.

A The Art House, 129 Bath St, **T** 0141-221 6789, **F** 0141-221 6777, www.arthousehotel.com. *Map 2, B4, p252* Stylish, sleek and individual hotel in a refurbished former education authority building. It's well located – *Sarti's* the excellent Italian restaurant is down below - and good value. The hotel itself features Scotlands's first Japanese Teppan-yaki grill.

A-C Corus Hotel, 377 Argyle St, **T** 0870-6096166, **F** 0141-221 1014, www.corushotels.co.uk/glasgow. *Map 2, F3, p252* This chain hotel has 121 en suite rooms, with satellite tv and clean, functional décor. There's a coffee shop and restaurant and it's about 5 minutes' walk from Central station.

B Glasgow Marriott, 500 Argyle St, **T** 0141-226 5577, **F** 0141-221 7676, www.marriott.co.uk/gladt. *Map 2, E1, p252* Just beside the M8 motorway is this huge 300-room hotel that's popular with business travellers. It's got good leisure facilities and a restaurant, and is handy if you're wanting to take day trips in the car to see the surrounding countryside.

B Holiday Inn Theatreland, 161 West Nile St, **T** 0141-352 8300, **F** 0141-332 7447, www.higlasgow.com. *Map 2, B7, p253* 113 rooms, convenient for the city's theatres.

B Malmaison, 278 West George St, **T** 0141-572 1000, **F** 0141-572 1002, www.malmaison.com. *Map 2, C2, p252* 72 rooms. Provides stylish urban accommodation. The chic rooms have CD players and the hotel's brasserie attracts plenty of diners.

B Milton Hotel and Leisure Club, Argyle St, **T** 0141-222 2929, **F** 0141-222 2626, www.miltonhotels.com. *Map 2, E1, p252* It has 141 rooms and aims to cater for those seeking a bit of luxury – though it doesn't exactly ooze character. There's a pool, sauna and gym, as well as a restaurant and business centre.

B Novotel, 181 Pitt St, **T** 0141-222 2775, **F** 0141-204 5438, www.novotel.com. *Map 2, B2, p252* Sleek and shiny city centre hotel, very convenient and comfortable, functional rooms.

B Saint Judes, 190 Bath St, **T** 0141-352 8800, **F** 0141-352 8801, www.saintjudes.com. *Map 2, B3, p252* An intimate and stylish boutique hotel with only 6 bedrooms and a fine dining restaurant. It's a good place for a romantic break, perhaps combined with a bit of shopping in the Italian Centre.

B Thistle Hotel, 36 Cambridge St, **T** 0870-333 8145, **F** 0870 333 9254, www.thistlehotels.com. *Map 2, A5, p252* There are 300 rooms in this large chain hotel.

C Bewleys Hotel, 110 Bath St, **T** 0141-353 0800, **F** 0141-353 0900, www.bewleyshotel.com. *Map 2, C6, p252* One of the well-known Irish chain hotels which opened in Jul 2000. It's a good central location and the 103 rooms, all priced at £59 year-round, represent great value.

C Holiday Inn, Bothwell St, **T** 0870-400 9032, **F** 0141-221 8986, www.holiday-inn.co.uk. *Map 2, D2, p252* A modern city centre hotel with 275 rooms.

C Pipers' Tryst Hotel, 30-34 McPhater St, **T** 0141-353 5551, **F** 0141-353 1570, www.thepipingcentre.co.uk. *Map 2, A5, p252* This well-established hotel, situated in the Piping Centre (see p65) has 8 cosy rooms. Located opposite the Theatre Royal.

C-D Adelaide's, 209 Bath St, **T** 0141-248 4970, **F** 0141-226 4247, www.adelaides.co.uk. *Map 2, B5, p252* Beautiful Thomson church restoration, with 8 rooms in the heart of the city centre. A chance to stay somewhere a bit different at a reasonable price.

C-D Premier Lodge, 10 Elmbank Gardens, **T** 0870 9906312, **F** 0870 9906313, www.premierlodge.com. Standard lodge accommodation, close to the King's Theatre. £46 per room per night, breakfast extra. The rooms have satellite TV. 278 rooms.

C-D Rennie Mackintosh Central, 59 Union St, **T** 0141-221 0050, **F** 0141-221 4580. *Map 2, E6, p252* 54 rooms, small Glasgow chain exploiting the name of one of the city's great architects.

D Cite, 37-39 Hope St, **T** 0141-248 2480, www.citehotel.co.uk. *Map 2, E5, p252* This contemporary hotel with 52 rooms is due to open when this book goes to press. They're catering for 30-somethings who want fresh, bright rooms but don't need lots of frills. There's a handy Indian restaurant next door for late night curry cravings.

D Greek Thomson, 140 Elderslie St, **T** 0141-332 6556, www.renniemackintoshhotels.com. *Map 2, F4, p252* 17 rooms. Named after Glasgow's less-famous architectural son. Good value, city centre guest house.

D **Ibis**, 220 West Regent St, **T** 0141-225 6000, **F** 0141-225 6010, www.ibishotel.com. *Map 2, B2, p252* 141 rooms. Reasonably priced lodge hotel with functional rooms. Satellite TV and central location.

D **Rennie Mackintosh Hotel**, 218-220 Renfrew St, **T** 0141-333 9992, **F** 0141-333 9995, www.renniemackintoshhotels.com. *Map 2, A2, p252* 24 rooms. A small hotel offering friendly service and superb value for money.

D **The Victorian House**, 212 Renfrew St, **T** 0141-332 0129, **F** 0141-353 3155, www.thevictorian.co.uk. *Map 2, A1/2, p252* 50 rooms. Large lodge close to the art college and the Tenement House. Superb location and the best value in the city centre.

Hostels

F **Euro Hostel**, 318 Clyde St, **T** 0141-222 2828, **F** 0141-222 2829, www.euro-hostels.com. *Map 2, G5, p252* 364 beds, all rooms with en suite facilities, includes continental breakfast. A huge multi-storey building overlooking the Clyde – the biggest hostel in the city.

F **Globetrotters Central**, 19 Dixon St, by St Enoch Sq, **T** 0141-221 7880, www.glasgowhostels.com/www.ukglobe trotters.com. *Map 2, G6, p252* An 80 bed hostel. Accommodation and breakfast at these for £9.50-12 per night.

Self-catering and serviced accommodation

The Spires, The Pinnacle, 1/10 160 Bothwell St, **T** 0141-572 0022, **F** 0141-572 0044, www.thespires.co.uk. *Map 2, D3, p252* 23 city centre apartments in a new building, all apartments have furniture especially imported from Italy. Nightly rates from £135, special weekend rates from £99.

Campus accommodation

C **Strathclyde Graduate Business School**, 199 Cathedral St, **T** 0141-553 6000, **F** 0141-553 6002, www.rescat.strath.ac.uk. *Map 2, D11, p253* 40 en suite rooms. Open all year. The more salubrious accommodation option.

C-E **The University of Strathclyde**, **T** 0141-553 4148, www.rescat.strath.ac.uk. *Map 2, D12, p253* Has a wide range of B&B accommodation available in its various halls of residence across the city, mostly in June to September, though a few are open all year round. D **Chancellors Hall** (Cathedral Street, on campus), 218 en suite rooms. E **Garnett Hall** (Cathedral Street on campus), 124 single rooms. Also self-catering, around £260-330 per week. E **Murray Hall** (Cathedral Street on campus, 70 single rooms. E **Forbes Hall** (Cathedral Street), 104 single rooms B&B or self catering flats from £300-355 per week. Further out of town, but the cheapest of the lot, is E **Jordanhill Campus** (76 Southbrae Drive), 130 rooms.

E **Glasgow Caledonian University**, 218 Dobbies Loan, Cowcaddens, **T** 0141-331 3980, **F** 0141-331 3957, accommodation@gcal.ac.uk. *Map 2, A8, p253* 100 flats in which rooms are let indivicually. Prices from £630-840 per week.

West End

Hotels

L **One Devonshire Gardens**, 1 Devonshire Gdns, **T** 0141-339 2001, **F** 0141-337 1663, www.onedevonshiregardens.co.uk. *Map 3, B1, p254* 36 rooms. Highly-acclaimed hotel which is still the very last word in style and comfort, with fragrant fresh flowers, deep baths to wallow in and staff who pay attention to every detail. There are few, if any, classier places to stay in the country. It's the hotel of choice for Tina Turner, George Clooney... in fact almost every big name who comes to Glasgow.

L-A Glasgow Moat House, Congress Rd, **T** 0141-306 9988, **F** 0141-221 2022, www.moathousehotels.com. *Map 3, L4, p255* 283 rooms. Massive multi-storey glass structure on the banks of the Clyde, next to the SECC and 'Armadillo' and conveniently situated opposite the glittering new Science Centre. A bit out of the city centre but good views of the river and 2 excellent restaurants, Mariner's and Dockside No 1.

L-B Hilton Glasgow Grosvenor, 1-10 Grosvenor Terr, Great Western Rd **T** 0141-339 8811, **F** 0141-334 0710, www.hilton.co.uk. *Map 3, D4, p254* 4-star Hilton with 96 rooms. A smaller, four star, version of the city centre Hilton situated in a traditional West End terrace. A good one for nature lovers as about half their rooms have views of the Botanic Gardens opposite.

A-C City Inn, Finnieston Quay, **T** 0141-240 1002, **F** 0141-227 1036, www.cityinn.com. *Map 1, F4, p250* 164 rooms. This contemporary hotel close to the river has light, contemporary bedrooms and does good-value, room-only deals. Emphasis is on providing business facilities, with ISDN and modem points in every room. It's convenient for the SECC.

B Kelvin Park Lorne Hotel, 923 Sauchiehall St, **T** 0870-6096138, **F** 0141-314 4888, www.corushotels.com. *Map 3, 14, p255* 100 rooms. Dependable old stalwart and well located for galleries, museums etc. Nothing exciting and could do with being refurbished.

B-C Manor Park Hotel, 28 Balshagray Dr, **T** 0141-3392143, **F** 0141-3395842. *Map 1, D3, p250* 10 rooms. This West End hotel in a cosy, traditional building is unusual in Glasgow in that Gaelic is spoken and actively promoted. Good for anyone wanting a rich taste of Scottish culture.

C Argyll Hotel, 973 Sauchiehall St, **T** 0141-337 3313, **F** 0141-337 3283, www.argyllhotelglasgow.co.uk. *Map 3, I4, p255* A traditional, 3-star hotel in a refurbished Georgian building by Kelvingrove Park. 38 rooms.

C Kirklee Hotel, 11 Kensington Gate, **T** 0141-334 5555, **F** 0141-339 3828, www.kirkleehotel.co.uk. *Map 3, D2, p254* 9 rooms. Lovely clean Edwardian townhouse with a beautiful garden that's widely admired. Close to bars and restaurants on Byres Road and the Botanic Gardens.

C Park House, 13 Victoria Park Gardens South, **T** 0141-339 1559, **F** 0141-576 0915, www.parkhouseglasgow.co.uk. *Map 1, D3, p254* Large Victorian townhouse with three rooms offering 4-star B&B. It's about a 10-minute drive into the city centre, so not ideal if you've only got a short time in the city. Open April to October.

C The Sandyford Hotel, 904 Sauchiehall St, **T** 0141-334 0000, www.sandyfordhotelglasgow.co.uk. *Map 3, I4, p255* 55 rooms. Comfortable and good value lodge convenient for the SECC, Kelvingrove Park and the Transport Museum.

C Wickets Hotel, 52 Fortrose St, **T/F** 0141-334 9334, www.wicketshotel.co.uk. *Map 1, E3, p255* 11 rooms. Overlooking the West of Scotland cricket ground and close to Partick rail station and Underground. With a conservatory bar/bistro and beer garden.

C-D Heritage Hotel, 4-5 Alfred Terr by 625 Great Western Rd, **T/F** 0141-339 6955, www.goglasgow.co.uk. *Map 3, E5, p254* 26 rooms. Good value Victorian townhouse, with simple décor, conveniently close to the West End action.

C-D Hillhead Hotel, 32 Cecil St, **T** 0141-339 7733, **F** 0141-339 1770, www.hillheadhotel.co.uk. *Map 3, E5, p254* 11 rooms. Small, friendly two-star guesthouse ideally placed for the Byres Rd nightlife and close to Hillhead Underground.

C-D Jury's Glasgow Hotel, Great Western Rd, **T** 0141-334 8161, **F** 0141-334 3846, www.jurysdoyle.com. *Map 3, A1, p254* 137 rooms. Nothing too fancy, but comfortable rooms and good facilities including pool, sauna and gym. Free parking. Very good value.

C-D Kelvin Hotel, 15 Buckingham Terr, Great Western Rd, **T** 0141-339 7143, **F** 0141-339 5215, www.kelvinhotel.com. *Map 3, E5, p254* 21 rooms. Comfortable two-star guesthouse in lovely Victorian terrace near Byres Rd and Botanic Gardens. Some rooms are en suite.

C-D Kirkland House, 42 St Vincent Cres, **T** 0141-248 3458, www.kirkland.net43.co.uk. *Map 3, J4/5, p255* 5 rooms. Small, guest house with that little bit extra. Close to Kelvingrove Park.

C-D The Townhouse, 4 Hughenden Terr, **T** 0141-357 0862, **F** 0141-339 9605, www.thetownhouseglasgow.com. *Map 3, B/C1, p254* 10 rooms. Just off the Great Western Rd. Lovely Victorian townhouse offering home from home comfort, hospitality and great value. There's a real fire on cold days and easy parking.

C-D The Townhouse Hotel, 21 Royal Cres, **T** 0141-332 9009, **F** 0141-353 2143, www.hotels.glasgow.com. *Map 3, J6, p255* 19 rooms. Restored Victorian townhouse, set back off Sauchiehall St and about 10 mins walk from the city centre. Good value.

D The Flower House, 33 St Vincent Cres, **T** 0141-204 2846, **F** 0141-226 5130, www.scotland2000.com/flowerhouse. *Map 3, J4/5, p255* This Grade A listed building has 4 rooms and is furnished with antiques – the rooms aren't en suite due to the age of the building.

D Kelvingrove Hotel, 944 Sauchiehall St, **T** 0141-339 5011, **F** 0141-339 6566, www.kelvingrove-hotel.co.uk. *Map 3, I4, p255* 4-star guesthouse with 22 en suite rooms. Non smoking.

Hostels

F Bunkum Backpackers, 26 Hillhead St, **T** 0141-581 4481, **F** 0141-581 6258, www.bunkumglasgow.co.uk. *Map 3, F5, p254* It has 36 beds, made up of 2 twin rooms with the rest in 6-bed dorm rooms. There are kitchen facilities, laundry, and car parking.

F Glasgow Backpackers Hostel, 17 Park Terr, **T** 0141-332 9099, www.scotlands-top-hostels. *Map 3, H6, p255* 90 beds. July to September. Independent hostel housed in halls of residence.

F North Lodge, 163 North St, **T** 0141-204 5470, **F** 0141-221 7880. *Near Charing Cross. Map 3, J8, p255* With 150 beds, all large dorms (open June to September only).

F SYHA Youth Hostel, 7/8 Park Terr, **T** 0870 0041119, www.syha.org.uk. *Open 24 hrs. It's a 10-min walk from Kelvinbridge Underground station, or take bus 44 or 59 from Central station and get off at the first stop on Woodlands Rd, then head up the first turning left (Lynedoch St). Map 3, H6, p255* 135 beds. This former hotel has been converted into a great 4 star hostel, all rooms with en suite facilities (being refurbished, opens June 2004). Price includes continental breakfast. It gets very busy in July and August so you'll need to book ahead.

Self-catering and serviced accommodation

City Apartments, 401 North Woodside Rd, **T** 0141-342 4060, **F** 0141-334 8159, www.glasgowhotelsandapartments.co.uk. *Close to Kelvinbridge Underground. Map 3, F7, p254* 4 apartments, including 1 studio apartment, to let from £330 per week, £48 per night.

Dreamhouse Inc, Lynedoch Cres, **T** 0141-332 3620, **F** 0141-303 7020, www.dreamhouseapartments.com. *Map 3, H8, p255* Several luxury serviced apartments in Victorian townhouses in Lynedoch Cres. Nightly rates range from £130-235.

Embassy Apartments, 8 Kelvin Dr, **T** 0141-946 6698, **F** 0141-945 5377, www.glasgowhotelsandapartments.co.uk. *Map 3, C4, p254* 6 apartments in a converted Victorian terrace house in the West End, about a mile from the city centre. All are en suite and sleep between 1 and 5 people. Weekly rates from £330.

The White House, 12 Cleveden Cres, **T** 0141-339 9375, **F** 0141-337 1430, www.whitehouse-apartments.com. *Map 3, A1, p254* This has 32 suites with a country house atmosphere. Weekly rates from £300-620.

Campus accommodation

E-F University of Glasgow, Conference and Visitor Services, 3 The Sq, **T** 0800-027 2030, or **T** 0141-330 5385, www.cvso.co.uk. *Map 3, I4, p255* There is a range of self-catering accommodation, available July until September. **Cairncross House** (20 Kelvinhaugh Pl, off Argyle St near Kelvingrove Park), has rooms to let, and **Kelvin- nhaugh Gate** and **Murano Street Village** have flats and rooms. It also has B&B accommodation (**E**) at **Dalrymple Hall** in the West End, from March to April and Juy to

September; **Wolfson Hall**, a modern block by Kelvin Conference Centre, available March and April and May to September; and **St Andrews Campus**, 6 miles from the West End, available April to May and mid-June to mid-August.

South of the Clyde

Hotels

A-B Sherbrooke Castle Hotel, 11 Sherbrooke Av, **T** 0141-427 4227, **F** 0141-427 5685, www.sherbrooke.co.uk. *Map 1, G4, p250* A small hotel (25 rooms) with a bit more character than the chains. It's a good base for exploring the attractions of the south side as it's only about a mile from the Burrell collection.

B Best Western Ewington, Balmoral Terr, 132 Queen's Dr, **T** 0141-423 1152, **F** 0141-422 2030, www.countryhotels.net. *Map 1, G5, p250* 43 rooms. Friendly and comfortable hotel in a secluded terrace facing Queen's Park. Their restaurant, *Minstrels*, is superb value and worth a visit in its own right.

B-C Swallow Hotel, 517 Paisley Rd West, **T** 0141-427 3146, **F** 0141-419 1602, www.swallowhotels.com. *Map 1, F4, p250* This chain is the largest on the south side and has 117 rooms. Is close to the Science Centre and also has its own pool – a good family option.

Around Glasgow

Hotels

A-B Balmory Hall, Ascog, Isle of Bute **T/F** 01700-500669, www.balmoryhall.com. 3 rooms. Elegant Victorian mansion offering a touch of class in palatial surroundings, 3 miles south of Rothesay. Their 7-course breakfast is an event in itself.

A-B Lake Hotel, Port of Menteith, **T** 01877-385258, www.lake-of-menteith-hotel.com. Situated on the lakeshore overlooking Inchmahome. Stylish, comfortable and very romantic hotel boasting a great setting and excellent dining room.

B Brisbane House Hotel, on the Esplanade, Largs, **T** 01475-687200, www.maksu-group.co.uk. Probably the most upmarket choice for those who wish to explore the area. It is comfortable and offers very fine Scottish cuisine at mid-range prices.

B Royal Hotel, Tighnabruaich, Cowal Peninsula, **T** 01700-811 239, **F** 01700-811300, www.royalhotel.org.uk. This waterfront establishment was taken over and totally transformed into a good-looking and tastefully decorated place to stay with an excellent restaurant serving the best of local produce and cheaper brasserie serving equally fine food all day.

D-E Ascog Farm, Ascog, Isle of Bute, **T** 01700-503372. Feng shui farmhouse offering excellent value. Very friendly, especially at breakfast when everyone sits down together.

Camping

Craigendmuir Park, Campsie View, Stepps, **T** 0141-779 4159, **F** 0141-779 4057, www.craigendmuir.co.uk. Located 4 miles northeast of the city centre and a 15-minute walk from Stepps station.

Eating and drinking

Even though such culinary delights as the deep-fried Mars bar, deep-fried pizza, deep-fried black pudding and deep-fried Cadbury's creme egg were all invented here, they certainly don't reflect the quality and variety of the food on offer – Glasgow has undergone a culinary renaissance and it continues unabated.

The city has always boasted a wide selection of ethnic eateries, particularly Indian, Chinese and Italian restaurants, and these have been joined by a growing number of cuisines from around the globe. Glasgow reflects the move away from strict culinary national boundaries and towards a more international style, with its many bistros and brasseries which feature wide-ranging menus. These also tend to be more lively and informal places to eat, as well as offering good value for money – and this is one of the city's great strengths. Compared to other cities (ie London), you can eat well and in some style without breaking the bank.

£ Price

Eating codes

£££	over £20
££	£10-£20
£	under £10

Prices refer to the cost of a two-course meal for one person. They do not include tax and tip.

Scottish cuisine is well represented, reflecting the trend of marrying traditional Scottish ingredients with continental and international flavours and styles. Meats like venison, pheasant, lamb and beef are often on the menu, and haggis may feature too. Fresh local fish is widely available, sometimes fashionably seared, sometimes served in an unusual sauce, and sometimes just fried with chips.

Vegetarians are well catered for with most places offering substantial and imaginative vegetarian options.

Glasgow prides itself on its café society and many of the new designer cafés make it seem more like Barcelona or Greenwich Village than the west coast of Scotland. There are many authentic Italian cafés where you can enjoy a fry-up washed down with frothy cappuccino. The city is also the home to the tearoom and those who insist on their mid-afternoon fix won't be disappointed.

The greatest concentration of eating places is around **Byres Road** in the West End, which is heavily populated by students and therefore the best area for cheap, stylish places to eat. The **Merchant City** contains most of the designer brasseries, which are more expensive, but many of the bars serve good food at reasonable prices. Some of the places listed also appear in the Bars and clubs chapter.

George Square and the Merchant City

Restaurants

£££ Etain, The Glass House, Springfield Court, **T** 0141-225 5630. *Mon-Fri 1200-1430, 1900-2200; Sat, 1900-2200, Sun 1200-1500. Map 2, F7, p253* This is Terence Conran's fine dining restaurant, which is already receiving good reviews. The menu features fresh, seasonal produce and might include a dish like roast pigeon with puy lentils, or seared scallops with bacon and black pudding. Great choice of cheeses too. Set lunches make it a more affordable option than in the evening.

£££ Rogano's, 11 Exchange Pl, **T** 0141-248 4055. *Daily 1200-1430, 1830-2230. Map 2, E7, p253* A Glasgow culinary institution. Designed in the style of the Cunard liner, *Queen Mary*, and built by the same workers. Looks like the set of a Hollywood blockbuster and you'll need a similar budget to pay the bill, but the seafood is truly sensational. Downstairs is **Café Rogano** (Sun-Thu 1200-1430, 1830-2230), which offers a less stylish alternative, but it's a lot easier on the pocket.

££ Arta, 13-19 Walls St, **T** 0141-5522101. *Wed, Thu and Sun 1700-2300, Fri, Sat 1700-2400. Bar open later. Map 2, G11, p253* Sister restaurant to the Corinthian (see p142). Spanish restaurant serving tapas, tortillas and meaty stews. Housed in the Old Cheese market, the décor is faux-Spanish with mosaics and huge candelabras.

££ Café Gandolfi, 64 Albion St, **T** 0141-552 6813. *Mon-Sat 0900-2330, Sun 1200-2330. Map 2, F11, p253* The first of Glasgow's style bistro/brasseries back in 1979, which almost makes it antique

Taste the difference
The Merchant City and West End in particular are full to bursting with cool cafés and buzzing style bars and the city is gaining an enviable reputation as one of the UK's leading culinary hotspots.

by today's contemporary design standards. The unusual wooden furniture was designed by Tim Stead. Still comfortably continental, relaxed and soothing. Good place for a snack or a leisurely late breakfast.

££ City Merchant, 97-99 Candleriggs, **T** 0141-553 1577. *Mon-Sat 1200-2230. Map 2, F10, p253* The best of Scottish meat and game but it's the fish and seafood which shine. Absolutely superb. It's at the top end of this price range but their 2- and 3-course set menus (available 1200-1830) are more affordable and excellent value. Very popular and a good atmosphere. No smoking area.

££ Corinthian, 191 Ingram St, **T** 0141-552 1101. *Mon-Thu 1700-2230, Fri, Sat, 1700-2300, bar open from 1200 Mon-Sat, 123- on Sun. Map 2, E8, p253* There's a sense of occasion about going to the popular Corinthian. There are several bars, a nightclub and private club as well as the restaurant. Food tends to be traditional with a modern twist and the puddings are very good.

££ Cuba Norte, 17 John St, **T** 0141-552 3505. *Mon- Sun 1200-2300. Map 2, E9, p253* As the name suggests there's a Latin American feel here, not just in the food but in the music. There's even dancing every night. Come just for cocktails or for a meal.

££ The Dhabba, 44 Candleriggs, **T** 0141-553 1249. *Daily 1200-2300. Map 2, G10, p253* Stylish new Indian restaurant with lots of polished wood and gleaming cutlery. It offers authentic Northern Indian cuisine.

££ Frango, 15 John St, **T** 0141-552 4433. *Mon-Sat 1200-2230. Map 2, E9, p253* Conveniently located in the Italian Centre this place is popular with business people and fashion-conscious shoppers. There's an all-day menu, with lots of fish dishes such as fish soup, tuna, and monkfish. Pudding might include a scrummy rosemary panacotta. Relaxed atmosphere.

££ Mao, 84 Brunswick St, **T** 0141-564 5161. *Mon-Fri 1200-2300, Sat 1200-2330, Sun 1300-2200. Map 2, F10, p253* Far Eastern and Oriental food in slick merchant city outlet. The décor features brightly coloured furniture and prints and fusion flavours are exciting.

££ Metropolitan, Merchant Sq, Candleriggs, **T** 0141-552 9402. *Map 2, F10, p253* This is a stylish, but slightly self consciously trendy, restaurant and bar – leather sofas and fashion tv on wide screen tv in the bar, and a sleek clientele. You can drink outside in the covered courtyard that was the old market. Food is contemporary with dishes like jerk chicken, steaks and pastas.

££ Schottische, 16-18 Blackfriars St, **T** 0141-5527774. *Tue-Sat 1830-2300.* ***Map 2, F11, p253*** Upstairs from the legendary *Babbity Bowsters* (see p123). Good French/Scottish food at very affordable prices. They use seasonal produce and you might find venison as well as haggis on the menu, so if you've never tried it, here's your chance. Make sure you leave enough room for their diet-busting puddings.

££ Smiths of Glasgow, 109 Candleriggs, **T** 0141-552 6539. *Tue-Sat 0930-2200, Sun, Mon 0930-1730.* ***Map 2, F10, p253*** There's a French tang to this Merchant City favourite which functions as a café by day and a restaurant by night. Dishes might include rump of lamb in gravy.

££ Strata, 45 Queen St, **T** 0141-2211888. *Daily 1200-2200, bar open later.* ***Map 2, F7, p253*** One of the city's coolest style bars, with good, Mediterranean style food too. Good place for a tasty sandwich or burger at lunchtime, or more unusual fare (ostrich has been spotted on the menu) in the evening.

£ Bargo, 80 Albion St, **T** 0141-553 4771. *Mon-Sat 1200-1900, Sun 1230-1900 (bar open until 2400).* ***Map 2, F10, p253*** Impressively stylish designer bar with lots of pinewood and portholes, serving excellent value bar snacks and meals of superior quality. Definitely a place to be seen in and flaunt your new Versace purchases.

£ The Italian Kitchen, 64 Ingram St, **T** 0141-572 1472. *Tue-Sun 1200-2200.* ***Map 2, F11, p253*** Newly opened Italian restaurant in the heart of the Merchant City. The décor features shiny wooden floors and red leather seats, and there's a large, wood-fired oven for authentic pizzas.

£ Khublai Khan, 26 Candleriggs, **T** 0141-552 5646. *Daily 1730-late. Map 2, G10, p253* The idea at this Mongolian restaurant is that you make your own dishes by selecting ingredients from a range of meats, vegetables, herbs and spices. Entertaining stuff provided you don't get too carried away with the spices.

£ OKO, 68 Ingram St, **T** 0141-572 1500. *Tue-Thu 1200-1500, 1800-2300, Fri 1200-1500, 1800-2400, Sun 1730-2230. Map 2, F10/11, p253* Sushi bar conveyor, lots of stainless steel and hot dishes like tempura, teriyaki and noodles.

Cafés

Babbity Bowster, 16-18 Blackfriars St, **T** 0141-5525055. *Mon-Sat 1200-2300, Sun 1000-2300. Map 2, F11, p253. See also p123 and p165* You can't get away from this place, and why would you want to? Buzzing café-bar housed in a magnificent 18th century building in the heart of the Merchant City. Traditional Scottish and French dishes served with flair. Outrageously good value. The bar is one of the city's perennial favourites (see p123).

Bibo Cibo, 5 Bell St, **T** 0141-552 3232. *Daily 0900-2100, bar open later. Map 2, G10, p253* Merchant City café/bar with extra seating out in the old Fruitmarket courtyard, a popular venue with local office workers. You can choose from bar fare like sandwiches and baked potatoes or opt for more filling options like lamb chops or lemon chicken.

Ichiban Japanese Noodle Café, 50 Queen St, **T** 0141-2044200. *Mon-Wed 1200-2200, Thu-Sat 1200-2300, Sun 1300-2200. Map 2, F7, p253* Excellent value, healthy Japanese specialities like sushi and tempura, washed down with saki.

Great if you've been indulging in too many local specialities – like Tunnock's Caramel Wafers or chips. There are communal tables and the surroundings are cool and modern. No smoking.

Noah, 84 Albion St, **T** 0141-552 3044. *Sun-Wed 1100-2100, Thu-Sat 1100-2200. Map 2, F11, p253* Relaxed and contemporary Merchant City café where you can relax with the papers and a toasted goats' cheese sandwich, or sit down to pan-fried chicken or fettucine in the evening.

Trongate to the East End

Restaurants

££ Café Cossachok, 10 King St, **T** 0141-553 0733. *Tue-Sat 1130-2230, Sun 1600-2230. Near the Tron Theatre. Map 2, G9, p253* Cosy, authentic-feeling Russian restaurant with a relaxed, informal atmosphere. Try a bowl of crimson borscht (beetroot and cabbage soup) – great on a damp Glasgow day, or a blini (pancake) stuffed with meat, spinach or even ice cream. The art gallery upstairs features the work of artists from around the world and exhibits change regularly. More than just a good meal, it's an entire cultural experience.

££ Esca, 27 Chisholm St, **T** 0141-553 0880. *Mon-Fri 1200-1500, 1700-2200, Sat 1200-2230, Sun 1700-2200. Map 2, H10, p253* Sleek, contemporary restaurant with a friendly, relaxed atmosphere, serving Mediterranean with a strong emphasis on pastas and steaks.

££ The Inn on the Green, 22 Greenhead St, **T** 0141-554 0165. *Mon-Fri 1200-1430, 1800-late, Sat, Sun 1800-late. Map 4, G3, p256* A well-established East End restaurant and hotel: it was once a seamen's mission. Good place for traditional good quality Scottish food, no mince and tatties here, but excellent steak, or delicious scallops. Dining is accompanied by piano music at night.

££ Pancho Villas, 26 Bell St, **T** 0141-552 7737. *Mon-Thu 1200-2230, Fri, Sat 1200-2300, Sun 1800-2230.* ***Map 2, G10, p253*** Cheery Mexican eaterie with good, adventurous food and colourful décor inspired by the Mexican festival, the Day of the Dead. Come here to sip Margaritas, slam tequilas and feast on fajitas.

££ Tron Theatre, Chisholm St, **T** 0141-552 8587. *Mon-Sat 1000-late; Sun 1100-late.* ***Map 2, H10, p253*** This refurbished restaurant offers a dining experience that's worth applauding. Food is described as modern European and portions are generous – no need for a bag of chips on the way home from here. There's a no-smoking area and the effortlessly stylish bar is perfect for that pre-prandial tipple.

£ Mono, Kings Court, King St, **T** 0141-553 2400. *Daily 1200-2220.* ***Map 2, H10, p253*** Clean and simple, this contemporary vegan restaurant is a welcome addition to the Glasgow culinary scene. No, it's not knit your own nut loaf territory, instead you'll find things like smoked tofu wantons with spicy apricot conserve or a delicate Thai curry. All the beers and wines are vegan so you can eat and drink with a sparkling clear conscience.

£ Trattoria Gia, 17 King St, **T** 0141-5527411. *Tue-Sat 1200-1400, 1700-2230, Sun 1700-2230.* ***Map 2, G10, p253*** Good value Italian eaterie. Checked tablecloths, friendly staff and a good choice of specials.

Cafés

Café Source, 1 St Andrews Sq (in the church), **T** 0141-548 6020. *Mon-Thu 1100-2300, Fri, Sat 1100-2400, Sun 1200-2300. (no food 1500-1700 Mon-Fri). Map 4, E1, p256* Great contemporary café in a former church offering everything from fishcakes to savoury vegetarian tart – sermons not on the menu. If you're not hungry you can just chill out with a latte and read the papers. Live music every Wed from 2100.

Buchanan Street to Charing Cross

Restaurants

£££ Brian Maule at Chardon d'Or, 176 West Regent St, **T** 0141-248 3801. *Map 2, C4, p252* Opulent venue catering very much to well lunched businessmen. Head chef was formerly at Le Gavroche in London. The place to come for crisp linen, delicious sauces and highly rate sirloin.

£££ Cameron's, 1 William St, **T** 0141-2045511. *Mon-Fri 1200-1400, 1900-2200, Sat 1900-2200. Map 2, D1, p252* In Glasgow's *Hilton Hotel*. Sublime Scottish/French cuisine with starters like mussels and scallops, and mains that include excellent Aberdeen Angus beef. Pricey but well worth it. No smoking area.

£££ Gamba, 225a West George St, **T** 0141-572 0899. *Mon-Sat 1200-1430, 1700-2230. Map 2, C4, p252* Popular fish restaurant, where you get the freshest fish cooked with flair and imagination. The décor is cool and discreet, and it's a great special occasion place. Try the fish soup to start.

£££ Ho Wong, 82 York St, **T** 0141-2213550. *Mon-Sat 1200-1400, 1800-2330, Sun 1800-2330. Map 2, F3, p252* Tucked away just off Argyle St, this Chinese restaurant doesn't look much from the outside but inside awaits a memorable Cantonese culinary experience and the city's finest Szechuan food. Not cheap but worth every penny. You can BYOB.

£££ Quigleys, 158 Bath St, **T** 0141-331 4060. *Mon-Sat 1200-1500, pre-theatre 1700-1900, 1900-2300. Map 2, B4, p252* Contemporary restaurant in the old Christie's showroom, offering imaginative fusion food for the slick set. Lots of mirrors so you can admire yourself while eating your lemon tart.

£££ St Judes, 190 Bath St, **T** 0141-3528800. *Mon-Fri 1200-1500, Daily 1800-2230. Map 2, B4, p252* Part of the chic small hotel but open to non residents. Very much the in-place for Glasgow's movers and shakers. Modern Scottish food with lots of chargrilled fish and meat and very good puddings.

£££ Two Five Seven, 257 West Campbell St, **T** 0141-572 4052. *Mon-Sat 1200-1430, 1800-2200. Map 2, B4, p252* Scottish produce with a French twist is on the menu at this new restaurant, on the site of Gordon Yuill's former eaterie. The chef is the same and the interior chic – though the service could be improved.

££ Amber Regent, 50 West Regent St, **T** 0141-331 1655. *Mon-Thu 1200-1415, 1730-2300, Fri 1200-1415, 1730-2330; Sat 1200-2330. Map 2, C5, p252* Plush and very upmarket restaurant serving classic Chinese cuisine. The aromatic crispy duck is particularly good. Those on a tight budget can also indulge themselves, with half price main courses before 1900 Wed-Fri and all night Mon/Tue. BYOB.

££ Baby Grand, 3-7 Elmbank Gardens, **T** 0141-248 4942. *Open Mon-Thu 0800-2400, Fri 0800-0200, Sat 1000-0200, Sun 1000-2400.* *Map 2, B1, p252* Chic jazz-café offering good bistro-style food when most other places have shut up shop. There's a changing 'specials' menu and a laid back atmosphere. Enjoy late night drinks and food and soothing jazz piano.

££ Bleu Ginger, 441 Sauchiehall St, **T** 0141-3325999. *Mon-Sat 1200-1430, 1730-0200, Sun 1730-0200.* *Map 2, B1, p252* This new Chinese restaurant offers classy dining in elegant surroundings – a large chandelier hangs from the ceiling and contemporary prints line the walls. Lots of 'chilli' dishes and several choices for veggies.

££ Bouzy Rouge, 111 West Regent St, **T** 0141-221 8804. *Sun-Thu 1200-2130, Fri, Sat 2400-2230.* *Map 2, C5, p252* Is one of a chain offering two types of dining – casual and gourmet. Gourmet choices are things like posh Scottish (venison and the like), casual has steaks and veggie options. Sleek wooden interior.

££ Fratelli Sarti, 121 Bath St, **T** 0141-204 0440. *Mon-Sat 0800-2230, Sun 1200-2230.* *Map 2, C5, p252* Everything you'd expect from a great Italian restaurant, and a lot more besides – it's a real Glasgow institution, practically everyone in the city must have eaten here at some time. Good value food in authentic Italian surroundings – lots of chatter and bustle. Their pizzas are delicious. No wonder it's always busy – be warned, service can be slow. No smoking area.

££ The Green Room, Glasgow Royal Concert Hall, 2 Sauchiehall St, **T** 0141-353 8000. *Open performance days only 1700-2130.* *Map 2, B7, p253* Much more than a good place to eat before the show. A superb restaurant in its own right where you can indulge in the finest of Scottish produce at reasonable prices. Good vegetarian selection. No smoking area.

££ Modern India, 51 West Regent St, **T** 0141-331 1980. *Mon-Thu 1200-2330, Fri, Sat 1200-0100, Sun 1600-2330. Map 2, C6, p252* This is a contemporary Indian restaurant featuring many dishes from Goa. Business lunches are a great bargain.

£ Canton Express, 407 Sauchiehall St, **T** 0141-332 0145. *Daily 1200-0400. Map 2, A1, p252* No-frills, cheap and filling Chinese fast food at any hour of the day or night. Popular with students and clubbers in need of an immediate monosodium glutamate hit.

£ Glasgow Noodle Bar, 482 Sauchiehall St, **T** 0141-333 1883. *Daily 1200-0500. Map 2, A1, p252* Handy central location for this refuelling stop serving Oriental fast food that you eat from disposable containers with plastic chopsticks or forks. Very cheap chow and great after a heavy night on the town.

£ Tempus at the CCA, 350 Sauchiehall St, **T** 0141-332 7959. *Daily 1100-2400 (last order for food 2130). Map 2, A3, p252* Set in the recently refurbished Centre for Contemporary Arts, this café/restaurant serves contemporary Scottish dishes. The menu is flexible and you can just drop in for a coffee and a snack if you don't want lunch. Upstairs (also reached via Scott St) is the **CCA Bar** which serves sandwiches and coffees. It is notable for its décor, designed by artist Jorge Pardo, which is a psychedelic creation with lots of bright colours and carved wood.

£ Wee Curry Shop, 7 Buccleuch St, **T** 0141-353 0777. *Mon-Sat 1200-1400, 1730-2230. Map 2, A4, p252* Son of *Mother India* (see p156). Small in every sense except flavour and value. Quite simply the best cheap curry this side of Mumbai, in a cosy, relaxed atmosphere. Good vegetarian options and incredible value 3-course buffet lunch. BYOB.

Cafés

Café Cosmo, 12 Rose St, **T** 0141-3326535. *Daily 1200-1700, bar open till 2100. Map 2, B4, p252* Part of the Glasgow Film Theatre (see 'Entertainment') this well preserved arty, art deco café is definitely worth knowing about, even if you're not a movie buff. It's a great cheap lunch venue, especially for vegetarians, with hearty soups, toasties and no nonsense slabs of cake on offer – good celeb spotting potential too.

The Doocot Café and Bar, The Lighthouse, 11 Mitchell La, **T** 0141-221 1821. *Map 2, E6, p252* There's a 1950s retro look at this café on the top of the Lighthouse (see p54) high above the shopping frenzy in the streets below. Stop for soups, sandwiches and light meals before immersing yourself in the world of architecture.

Miss Cranston's Tearooms, 33 Gordon St, **T** 0141-204 1122. *Map 2, E6, p252* You could miss this traditionally run tea-shop as it's hidden above a baker's shop, but it's worth seeking out if you fancy something rather more genteel than a skinny cappuccino on the run. This is the place to come for a full blown afternoon tea with sandwiches, scones, cakes, milk in jugs and gallons of tea.

Starbucks at Borders, 98 Buchanan St, **T** 0141-222 7700. *Mon-Sat 0830-2200, Sun 1000-2000. Map 2, E7, p253* Handy Starbucks inside *Borders* bookshop. Good for those who can't tear themselves away from the books, and it also offers fantastic people-watching potential if you grab a seat overlooking the floor below. As you'd expect there are plenty more Starbucks outlets scattered throughout the city.

Where the Monkey Sleeps, 182 West Regent St, **T** 0141-226 3406. *Mon-Sat 0700-1900, Sat 1000-1800.* *Map 2, C4, p252* This is a relaxed exhibition space and trendy café run by former art students. Relax on a comfy sofa, read the paper and tuck into a bagel or a sandwich. Exhibits and sells works of new artists, including graduates of Glasgow and London schools of art.

Willow Tea Rooms, 217 Sauchiehall St, **T** 0141-3320521. *Mon-Sat 0900-1630, Sun 1200-1530.* *Map 2, B4, p252* A careful recreation of the original Miss Cranston's Tearooms, secreted away above a jeweller's and designed by Charles Rennie Mackintosh. It's filled with many of his original features and looks striking with its high backed chairs. Most visitors come here for the design, but they also offer a selection of sandwiches and cakes, as well as hot meals. There's also a sister branch at 97 Buchanan St (**T** 0141-2045242. *Mon-Sat 0930-1700, Sun 1200-1700*), which is licensed. No smoking area.

West End

Restaurants

£££ The Buttery, 652 Argyle St, **T** 0141- 221 8188. *Tue-Fri 1200-1400, 1900-2200; Sat 1800-2200.* *Map 3, L8, p255* Victoriana abounds in this old favourite with its clubby atmosphere. Consistently rated as one of the best in the city, with an emphasis on the finest Scottish fish, seafood and game. Good high-quality wine list.

£££ The Cabin, 996-998 Dumbarton Rd, **T** 0141-5691036. *Tue-Sat, lunch Tue-Fri 1200-1400. Closed Mon/Sun. BYOB.* *Map 3, G0, p255* If your idea of a good night out is piles of the finest Scottish food followed by a post-dinner cabaret by Wilma, the legendary singing waitress, then this is the place for you. A truly one-off experience and great fun. Not to be missed. The only drawback is there's only one dinner sitting, at 1930.

£££ The Cook's Room, 13 Woodside Crescent, **T** 0141-353 0707. *Mon-Sat 1200-1430 and 1800-2200.* *Map 3, I8, p255* This former southside favourite has now moved to the West End, taking over Nick Nairn's old premises. They serve good modern Scottish food in clean blue and cream surroundings. Look out for dishes like tarragon chicken and leave room to try their great puddings. Sunday brunch is good value and you can eat more cheaply at lunchtime than in the evening.

£££ Dining Room, 41 Byres Rd, **T** 0141 339 3666. *Map 3, G2, p255* Acclaimed, imaginative food at this West End restaurant. Mains might include a creamy asparagus and pea risotto, and warm carrot cake with marmalade ice cream for dessert.

£££ La Parmigiana, 443 Great Western Rd, **T** 0141-334 0686. *Mon-Sat 1200-1430, 1800-2300.* *Map 3, F6, p254* This sophisticated, very traditional, Italian restaurant is one of Glasgow's finest eating establishments. Mains might include sausage ragu with polenta – you don't nip in here for a quick pizza. Recommended for a special occasion.

£££ Stravaigin, 28-30 Gibson St, **T** 0141-334 2665. *Tue-Thu, 1700-2230, Fri-Sun 1200-1430, 1700-2300.* *Map 3, G6, p255* Hard to define but difficult to resist. An eclectic mix of flavours and prime Scottish ingredients to produce the most sublime results. Expensive but you won't get better value for money in this category and it totally justifies its many awards. Upstairs is a café-bar where you can sample some of that fabulous food at more affordable prices.

£££ Two Fat Ladies, 88 Dumbarton Rd, **T** 0141-3391944. *Mon-Sat 1200-1500, 1730-2230; Sun 1730-2230. Map 3, G1, p255* Fantastic fish and seafood in the humblest of surroundings, tucked away in an unfashionable corner of the West End. Prepare your tastebuds for smoked haddock, baked sole or scallops.

£££ The Ubiquitous Chip, 12 Ashton La, **T** 0141-334 5007. *Mon-Sat 1200-1430, 1730-2300; Sun 1230-1500, 1830-2300. Map 3, F3, p254* 'The Chip', as it's known locally, is a ground-breaking, multi award-winning restaurant and still the city's favourite place for Mctastic Scottish food, especially venison and seafood. All served in a plant-filled, covered courtyard patio. Upstairs is their bistro, **Upstairs at the Chip** (*daily 1200-2300*), which doesn't make you feel quite as special but is much easier on the wallet.

££ Air Organic, 36 Kelvingrove St, **T** 0141-5645200. *Sun-Thu and Sun 1200-2200, Fri-Sat 1200-2230. Map 3, I6, p255* Ultra-cool, futuristic looking bistro in the West End. The type that could only really exist in Glasgow. Styled on Miami International Airport and serving organic and orgasmic fusion food like prawn and lemon linguine. Try their Thai or Japanese offerings. No smoking area.

££ Ashoka Ashton Lane, 19 Ashton La, **T** 0141-337 1115. *Mon-Thu 1200-2400; Fri/Sat 1200-0030; Sun 1700-2400. Map 3, E4, p254* First-class Indian restaurant, part of the famous west coast chain. Very popular with students and Byres Road trendies.

££ Ashoka West End, 1284 Argyle St, **T** 0141-339 3371. *Sun-Thu 1700-0030, Fri,Sat 1700-0100. Map 3, 14, p255* The oldest in this ever-popular chain of excellent Indian eateries. Great value and a vegetarian-friendly menu.

££ The Bothy, 11 Ruthven La, **T** 0141-334 4040. *Daily 1200-2400. Map 3, E2, p254* New kid on the culinary block. Owned by the same people at Corinthian, it offers traditional Scottish food in rustic surroundings – all done in a modern, ironic West End sort of way.

££ Brel, 39-43 Ashton La, **T** 0141-3424966. *Daily 1200-2230, bar open later. Map 3, F3, p254* Another stylish continental eating establishment in Glasgow's hippest culinary quarter. This time it's Belgian so delicious beers, and moules frites are on the menu. Great food and great value, especially during the half-price happy hour (1700-1900).

££ Café India, 171 North St, **T** 0141-248 4074. *Mon-Thu 1200-2400, Fri-Sat 1200-0030, Sun 1500-2400. Map 3, J8, p255* Cavernous Indian restaurant that's big on style and has a deserved reputation for fine food. Dishes are mainly Punjabi. Good value buffet downstairs (1200-1400 Mon-Fri, daily 1800-2230).

££ Cottier's, 93-95 Hyndland St, **T** 0141-357 5825. *Mon-Thu 1200-1600, 1700-2230, Fri-Sat 1200-1600, 1700-2300; Sun 1200-2230. Map 3, F1, p254* Very elegant Caribbean style restaurant housed in a converted church. The food is heavenly and the ambience spiritually rewarding. These dear souls are also great with kids, bless them. Stylish bar and theatre downstairs on the ground floor where you can often hear live music (see p185).

££ Cul de Sac, 44-46 Ashton La, **T** 0141-334 6688. *Sun-Thu 1200-2300, Fri-Sat 1200-2400. Map 3, F3, p254* Effortlessly fashionable, laid back and oh, so boho. A great place to sit back, soak up the atmosphere and enjoy good French-style food. Their famous crêpes are half price between 1700 and 1900, as are the tasty burgers and pasta. Good vegetarian choices too, and it's a great place to work off last night's excesses with a hearty Sunday brunch.

££ Gingerhill, 1 Hillhead St, **T** 0141-956 6515. *Wed-Sun 1930-2130. Map 1, D3, p250* Well off the beaten track in posh Milngavie, but well worth the trip. Has a reputation as one of Glasgow's best seafood restaurants. It's an awfy wee place so you'll have to book well in advance. No smoking. BYOB (no licence).

££ Gong, 17 Vinicombe St, **T** 0141-576 1700. *Mon-Thu 1700-2230, Fri, Sat, 1200-1500, 1700-0200, Sun 1200-1500, 1700-2230, bar open longer. Map 3, E4, p254* Sleek new venture housed in an old cinema that is already proving popular with the locals. Lots of sharing platters and Italian and Mexican influences. Brunch served at weekends.

££ Killermont Polo Club, 2022 Maryhill Rd, **T** 0141-9465412. *Daily 1200-2300. Map 1, C4, p250* An exclusive, elegant Indian restaurant that offers a genuinely new culinary experience with their astonishing Dum Pukht (slow-cooked) menu. A bit out of the way, but worth it for something out-of-the-ordinary.

££ Mother India, 28 Westminster Terr, Sauchiehall St, **T** 0141-221 1663. *Mon, Tue 1730-2230, Wed,Thu 1200-1400, 1730-2230, Fri 1200-1400, 1700-2300, Sat 1300-2300; Sun 1630-2200. Map 3, J6, p255* Exquisite Indian cooking in chic, bistro-style surroundings. Among the unusual dishes on the menu is smoked haddock in Punjabi spices. Surprisingly affordable prices that won't put undue strain on your wallet. There's a friendly and informal atmosphere and a refreshingly strong vegetarian selection. Cheap set lunch and good banquet menus. BYOB.

££ Mr Singh's India, 149 Elderslie St, **T** 0141-204 0186. *Mon-Sat 1200-2400 Sun 1430-2400. Map 3, J7, p255*
Imagine good Punjabi cooking brought to you by kilted waiters with a background wallpaper of disco music. If that sounds like your cup of char then get on down here and join in the fun. Many celebs have, so you never know who might pop in for a poppadum. Very child friendly.

££ Oblomov, 372-374 Great Western Rd, **T** 0141-339 9177. *Mon-Fri 1600-2200, Sat, Sun 1100-2200, bar open later. Map 3, F7, p254* An arty West End crowd fills this eaterie, named after a novel by 19th-century Russian writer Ivan Goncharov. That's pretty well where the East European theme ends as food is more modern bistro style with some more exotic dishes like Japanese-style chicken, as well as mains like pasta and burgers. There's also a very popular brunch menu available at weekends.

££ Shish Mahal, 66-68 Park Rd, **T** 0141-339 8256. *Mon-Thu 1200-1400, 1700-2330, Fri, Sat 1200-1145, Sun 1700-2330. Map 3, F7, p254* 'The Shish' has long been a byword for great curry in Glasgow – they've been here since 1964 and are still satisfying the locals. The Pakistani food's imaginative and there's loads of choice. Worth trying one of the house specialities like chilli and garlic nishilee. You can BYOB.

££ Stazione, 1051 Great Western Rd, **T** 0141-576 7576. *Mon-Fri 1200-1430, 1700-2230, Sat, Sun 1200-2200. Map 1, D3, p250* Housed in a converted Victorian train station, this is most definitely the "rail" thing. It's stylish and comfortable, serves excellent Mediterranean food (there are strong Moroccan influences) and has great service. Good vegetarian selection, too. No smoking area.

Cafés

The Bay Tree, 403 Great Western Rd, **T** 0141-334 5898. *Mon-Sat 0930-2100; Sun 1000-2000.* *Map 3, F7, p254* Rather basic, but good value, self-service café serving food with a Middle Eastern emphasis. Come for a fry-up or something more exotic.

Brasserie Metro, 8 Cresswell La, **T** 0141-338 8131. *Mon-Sat 0800-1800; also opens Sun.* *Map 3, E4, p254* Big and bright West End café just off Byres Rd that's popular with students. Wide-ranging menu makes it a good, cheap choice for lunch with things like homemade soup, cauliflower bake or fish cakes. No smoking area.

Grassroots Café, 97 St Georges Rd, **T** 0141-3330534. *Daily 1000-2200.* *Map 3, I8, p255* Vegetarian and vegan organic food at this cool, intimate café near St Georges Cross. There are strong North African and Middle Eastern influences which provide a welcome change for jaded vegetarian palates. Lots of soups and salads and filling main courses like tajines with apricot, lemon and pistachio couscous or no nonsense veggie bangers with mash.

Grosvenor Café, 31 Ashton La, **T** 0141-339 1848. *Mon, Tue 0900-1600; Wed-Sat 0900-2200; Sun 1000-1800. Behind Hillhead Underground.* *Map 3, F3, p254* A perennial favourite with local students who come for the wide selection of cheap food (filled rolls, soup, burgers, pizzas, etc). Cosy and friendly atmosphere.

Little Italy, 205 Byres Rd, **T** 0141-339 6287. *Mon-Thu 0800-2200, Fri, Sat 0800-1145, Sun 1000-2200.* *Map 3, F3, p254* A convenient and buzzy refuelling stop that never seems to close. Great pizza and strong espresso. A favourite with everyone from West End trendies to scruffy students.

North Star, 108 Queen Margaret Dr, **T** 0141-946 5365. *Mon 0800-1800, Tue-Thu 0800-1900, Fri, Sat 0800-2000, Sun 1100-1800.* *Map 3, B6, p254* Portugese café/deli that has an extremely loyal following. Good speciality treats.

Otago, 61 Otago St, **T** 0141-337 2282. *Daily 1100-2200.* *Map 3, F6, p254* There's a cool, minimalist look to this Mediterranean bistro where the West Ends boho population come to read the newspapers and chat. The menu offers lots of veggie choices like asparagus risotto and there are filling meaty mains too. There's a good selection of wines on offer.

Tinderbox, 189 Byres Rd, **T** 0141-339 3108. *Mon-Sat 0745-2300, Sun 0845-2300.* *Map 3, F3, p254* Coffee shop which looks and feels more like a style bar. Great coffee, good magazines to read and a large no smoking, child-friendly area.

TchaiOvna, 42 Otago La, **T** 0141-357 4524. *Daily 1100-2300.* *Map 3, G6, p255* Laid back Czech inspired café, where you'll find a relaxed boho atmosphere, light meals and a huge selection of teas to choose from.

University Café, 87 Byres Rd, **T** 0141-339 5217. *Mon-Thu 0900-2200; Fri, Sat 0900-2230, Sun 1000-2200.* *Map 3, G2, p254* A gloriously authentic Italian art deco café, where grannies and students sit shoulder-to-shoulder enjoying real cappuccino, great ice cream and good, honest and cheap mince and tatties, pie and chips, sausage rolls, gammon steak and all the other golden oldies.

South of the Clyde

Restaurants

££ **Arigo**, 67 Kilmarnock Rd, **T** 0141-636 6616. *Mon-Fri 1200-1430, 1700-2230, Sat, Sun 1200-2230.* *Map 1, H4, p250* Good Italian restaurant offering high quality fresh food and generous portions that make you think twice about indulging in a dessert. The sort of place that doesn't need to advertise.

££ **Ashoka Southside**, 268 Clarkston Rd, **T** 0141-637 0711. *Fri,Sat 1700-2400; Sun-Thu 1700-2300.* *Map 1, H6, p250* Small and intimate Southside version of this venerable chain of Glaswegian Indian restaurants. All the usual suspects are on the menu, together with some more interesting options like massala lamb chops.

££ **The Greek Golden Kebab**, 34 Sinclair Drive, **T** 0141-649 7581. *Thu-Sun 1700-0100.* *Map 1, H6, p250* It might sound like a takeaway but this is a restaurant and an enduring favourite with those who come for the home cooked Greek food. Squeeze inside – it's only small, and try one of the many lamb dishes, or a rich aubergine and tomato veggie bake.

££ **Spice Garden**, 11-17 Clyde Pl, **T** 0141-429 4422. *Daily 1800-0430.* *Map 1, F5, p250* There's an enormous choice at this popular Indian restaurant that prides itself on its cleanliness. Although its location isn't immediately glamorous (by the railway), the food is good and it's conveniently open all night – so good for those desperate for a post-club curry.

£ Buongiorno, 1021 Pollokshaws Rd, **T** 0141-649 1029. *Mon-Sat 0900-2300; Sun 1000-2200. Map 1, G5, p250* The best pizza in Glasgow – at these prices? Impossible, surely. Well, check it for yourself. Impeccable Italian family cooking, with cosy ambience to match. They even have a pre-theatre two-for-one deal! Are they crazy? Simply unbeatable, so book ahead.

Cafés

Art Lovers' Café, Bellahouston Park, Drumbreck Rd, **T** 0141-353 4779. *Daily 1000-1700. Map 1, F3, p250* Housed in CRM's exquisite House for an Art Lover, see p90. A nice place to chill and a good selection of light snacks and hot or cold meals. Some imaginative veggie choices like roasted parsnip, spinach and parmesan risotto, as well as tasty meaty mains. No smoking.

Around Glasgow

££ Bistro@Bute Discovery Centre, Winter Gardens, Rothesay, **T** 01700-500505. Offers good-value lunches and dinners.

££ Ristorante La Vigna, 40 Wellgate, Lanark, **T** 01555-630351. *Open daily for lunch and dinner.* Italian restaurant of some renown and the best place to eat in town. It is popular, so book in advance.

Cafés

Nardini's, on the Promenade, Largs, **T** 01475-674555. *Daily 2230 in summer.* Don't leave town without visiting this authentic 1950s Italian café. It's an institution and is reckoned by some to be the best café in Scotland. Though it has changed hands in recent years, it still pushes all the right buttons. The ice cream is worth the trip alone but it also does good Italian food and coffee.

West End Café, 1-3 Gallowgate, Rothesay, **T** 01700-503596. *Easter-Sep 1200-1400 and 1600-2400 (closed Mon).* It is an absolute must while you are on Bute to sample the superb fish and chips at this award-winning chippie. It's open for takeaways all year round, and for sit-down meals. Phone ahead from your hotel or B&B to avoid the massive queues.

Bars and clubs

Glasgow comes alive after dark with a buzzing nightlife culture, from live music and bars to cafés and clubs. Glasgow definitely has something for everyone, whether it's hands-in-the-air dancing, checking out some new bands or catching one of the big names on their world tour.

The city is bursting at the seams with bars, many of which are excellent pre-club venues to get you in the mood for a night's clubbing. The DJ sets normally start at 2100 and carry on until 2400 but some start earlier depending on the DJs. Entry is normally free, with some charging after 2300. Clubbers of all tastes and styles are catered for, with some of the UK's biggest and best club nights.

There are also many places to hear live music and with so many venues to play in, its no surprise that Glasgow has produced a mass of excellent bands. The biggest names over the years have included Travis and Texas as well as smaller indie bands such as Belle & Sebastian and Teenage Fanclub, to name just a few.

Club opening times are pretty much the same all over, with doors opening from 2300 until 0300. Entry costs can vary from £2-5 for the smaller venues, and £5-10 for the bigger venues, while you can pay up to £20 from some of the special club nights with top class DJs.

The bars are open from around 1100-2300 during the week and 1100-2400 on Friday and Saturday, with music-only venues normally opening around 1900 before support bands come on.

George Square and the Merchant City

Pubs and bars

Babbity Bowster, 16-18 Blackfriars St, **T** 0141-552 5055. *Mon-Sat 1100-2400, Sun 1000-2400. Map 2, F11, p253. See also p123 and p144* Prime Merchant City pub in an 18th-century townhouse, this is a place that has everything; lively atmosphere, wide selection of real ales and good food.

Bar 91, 91 Candleriggs, **T** 0141-552 5211. *Mon-Sat 1100-2400, Sun 1200-2400. Map 2, F10, p253* This cool bar in the Merchant City manages to cater for the after-work crowd as well as pre-clubbers. It's comfortable, relaxed and a good place to eat. Happy-hour specials 1700-2000.

Bargo, 80 Albion St, **T** 0141-553 4771. *Mon-Sat 1200-2400, Sun 1230-2400. Map 2, F10, p253* Stylish and spacious Merchant City bar/bistro with surprisingly good food and a high posing quotient. Can be a bit empty, especially during the week. (See also 'Eating').

Blackfriars, 36 Bell St, **T** 0141-552 5924. *Mon-Sat 1200-2400, Sun 1230-2400. Map 2, G10, p253* Merchant City favourite which pulls in the punters with its vast range of international beers and lagers. Real ales, Belgian beers and a dark traditional interior. Also a wide range of excellent grub, live music and comedy at weekends and that inimitable Glasgow atmosphere (see p182 and p184).

Rab Ha's, 83 Hutcheson St, **T** 0141-572 0400. *Mon-Sat 1100-2400, Sun 1230-2400.* ***Map 2, F9, p253. See also p123*** This old Merchant City stalwart still packs 'em in. It has an enviable reputation for its food and is above the restaurant of the same name. Décor is cosy with lots of dark wood panelling, while regulars include cheery, well-lunched men in suits.

Strata, 45 Queen St, **T** 0141-221 1888. *Daily 1200-2400.* ***Map 2, F7, p253*** Another horizontally cool but nicely relaxed bar, slap bang in the city centre, where you can strut your stuff before heading off to the clubs.

Vespa, 17 John St, **T** 0141-552 4017. *Daily 1000-2400.* ***Map 2, E9, p253*** As the name suggests there's a contemporary Italian theme at this slick bar next to Glasgow's branch of Armani. Good range of pastas to eat, and outdoor seats for posing on fine days.

Yang, 33 Queen St, **T** 0141-248 8484. ***Map 2, F7, p253*** A 3-bar venue with DJs to get you in the mood for *Archaos* next door or for their own bar/club downstairs.

Clubs

Archaos, 25 Queen St, **T** 0141-204 3189. ***Map 2, F7, p253*** A younger, more dressy crowd head out to Archaos for house, techno and club classics in this massive venue.

Babaza, 25 Royal Exchange Sq, **T** 0141-204 0101. ***Map 2, E7, p253*** An unusual club venue with drapes and booths as well as an 'up for it' crowd who love their R&B and hip hop.

MAS, 29 Royal Exchange Sq, **T** 0141-221 7080. *Map 2, E7, p253* As well as being the temporary home of the Sub Club nights which include the incredibly popular and weekly Sub Culture and Optimo, it is also holds its own nights including a staff night for all hardworking bar and club staff, and hip hop nights.

Trongate to the East End

Pubs and bars

13th Note Café, 50-60 King St, **T** 0141-553 1638. *Daily 1200-2400.* *Map 2, H9, p253* Established East End hang out attracting students and arty types. Good helpings of vegan and veggie food, and a buzzy live music venue (see also p171).

McChuills, 40 High St, **T** 0141-552 2135. *Map 2, G11, p253* A great place to drink, chat or meet before going to a gig at the Barrowlands or pre-clubbing. DJs play everything from hip hop to funk.

The Scotia Bar, 112 Stockwell St, **T** 0141-552 8681. *Mon-Sat 1100-2400, Sun 1230-2400.* *Map 2, H8, p253* This East End pub claims to be the oldest in town, and its low ceilings and wooden beams support a convincing argument. It's also the best place in town for folk music (see p187), and much-frequented by writers, poets and drinking thinkers (or thinking drinkers).

The Victoria Bar, 159 Bridgegate, **T** 0141-552 6040. *Mon-Sat 1100-2400, Sun 1230-2400.* *Map 2, I8, p253* Real traditional howff in one of Glasgow's oldest streets. Seemingly unchanged since the late 19th century and long may it stay that way. One of the city's great pubs, where entertainment is provided free, courtesy of the local wags.

Buchanan Street to Charing Cross

Pubs and bars

Ad Lib, 111 Hope St, **T** 0141-248 6645. *Map 2, D5, p252* Bar and food by day, bar and club by night. A trendy crowd with good weekend DJs.

The Arches, 253 Argyle St, **T** 0901-022 0300. *Daily 1200-2000; bar open 1100-2400. Map 2, F5, p252* Part of the legendary club, this stylish basement bar is the ideal place to get hyped before heading in to one of their many popular club nights. Also the perfect place to linger over a Belgian beer or enjoy their food. See p.

Bar 10, 10 Mitchell St, **T** 0141-572 1448. *Mon-Sat 1000-2400, Sun 1200-2400. Map 2, F6, p252* This converted warehouse is Glasgow's original style bar and still as cool as ever. Good food on offer and a popular pre-club meeting place at weekends with regular DJs.

Bar Soba, 11 Mitchell La, **T** 0141-204 2404. *Mon-Sat 1000-2400, Sun 1100-2400. Map 2, E6, p252* There's a 1970's feel to this bar on the ground floor of *The Lighthouse*. Soba manages to combine being a bar with a great club feel. Food is Asian fusion and the cocktails are good.

Bloc, 117 Bath St, **T** 0141-574 6066. *Mon-Thu and Sun 1200-2400 (food served until 1900), Fri, Sat 1200-0200 (food served until late). Map 2, C5, p252* Another Bath Street style bar, with good DJs and food that's a mix of Eastern European and Far Eastern flavours. It gets nice and buzzy attracting a lively pre-club crowd.

Candy Bar, 185 Hope St, **T** 0141-353 7240. *Mon-Sat 1200-2400, Sun 1600-2400. Map 2, C5, p252* Billed as one of the city's coolest bars (Prince William has been spotted at its sister venue in

Edinburgh), this is the place to flaunt those new clothes you splashed out on in the Italian Centre. Exotic bites, pasta dishes and lots of posing - a long way from spit and sawdust.

The Griffin, 226 Bath St, **T** 0141-331 5171. *Mon-Tue 1200-2300, Wed-Sat 1200-2400, Sun 1230-2300. Map 2, B1, p252* Opposite the King's Theatre. Turn of the century pub (not t he most recent one) recently renovated but losing none of its style. Still the best place in the city for pie and chips and a drink. Also a good place to meet the locals. Other traditional dishes, plus vegetarian are served at amazing value.

The Horse Shoe Bar, 7 Drury St, **T** 0141-229 5711. *Between Mitchell St and Renfield St, near the station. Map 2, D6, p252* Classic Victorian Gin Palace that is still one of the city's favourites. Its much-copied island bar is the longest continuous bar in the UK, so it shouldn't take long to get served, which is fortunate as it gets very busy. Incredibly good-value, no nonsense food served Mon-Sat 1200-1930, Sun 1230-1700 and perhaps the cheapest pint in town. If you only visit one pub during your stay, then make sure it's this one.

Kelly Cooper Bar, 158-166 Bath St, **T** 0141-331 4060. *Mon-Wed 1200-0100, Thu 1200-0200, Fri, Sat 1200-0300, Sun 1300-0100. Map 2, B4, p252* Style conscious newcomer on the Glasgow scene – full of hot to trot locals and the odd celeb, so dress to impress. Upstairs is *Lowdown*, see below.

Lowdown, 158-166 Bath St, **T** 0141-331 4061. *Mon-Thu 1700-0100, Fri, Sat 1700-0300, Sun 2100-0300. Map 2, B4, p252* Another cool hangout that majors on cocktails. It also does a tasty line in tapas and R&B sounds on Sundays and Thursdays.

Moskito, 200 Bath St, **T** 0141 331 1777. ***Map 2, B3, p252*** A newish addition to the bar scene in Glasgow, with DJs at the weekends.

Nice 'n' Sleazy, 421 Sauchiehall St, **T** 0141-333 9637. ***Map 2, A1, p252*** A tongue-in-cheek and eclectic mix of people and music, with pre-club DJs such as Bitch School who play a mix of rock and metal on Sun afternoons and a more laid back funky feel at other times.

Nicos, 395 Sauchiehall St, **T** 0141-332 5736. ***Map 2, A2, p252*** A well-known and long-standing bar in Sauchiehall St with DJs playing pre-club pop, hip hop and garage at weekends.

The Pot Still, 154 Hope St, **T** 0141-333 0980. *Mon-Thu 1100-2300, Fri, Sat 1100-2400, Sun 1230-2300.* ***Map 2, C5, p252*** Edwardian pub with lots of original features, justly famous for its massive range of malts (there's around 500 of them so you'll need more than one visit). They also have a selection of cask ales and decent pub grub during the day.

St Judes, 190 Bath St, **T** 0141-352 8800. ***Map 2, B4, p252*** The haunt of Glasgow's trendy media types with fine cocktails and occasional but top-notch DJs.

Spy Bar, 153 Bath St, **T** 0141-221 7711. *Mon-Sat 1200-2400, Sun 1800-2400.* ***Map 2, B4, p252*** A sleek bar with lots of mirrors and wacky colours. A popular pre-club haunt with a trendy crowd wanting jazz, funk, house and soul from Thursday to Sunday. Food ranges from sandwiches and soups to more substantial fare. Monday to Saturday 1200-2400 (food until 2000).

Tom Tom, 207 Bath St, **T** 0141-248 2123. *Daily 1200-2400.* ***Map 2, B3, p252*** New classy-looking bar with lots of light wood and airy space upstairs, and a cosier, more snug feel downstairs. DJs play chilled sounds at night.

Variety Bar, 401 Sauchiehall St, **T** 0141-332 4449. *Map 2, A1, p252* An atmospheric art deco bar with as varied a crowd as the music policy and DJ sounds. Various drink promotions and happy hours with good music.

Zinc, Princes Sq, **T** 0141-225 5620. *Mon-Sat 0900-2400, Sun 1200-2400. Map 2, E/F7, p253* Terence Conran designed style bar in the elegant Princes Square shopping mall. Convenient and chilled shopping stop that serves bistro style food.

Clubs

13th Note Club, 260 Clyde St, **T** 0141-243 2177. *Map 2, H6, p252* A fine club that not only has two bars over two floors but also holds live music and club nights. A laid-back space with a smorgasbord of musical tastes from electro and hip hop to jazz and indie. See also p167.

Alaska, 142 Bath La, **T** 0141-248 1777. *Map 2, B4, p252* A happening club with monthly nights Foot Therapy, Homebass from the Jengaheads and Freelance Science from the Slam boys, Orde Meikle and Stuart McMillan.

Arches, Midland St, **T** 0901-022 0300. *Map 2, F5, p252* This venue is home to some of Glasgow's best club nights including top-notch DJs Paul Oakenfold and Carl Cox at Colours, Judge Jules at Inside Out, and the Slam boys at Pressure, as well as Traxx and the Sunday Social which includes DJs and live music.

Asylum, 70 Cowcaddens Rd, **T** 0141-332 0681. *Map 2, A6, p252* This club is set in Caledonian University and as well as being a student union it is also a club with a regular alternative indie night.

Cathouse, 15 Union St, **T** 0141-248 6606. *Map 2, F5, p252* If you like all things rock this is definitely the place for you, with two floors devoted to metal, grunge, thrash and a good bit of moshing.

Destiny, 18 Cambridge St, **T** 0141-353 6555. *Map 2, A5, p252* A dressed-up club for a slightly older crowd wanting to party to the latest dance tracks.

CCA, 350 Sauchiehall St, **T** 0141-352 4900. *Map 2, A3, p252* The Centre for Contemporary Arts mixes music, art and visuals on their popular club nights Future World Funk and Sonic Mook Experiment.

Club Budda, 142 St Vincent St, **T** 0141-221 5660. *Map 2, D4, p252* A small, trendy club with loads of house, garage, soul and funk at the weekends from resident DJs. Downstairs Budda, an ideal place to get ready for a night's clubbing, with DJs to keep you going.

Fury Murrys, 96 Maxwell St, **T** 0141-221 6511. *Map 2, H7, p253* A busy club, full of students who like a bit of party and chart music.

g2, 474 Sauchiehall St, **T** 0141-353 3111. *Map 2, A1, p252* A weekend haunt for clubbers in search of a good dance to anything from party anthems and disco to funk and soul.

Garage, 490 Sauchiehall St, **T** 0141-332 1120. *Map 2, A1, p252* A student 'must' with several club rooms to enjoy the cheap drink. Check out the weird décor and dance to chart and dance tunes.

Glasgow School of Art, 167 Renfrew St, **T** 0141-332 0691. *Map 2, A4, p252* A venue with a varying club night schedule including the weekly Divine Funk and Northern Soul night as well as the techno My Machines night. Popular nights for students and clubbers young and old.

Havana, 50 Hope St, **T** 0141-248 4466. *Map 2, E5, p252* Is it a bar, is it a restaurant, or is it a club? All three, in fact. Latin grooves, Latin food and Latin spirit, all rolled into one. Cocktails, cigars and salsa. Coming here is like stepping into a Bacardi advert.

Privilege, 69 Hope St, **T** 0141-204 5233. *Map 2, F5, p252* A crazy club with busy club nights, but none more so than Shagtag – a very appropriately named night with house and trance music and the chance to meet the person of your dreams, or not as the case may be.

Reds, 375 Sauchiehall St, **T** 0141-331 1635. *Map 2, A1/2, p252* A small but popular club offering a wide range of musical styles.

Riverside Club, 33 Fox St, **T** 0141-569 7287. *Map 2, H6, p252* Home to hard-core rave club Shake the Disease and electro club Spanner. It also doubles as a ceilidh venue.

Shack, 193 Pitt St, **T** 0141-332 7522. *Map 2, B2, p252* This venue is huge, in fact it's an old converted church, which is popular with students and young clubbers alike. Chart and dance tunes abound.

Strawberry Fields, 56 Oswald St, **T** 0141-221 7871. *Map 2, F4, p252* A club playing music from the 60s through to present-day chart stuff.

Sub Club, 22 Jamaica St, **T** 0141-248 4600. *Map 2, G5, p252* The 'Subby' suffered from severe smoke and water damage over a year ago after a fire broke out in the adjoining building. It is undoubtedly one of Glasgow's best-loved clubs and the regulars are eagerly awaiting its return. They will be home again to their popular club nights including Sub Culture and Optimo which are temporarily at MAS.

Twenty-four hour party people
Glasgow's image as a place of hard drinking and alcohol-fuelled fighting has been hard to shake off but, slowly, the city is becoming better known for its wild club nights than drunken brawls. People are now hitting the dancefloor instead of each other.

Trash, 197 Pitt St, **T** 0141-572 3372. *Map 2, B2, p252* A club made up of several rooms offering a mix of music but mainly focusing on the studenty house and R&B gang.

Tunnel, 84 Mitchell St, **T** 0141-204 1000. *Map 2, E6, p252* One of Glasgow's posiest and best-dressed clubs with a regular crowd who know their DJs and their favourite house style.

Velvet Rooms, 520 Sauchiehall St, **T** 0141-332 0755. *Map 2, A6, p252* A popular Sauchiehall Street haunt for students and dressed-up drinkers who want to enjoy everything from R&B and soul to more commercial sounds.

West End

Pubs and bars

Air Organic, 36 Kelvingrove St, **T** 564 5201. ***Map 3, I6, p255***
A popular West End place to be seen in and to enjoy some of the best DJs before you head into town.

Brel, 39 Ashton La, **T** 0141-342 4966. ***Map 3, F3, p254***
Belgian-themed bar in the West End which has DJs on several nights a week playing laid-back sounds as well as hip hop and soul.

Cul de Sac, Ashton La, **T** 0141-334 8899. ***Map 3, F3, p254***
Situated in the lively Ashton La, the Sac is an atmospheric bar where DJs play a wide selection of sounds and styles but all of which are designed to create a good vibe.

Firebird, 1321 Argyle St, **T** 0141-334 0594. *Mon-Thu 1130-2400, Fri, Sat 1130-0100, Sun 1230-2400.* ***Map 3, I4, p255*** A cool place to hang out in the West End and have food, drinks and listen to some of Glasgow's finest DJs on Thu-Sun. Has the advantage of providing excellent food, especially their crispy pizzas. Itis got a Mediterranean, terracotta interior and its large windows make it light and bright – as well as giving you great views of Kelvingrove.

The Halt Bar, 160 Woodlands Rd, **T** 0141-564 1527. *Mon-Sat 1100-2400, Sun 1230-2400.* ***Map 3, H8, p255*** This erstwhile tram stop (hence the name) is one of Glasgow's great, endearingly scruffy, unspoiled pubs with many of the original Edwardian fixtures intact. It is also a great place to see live music two or three times a week or watch a match on the big screen TV (unless you're supporting England of course).

Lock 27, 1100 Crow Rd, **T** 0141-958 0853. *Map I, D3, p250* If the weather's fine (and it sometimes is), there are few nicer places to enjoy a spot of al fresco eating and drinking than this place by the Forth and Clyde Canal in Anniesland. Good food served until 2100 and kids are made welcome. You could take a stroll along the towpath afterwards.

McChuills Way Out West, 10-14 Kelvinhaugh St, **T** 0141-576 5018. *Map 3, J5, p255* Sister bar to the East End fave, this West End version plays host to a more studenty crowd as well as weekend DJs.

The Tap, 1055 Sauchiehall St, **T** 0141-339 0643. *Mon-Thu 1200-2300, Fri, Sat 1200-2400, Sun 1230-2300. Map 3, I4, p255* Classic student haunt, within easy skiving distance of the university. Convivial atmosphere, very cheap food and a good selection of ales on tap are all major attractions.

Tennent's, 191 Byres Rd, **T** 0141-341 1024. *Map 3, F3, p255* Big, no-nonsense, old West End favourite, serving a range of fine ales and about 15 different malt whiskies to a genuinely mixed crowd. It's also a great place for a chat (no music) and some very cheap food.

Uisge Beatha, 232 Woodlands Rd, **T** 0141-564 1596. *Map 3, G7, p255* The "water of life" is one of those pubs where you go for a wee drink and you're still there many hours later, the day's plans in ruins around your feet. Looks and feels like a real Highland hostelry. Cosy and welcoming and serving ridiculously cheap food. Scottish in every sense, and 135 whiskies to choose from too.

West is best
The city's West End is a great place to hang out. The narrow cobbled lanes around Byres Road are lined with quirky independent shops, bars and cafés and lots of top-notch restaurants.

Clubs

Cleopatra's, 508 Great Western Rd, **T** 0141-334 0560. *Map 3, E6, p254* This Glasgow institution has been around for years and is well known for its lively clubbers and packed dance floor for chart tunes.

Queen Margaret Union, 22 University Gardens, **T** 0141-339 9784. *Map 3, F4, p254* A student union that doubles up as a club and music venue. In club terms it is known for its regular nights as well as Glasgow's Bugged Out! Night of techno.

Along the Clyde

Clubs

Renfrew Ferry, Clyde St, **T** 0141-227 5511. As the name suggest this is a ferry which holds one-off club nights, including the fantastically kitsch Vegas night when you can dress up in all your finery, have a go at the gambling tables and dance the night away to some excellent easy listening tunes.

South of the Clyde

Pubs and bars

Samuel Dow's, 69-71 Nithsdale Rd, **T** 0141-423 0107. *Map1, G5, p250* Sammy Dow's (as it's known by its many Shawlands regulars) is a friendly Southside local serving good real ales (Deuchars, plus a selection of guest ales) and cheap bar food. Also hosts regular live music nights and a Thu jam session.

The Taverna, 778 Pollokshaws Rd, **T** 0141-424 0858. *Map 1, G5, p250* Popular Southside venue near the Tramway Theatre and Queen's Park. Nice, bright Mediterranean look and feel which extends to their love of kids. Good selection of ales and European beers, with everything from Belgian, Czech and German brands to choose from. They also do good value Mediterranean food, especially their pre-theatre dinner.

Tusk, 18 Moss Side Rd, **T** 0141-649 9199. *Map 1, H4, p250* Opulent Asian interior at this popular Southside style bar –a huge Buddha watches over proceedings. They've got a restaurant too.

Arts and entertainment

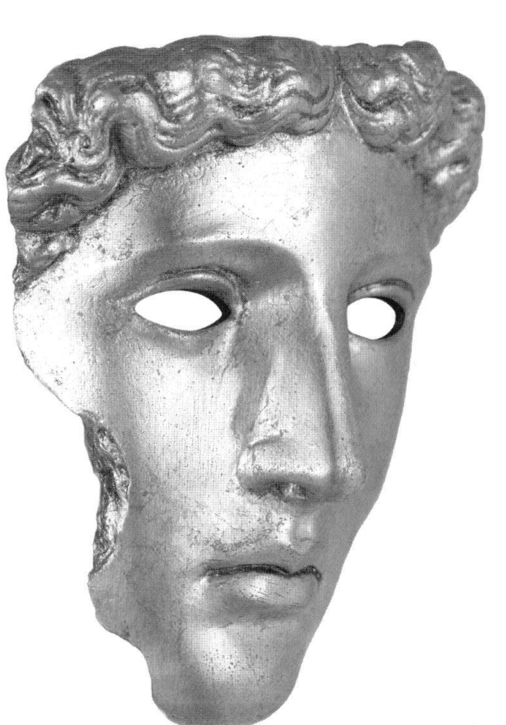

Glasgow enjoys a wide span of art, theatre, film and music. The majority of the larger theatres, concert halls and cinemas are concentrated in the city centre, though its two most renowned theatres – The Citizens' and the Tramway – are to be found south of the Clyde. The city is also a hotbed of live music which has gone from strength to strength over the years. There are now more bands than you can shake your booty at and countless live music venues ready to give everyone a stage.

Details of all the city's events are listed in the two local newspapers, *The Herald* and the *Evening Times*. Another excellent source of information is the fortnightly listings magazine *The List*, www.list.co.uk, which also covers Edinburgh. To book tickets for concerts or theatre productions, call at the **Ticket Centre**, City Hall, Candleriggs **T** 0141-287 4000. Note that some venues don't have their own box office. For tickets and information go to Tower Records, on Argyle St, **T** 0141-204 5788.

Cinema

Bombay Cinema, 5 Lorne St, Ibrox, **T** 0141-419 0722. *Map 1, E3, p250* Some of Bollywood's films are made in Scotland, so it's entirely fitting that there should be a dedicated cinema screening contemporary Bollywood hits.

Glasgow East Showcase, Barrbridge Leisure Centre, Langmuir, **T** 01236-438880. For mainstream films.

Glasgow Film Theatre (GFT), 12 Rose St, **T** 0141-3326535, www.gft.org.uk. *Map 2, B4, p252* There are plenty of cinemas in the city, but this one is in a league of its own. It's the city's leading independent cultural cinema, which looks as good inside as it does from the outside. There's always something interesting to see here, from top US indie hits to European cinema, and also a programme of World Film Festivals. Café Cosmo by the foyer (see p151) is a great place for a post-movie discussion or a cheap lunch.

Grosvenor, 31 Ashton La, **T** 0141-339 4298. *Map 3, F3, p254* A small cinema screening less mainstream films.

IMAX, Glasgow Science Centre, Pacific Quay, **T** 0141-420 5000. *Map 1, F4, p250* See p79 and p225.

Odeon City Centre, 56 Renfield St, **T** 0870-5050007, www.odeon.co.uk. *Map 2, C6, p252* For the usual Hollywood offerings. There's also an Odeon at the Quay, (Springfield Quay, Paisley Rd, **T** 0870-5050007, www.odeon.co.uk.)

UGC, 145 West Nile St, **T** 0870-907 0789. *Map 2, B7, p253* Mainstream filmic fare. There is another UGC at The Forge, (Parkhead, **T** 0870-1555136.)

Comedy

In the city that gave us Billy Connolly, Jerry Sadowitz and Rab C Nesbitt, you'd expect a thriving comedy scene. But although the streets of this city are where you can hear the funniest lines (for free), there are also a few clubs where you can sit down in comfort and listen to people who are paid to be funny.

Blackfriars, 36 Bell St, **T** 0141-552 5924. *Map 2, G10, p253* Regular slots on Sun nights. Also live jazz (see p184).

Jongleurs, UGC Development, Renfrew St, **T** 0870-7870707, www.jongleurs.com. *Map 2, B6, p252* Glasgow's own branch of the national laughter chain, on the site of the former Glasgow Apollo. Comedy Thu-Sun, tickets £7-13 depending on night.

Stand Comedy Club, 333 Woodlands Rd, **T** 0870-6006055, www.thestand.co.uk. *Map 3, G7, p255* Here you can see Scottish and international comedy acts every week, from Thu to Sun. It's very popular so you're advised to book in advance.

The State Bar, 148 Holland St, **T** 0141-332 2159. *Map 2, B2, p252* Good comedy club on Sat nights. Also live blues on Tue and a good selection of real ales.

Music

Glasgow has a number of venues for classical music and opera and is the home of **Scottish Opera**, the **Royal Scottish National Orchestr**a and the **BBC Scottish Symphony Orchestra**. The city attracts talent from all over the world. Traditional Scottish music is performed by the **Scottish Fiddle Orchestra** (www.sfo.org.uk) who perform at various venues in Glasgow to raise funds for a wide variety of charitable causes.

As for contemporary rock, pop and indie music, **The Barrowlands**, with its old-ballroom style décor and incredible atmosphere, has seen an amazing selection of bands over the years including home-grown talent as well as international bands. The **Scottish Exhibition and Conference Centre** (SECC) offers a larger arena-style venue for bigger tours.

The best places to see smaller gigs are at the **Garage**, **Cathouse**, **King Tuts Wah Wah Hut**, **13th Note** and **Nice'n'Sleazy's**, all of which play host to signed and unsigned talent from Glasgow and further afield.

The larger and well-known gigs cost anything from £10-25 in the SECC, Barrowlands and Glasgow Royal Concert Hall with the smaller gigs in bars ranging from free entry to about £10 for bigger bands.

Classical and opera

Glasgow Royal Concert Hall, 2 Sauchiehall St, **T** 0141-353 8080, www.grch.com. *Map 2, B7, p253* Prestigious venue for orchestras and big-name rock, pop and soul acts.

City Hall, Candleriggs, **T** 0141-287 5024, www.glasgow.gov.uk. *Map 2, F10, p253* Another fine concert hall that also hosts the BBC Symphony Orchestra every season. Classical concerts are also occasionally performed here by the **Scottish Chamber Orchestra** (**T** 0131-5576800, www.sco.org.uk).

Henry Wood Hall, 73 Claremont St, **T** 0141-225 3555, www.rsno.org.uk. *Map 3, J6, p255* A classical music venue set in a former church that is now home to the Royal Scottish National Orchestra, and also hosts a variety of concerts.

The Royal Scottish Academy of Music and Drama, 100 Renfrew St, **T** 0141-332 4101, www.rsamd.ac.uk. *Map 2, A5, p252* Varied programme of international performances.

Theatre Royal, Hope St, **T** 0141-332 3321, www.theatreroyalglasgow.com. *Map 2, A6, p252* The home of the generally excellent Scottish Opera and Scottish Ballet, also regularly hosts large-scale touring theatre and dance companies and orchestras.

Rock, pop, folk, country and jazz

13th Note Café, 50-60 King St, **T** 553 1638. *Map 2, H9, p252* Downstairs at the Note is a superb venue which showcases unsigned bands and new talent. It supports everything from indie to metal and is worth wandering down to just to sample some new talent, both local and from further afield. See also p167.

13th Note Club, 260 Clyde St, **T** 0141-243 2177. *Map 2, H6, p252* Like the café, the club also plays host to unsigned bands as well as some more well-known names who need a slightly bigger space.

Arches, 253 Argyle St, **T** 0901-0220300. *Map 2, F5, p252* Underneath the railway tracks of Glasgow Central station lies this venue which houses a theatre, bar, restaurant and club. It regularly has live bands either performing a small gig, as part of a festival, or taking part in one of their famous club events such as the Sunday Social.

Barrowlands, 244 Gallowgate, **T** 0141-552 4601. *Map 4, E2/3, p256* The 'Barras' is the best place in Glasgow, if not the UK, to see a live gig. Its previous use was as a ballroom so it has everything just right to create a fantastic atmosphere with bands.

Blackfriars, 36 Bell St, **T** 0141-552 5924. *Map 2, G10, p253* A Merchant City favourite featuring live jazz in the basement Thu-Sat.

Bourbon Street, 108 George St, **T** 0141-552 0141. *Map 2, E10, p253* This bizarre bar and restaurant has live music events which you can enjoy while dining. The bands are normally tribute bands to Abba, The Beatles and the like.

Cathouse, 15 Union St, **T** 0141-248 6606. *Map 2, F5, p252* Glasgow's only rock club also plays host to many a smaller rock gig before the club opens. Ideal for seeing bands before they make it big.

Clyde Auditorium, Finnieston Quay, **T** 0141-287 7777. *Map 3, L4, p255* Also known as the Armadillo for obvious reasons, this eye-catching venue looks like a mini Sydney Opera House and tends to feature more highbrow, big-name acts.

Cottiers, 93-95 Hyndland St, **T** 0141-357 3868. *Map 3, G1, p254* This venue in the West End of the city has a bar, restaurant and theatre which also puts on live performances.

Clutha Vaults, 167 Stockwell St, **T** 0141- 552 7520. *Map 2, I8, p258* One of Glasgow's well known and established pubs that has live music nights from a whole host of local talent.

Fury Murrys, 96 Maxwell St, **T** 0141-221 6511. *Map 2, H7, p253* Fury's hosts gigs by popular bands before the club opens. Music can range from local rock and pop to small tours.

The Garage, 490 Sauchiehall St, **T** 0141-332 1120. *Map 2, A1, p252* This is the place which books you if you're a band that can't quite fill the Barrowlands or you are too big for the Cathouse. It has seen a whole host of rock stars on their way up as well as on the way down. It also doubles as a very busy club later in the night.

Glasgow Royal Concert Hall, 2 Sauchiehall St, **T** 0141-287 5511. *Map 2, B7, p253* Just as its name suggests, the Concert Hall puts on all sorts of concerts from classical to rock and pop. It's a somewhat subdued venue and all-seated, but you can see everyone from Kenny Rogers to Mel C, as well as being the home to the Celtic Connections music festival (see p193).

Glasgow School of Art, Renfrew St, **T** 0141-353 4530. *Map 2, A3, p252* The School of Art sees bands playing a more eclectic mix of music. This venue also holds club nights by night as well as being an art school by day.

Grand Ole Opry, 2 Govan Rd, **T** 0141-429 5369. *Map 1, F4, p250* Homage to Nashville in the heart of Govan. Perfect for a fix of C&W and a spot of line dancing.

Halt Bar, 160 Woodlands Rd, **T** 0141-564 1527. *Map 3, H8, p255* The Halt is a well-known and long-standing bar in the West End. It offers a mix of musical styles and abilities from local bands as well as an open-stage night for all wannabes.

King Tut's Wah Wah Hut, 272a St Vincent St, **T** 0141-221 5279. *Map 2, C2, p252* Upstairs at Tut's is an excellent venue to see live music from both unsigned and signed bands. There is music on most nights of the week and it's worth a visit on spec to check out new talent. A claim to fame is that Oasis were performing there on the night that they were discovered by Alan McGee, boss of record label, Creation records.

McChuills, 40 High St, **T** 0141-552 2135. *Map 2, G11, p253* Weekends at McChuills sees live music from a selection of local bands and all for free.

Nice'n'Sleazy, 421 Sauchiehall St, **T** 0141-333 9637. *Map 2, A1, p252* Sleazy's is a fantastic bar and music venue with a kitsch art deco style. Downstairs bands play everything from indie to rock while upstairs the bar is frequented by muso bods.

Old Fruitmarket, Albion St, **T** 0141-287 5511. *Map 2, F10, p253* Underused larger venue which mostly plays host to jazz and blues giants.

Queen Margaret Union, University Gardens, **T** 339 9784. *Map 3, F4, p254* Mostly the QMU is a university student union bar and club, but it is used as a live-music venue by touring bands and is also used as part of the *NME* tour.

The Renfrew Ferry, Clyde Pl, **T** 0141-287 5511. The Ferry is just that – a ferry, but it is also used as a club and live-music venue for one-off events.

Scottish Exhibition and Conference Centre (SECC), Finnieston Quay, **T** 0870-0404000. *Map 3, L4, p255* The SECC is like a big metal barn and is Glasgow's biggest music arena which has had many a famous name pass through it's dressing rooms. It has played host to all the big UK and international bands, as well as the occasional classical concert.

Samuel Dows, 67-91 Nithsdale Rd, **T** 0141-423 0107. *Map I, G4, p250* This pub is on the south side of the city and is a well-known place to hear local live music including pop and blues as well as a selection of cover bands.

The Scotia Bar, 112-114 Stockwell St, **T** 0141-552 8681. *Map 2, H8, p253* This bar is one of Glasgow's 'institutions' alongside its sister bars the Victoria and Clutha Vaults. It is most familiar as a folky bar but is also known to go a bit more rocky on occasion.

Strawberry Fields, 56 Oswald St, **T** 0141-221 7871. *Map 2, F4, p252* An unsigned-band venue, which can be anything from pop to rock. Hang around for when it turns into a club later in the night.

Studio One, Grosvenor Hotel, Grosvenor Terr, Byres Rd, **T**0141-341 6516. *Map 3, D4, p254* As part of the Grosvenor Hotel this is a bizarre place to find live music – but live music it has on several nights of the week. Mainly local talent and covers bands.

Theatre

For many years the most famous theatre in Glasgow was the **Glasgow Empire**, a variety theatre whose audience had forthright ways of voicing their displeasure with acts – particularly with comics. These days audiences are more polite and the city has a thriving theatre scene where you have the opportunity to see everything from traditional panto to contemporary plays.

Traditional theatre

King's Theatre, 297 Bath St, **T** 0141-248 5153, www.glasgow.gov.uk. *Map 2, B1, p252* The city's main theatre which stages big-name touring musicals, the annual panto and a number of amateur performances.

Theatre Royal, Hope St, **T** 0141- 332 3321, www.theatreroyalglasgow.com. *Map 2, A6, p252* The home of Scottish Opera. It also stages major productions by Scottish Ballet and visiting companies such as the Royal Shakespeare Company and the Royal National Theatre.

Citizens' Theatre, 119 Gorbals St, **T** 429 0022, www.citz.co.uk. *Map 1, F6, p250* A famous theatre which has a Victorian auditorium and two modern studio theatres. The resident theatre company presents British and European classic plays, as well as popular Christmas shows.

Pavilion Theatre, 121 Renfield St, **T** 0141-332 1846. *Map 2, B6, p252* Victorian theatre continuing the Glasgow tradition of staging variety shows. Seating 1,800, it stages an annual panto, musicals and also hosts an extraordinary range of visiting performers from hypnotists to American wrestlers. Over the years audiences have seen acts as varied as Lulu, Shania Twain, Billy Connolly, Jim Davidson, Bernard Manning, Ardal O'Hanlon and Roy 'Chubby' Brown.

The Royal Scottish Academy of Music and Drama, 100 Renfrew St, **T** 0141-332 4101. *Map 2, A5, p252* Has a varied programme of international performances. This is Glasgow's major theatre school and puts on work by its various student companies. Cheap tickets for students.

Contemporary theatre

The Arches, 30 Midland St, **T** 0141-565 1023. *Map 2, F5, p252* In the railway arches under Central station. Presents more radical and experimental theatre. Also home to one of the city's major clubs (see p168).

Centre for Contemporary Arts (CCA), 350 Sauchiehall St, **T** 0141-352 4900. *Map 2, A3, p252* Hosts contemporary dance and theatre, as well as staging various art exhibitions.

Citizens' Theatre, 119 Gorbals St, **T** 0141-429 0022, www.citz.co.uk. *Map 1, F6, p250* Just across the river. Home to some of the UK's most exciting and innovative dramatic performances. Main auditorium and two smaller studios. Big discounts for students and the unemployed.

G12, 9 University Av, **T** 0141-330 5522. *Map 3, G4/5, p255* Glasgow University's Gilmorehill Centre for Film, Theatre and TV also has its own theatre, housed in a Norman gothic church. It screens short films, stages contemporary dance and puts on plays such as *The Steamie*, and *Look Back in Anger*.

Mitchell Theatre, 6 Granville St, **T** 0845 3303501. *Map 3, J8, p255* At Charing Cross. Stages various drama productions as well as the occasional jazz concert.

Tramway Theatre, 25 Albert Dr, **T** 0845-3303501. *Just off Pollokshaws Rd. Map 1, G5, p250* Internationally-renowned venue with varied programme of innovative and influential theatre, dance, music and art exhibitions. You can always expect a challenging and provocative evening here.

The Tron Theatre, 63 Trongate, **T** 0141-552 4267, www.tron.co.uk. *Map 2, G10, p253* One of Glasgow's leading theatres, presenting a mixed programme of drama, comedy, music and dance. It's also got a trendy bar and restaurant where the city's cool and arty crowd hang out.

Festivals and events

Glasgow may not be able to boast such a dazzling event as the world famous Edinburgh Festival, but it doesn't like to be overshadowed by its arch rival in the east, and so it has a few notable festivals of its own. The atmosphere's always good and they're a good way of meeting visitors to the city as well as local people. A strong musical heritage and great choice of venues means that there are several well-established music festivals to choose from, ranging from Celtic Connections – which not surprisingly celebrates all types of celtic music - to a Jazz Festival. Never a city to rest on its laurels, Glasgow also has some recent additions to its cultural scene with an International Comedy Festival and a Merchant City Festival. There's also a lively celebration of lesbian and gay culture in the annual Glasgay festival. Booking in advance for major events is recommended, but it's still possible to leave things until you arrive in the city and see what tickets you can get. A useful website is www.summerinthecity.org which goes online around June and gives details of summer events. Otherwise check out www.seeglasgow.com.

January

Celtic Connections, (last 2 weeks). **T** 0141-353 8000, www.celticconnections.co.uk. Festival featuring celtic rock, traditional music and ceilidhs. International artists perform around the city.

March

International Comedy Festival (last 2 weeks). **T** 0141-339 6208, www.glasgowcomedyfestival.com. Massively popular event with around 130 shows at 15 venues in the city.

April

Glasgow Art Fair (mid-month). **T** 0141-5526027, www.glasgowartfair.com. The largest art fair in the UK outside London. George Square is the focus and there are visual arts events throughout the city over three days. Art dealers display and sell works of art.

June

Glasgow Jazz Festival (late Jun-early Jul). **T** 0141-552 3552, www.jazzfest.co.uk. George Square is the focus of this jazz festival held in various venues around the city.

Royal Scottish National Orchestra Proms (last 2 weeks). **T** 0141-353 8000, www.rsno.org.uk. Serious classical works for those who like their music highbrow.

West End Festival (mid-month). **T** 0141-341 0844, www.westendfestival.co.uk. Well-established festival involving lots of arts events in various venues. There's poetry, music, book readings and it all culminates in a Midsummer Carnival.

July

Bard in the Botanics (mid Jun-mid Jul). **T** 0141-3343995, www.glasgowrep.org. Shakespeare's works performed in the Botanic gardens by the Glasgow Repertory Company.

August

Glasgow International Piping Festival (mid-Aug). **T** 0845-241 4400. A week-long celebration of the bagpipes culminating in the long established World Pipe Band Championships at Glasgow Green.

September

Victorian Fair (early Sep). **T** 01555-661345. In New Lanark, featuring street theatre and music.

Merchant City Festival (mid-month). **T** 0141-287 8402, www.glasgowmerchantcity.net. This festival celebrates the heritage of the city's former commercial heart.

October

Glasgay (late Oct). **T** 0141-334 7126, www.glasgay.co.uk. Britain's largest lesbian and gay festival held in various venues throughout the city. There's music, comedy, visual arts and lots more. See also p221.

December

Hogmanay (31st). www.hogmanay.net. Various rock, pop and dance acts perform live at stages across the city centre, and in George Square there's a massive dance party featuring top DJs.

Shopping

Glasgow is a shopaholic's paradise – particularly for anyone seeking new clothes. Glaswegians love fashion and are happy to spend their money on good clobber. Glasgow is the best shopping city in the UK after London and there are endless opportunities for retail therapy. The **Merchant City** is the city's most upmarket shopping area, and fashionistas should click their Manolo Blahnik clad feet over to the classy **Italian Centre**, which has branches of Armani and Versace. There are some huge shopping malls too, like the Buchanan Galleries near Queen St station, which has all the usual high street suspects. There's the ever classy **Princes Square**, which has a good mix of designer stores and gift shops. **Buchanan Street** is the most upmarket of the city's central retail thoroughfares, while cheaper outlets are focused on Sauchiehall Street and Argyle Street. The West End is the place to go for more off-beat and quirky purchases, with designer jewellers, vintage and individual clothes shops, and second-hand bookshops.

Art and antiques

Glasgow Print Studio Galleries, 22 and 25 King St, **T** 0141-5520704, www.gpsart.co.uk. *Tue-Sat 1000-1730. Map 2, H9, p253* One of the largest publishers of original prints in the UK. They display and sell etchings, lithographs and screenprints by over 300 artists including well known names like Elizabeth Blackadder, Ken Currie, Peter Howson and Adrian Wiszniewski.

Hutcheson's Hall, 158 Ingram St, **T** 0141-552 8391. *Map 2, E9, p253* A good place to find original crafts by Scottish designers. Worth browsing for unusual gifts – real Glasgow Style.

Victorian Village, 93 West Regent St, **T** 0141-332 0808. *Mon-Sat 1000-1700. Map 2, C5, p252* Has a selection of individual traders who sell costume jewellery, antiques and retro clothing. Also on West Regent Street are a couple of worthwhile art galleries: **Compass Gallery** (number 178, **T** 0141-2216370. *Mon-Sat 1000-1730*); and **Cyril Gerber Fine Art** (number 148, **T** 0141-2213095. *Mon-Sat 0930-1730*). Farther north, near the Glasgow School of Art is **Fireworks** (35a Dalhousie St, **T** 0141-3324969, *Tue-Sat 1000-1800*), a ceramic gallery and workshop.

Books

Borders, 98 Buchanan St, **T** 0141-222 7700. *Mon-Sat 0830-2200, Sun 1000-2000. Map 2, E7, p253* Great selection of books on Glasgow and Scotland, as well as hefty sections on travel and fiction. Lots of magazines and newspapers and there's a café and toilet.

Hyndland Bookshop, 143 Hyndland Rd, **T** 0141-334 5522. *Mon-Sat 1000-1800, Sun 1300-1700. Map 3, E1, p254* Has lots of books on Scotland and Glasgow.

Ottakars, 6 Buchanan Galleries, **T** 0141-353 1500. *Mon-Wed, Fri, Sat 0900-1800, Thu 0900-2000, Sun 1100-1730.* *Map 2, C7, p253* Good children's section and a coffee shop with squashy sofas.

Oxfam, 330 Byres Rd, **T** 0141-338 6185. *Mon-Wed 0930-1730, Thu-Sat 0930-1800, Sun 1200-1800.* *Map 3, E4, p254* Good selection of well-thumbed secondhand books, very popular with West Enders.

Voltaire and Rousseau, 12-14 Otago La, **T** 014-339 1811. *Mon-Sat 1000-1800.* *Map 3, G6, p255* An old established antiquarian bookstore and a favourite with students The two resident cats are an added attraction and have their own unofficial fan club.

Collectables

Relics, Dowanside La, **T** 0141-341 0007. *1030-1800 Mon-Sat, Sun 1230-1800.* *Map 3, F3, p254* A great place to rummage for well, anything really – quirky items, antiques, you name it, it's probably here.

Clothes and shoes

Buchanan Street, *Map 2, D7-F6, p252-253* Pedestrianised Buchanan Street has plenty of good clothes and shoe shops, most of which have a 1900 late night opening on Thursdays and a midday to 1700 opening on Sundays, in addition to the normal opening hours during the rest of the week. The street offers **Dune** for footwear, **Nine West** for shoes and bags, Diesel for trendy clothes and accessories, **Jaeger** for clothes, **Jones Bootmaker** for footwear, **Karen Millen** for slightly pricey but beautiful womenswear, **Miss Sixty** again slightly pricey clothes, but catering more for young female adults and teenagers, **Planet**, classy couture, **Boss**s for menswear and **Office** for the latest in trendy footwear.

Designer Exchange, off 17 Royal Exchange Sq near Rogano, **T** 0141-221 6898. *Tue-Sat winter 1030-1630, summer 1000-1700. Map 2, E7, p253* It has loads of nearly-new designer clothes, samples and accessories. Great place for a bargain.

Flip, 15 Bath St, **T** 0141-353 1634. *Map 2, C7, p253* Fans of American retro and vintage sports gear will head straight here for a diverse selection or urban, skate and fetish gear at the Hellfire Club. Cheap and cool.

Italian Centre, Merchant City. *Map 2, E9, p253* Has branches of **Armani**, (19 John St, **T** 0141-552 2277, *Mon-Wed and Fri 1000-1800, Thu 1000-1900, Sat 1000-1830* and **Versace** (162 Ingram St, **T** 0141-552 6510) as well as some other upmarket shops, cafés and restaurants. Friendly staff make these less intimidating than they are in other cities – though you still wouldn't want to come on a 'fat day'. There's also a **Cruise** (180 Ingram St, T 0141-572 3232, Mon-Wed 0930-1800, Thu 1000-1900, Fri 0930-1900, Sat 0900- 1800 and Sun 1200-1700) – the hottest outlet for designer gear in the city stocking everything from Prada and Gucci to Oki-ni and Boyd.

Moon, 10 Ruthven La, **T** 0141-339 2315. *Mon-Sat 1000-1730. Map 3, E3, p254* Good outlet for women's designer clothes, stocking names like Betty Jackson.

Mr Ben, Studio 6 Kings Court, Kings St, **T** 0141-553 1936. *Mon-Sat 1030-1730, Sun 1230-1700. Map 2, H9, p253* Good range of retro clothing. They'll kit you out with jeans, ballgowns – or even old nylon y-fronts.

Pink Poodle, 181 Byres Rd, **T** 0141-357 3344. *Mon-Sat 1000-1800, Sun 1200-1700. Map 3, F3, p254* Women's fashion labels like Miss Sixty and others which will really put some go into your wardrobe.

Saratoga Trunk, Unit 10, 61 Hydepark St, **T** 0141-221 4433. *Mon-Fri 1030-1700. Map 3, L7, p255* For the widest range of vintage and retro clothing. It's an enormous Aladdin's cave of a warehouse stuffed with the most extraordinary range of clothes, from beautiful beaded dresses to swirly 60s gear. The staff are very friendly and they also have brilliant jewellery and accessories. They supply gear for film and TV crews. Well worth the journey if you like a good rummage. Also has a small outlet in Victorian Village.

Slaters, 165 Howard St, **T** 0141-552 7171. *Mon-Wed, Fri, Sat 0830-1730, Thu 0830-1930, Sun 1130-1630. Map 2, H8, p253* A famous and enormous menswear store which has become something of a Glasgow institution.

Starry Starry Night, 19 Dowanside La, T 0141-337 1837. *1000-1730 Mon-Sat. Map 3, F3, p254* Has a wide range of old and vintage clothes from the 80s back to Victorian times (see p202).

Urban Outfitters, 157 Buchanan St, **T** 0141-248 9203. *Mon-Wed and Fri, Sat 0930-1830, Thu 0930-1800, Sun 1200-1800. Map 2, D7, p253* A trendy's paradise, full of '70s items and retro gear.

Department Stores

Fraser's, 21-45 Buchanan St, **T** 0141-221 3880. *Mon-Wed and Fri, Sat 0930-1800, Thu 0930-2000, Sun 1200-1730. Map 2, F6, p252* Traditional department store with a good range of designer clothes.

John Lewis, 220 Buchanan St. *Map 2, C7, p253* See Buchanan Galleries, p203.

Food and drink

Grassroots, 20 Woodlands Rd, **T** 0141-353 3278. *Map 3, I8, p255* A great veggie deli.

Heart Buchanan, Byres Rd, **T** 0141-334 7626. *Mon-Sat 0830-2130, Sun 1200-1900. Map 3, D4, p254* A brilliant deli with lots of fresh sandwiches and cakes. They specialise in restaurant quality take-home meals to reheat – there's a veggie meal each day.

Ian Mellis, 492 Great Western Rd, **T** 0141-339 8998. *0930-1800 Mon-Wed, Thu 0930-1830, Fri 0930-1900, Sat 0900-1800, Sun 1100-1700. Map 3, E6, p254* Wonderful cheese shop full of unusual varieties of cheese ranging from strong blues, to creamy bries. Choose from around 45 types. Great range of Scottish cheeses like Isle of Mull cheddar or Criffel, a soft cheese, and plenty of Irish cheeses too such as the unusual Coolea.

North Star Provisions, 108 Queen Margaret Dr, **T** 0141-946 5365. *Map 3, B6, p254* Portuguese specialities.

Peckham's, 124 Byres Rd, **T** 0141-357 1454. *0900-2400 daily. Map 3, E3, p254* Great outlet stocking fine wines and all sorts of scrummy foods for posh picnics and treats.

Homewares

Felix and Oscar, 459 Great Western Rd, **T** 0141-339 8585. *Mon-Sat 1000-1730, Sun 1200-1700. Map 3, F6, p254* Trendy lifestyle shop stocking Alessi, Cath Kidston and Nigella Lawson ware. Designer children's clothing and cute toys. Next to their lifestyle store.

Inhouse, 24-26 Wilson St, **T** 0141-552 5902. *Mon-Wed, Fri 1000-1800, Thu 1000-1900, Sat 0930-1730. Map 2, F9, p253* Lots of contemporary designer homeware by names like Alessi. Also stocks cool furniture.

Jewellery

De Courcey's Arcade, 5-21 Cresswell La, **T** 0141- 334 6673. *Map 3, E4, p254* Has a brilliant selection of goods from different traders. You can find jewellery, as well as antiques, pottery, 'Glasgow Style' artefacts and the like.

Orro, 49 Bank St, West End, T 357 6999 *Tue-Sat 1030-1730. Map 3, F6, p254* A sleek contemporary jewellers' with another branch in the Merchant City (12 Wilson St, **T** 552 7888, Tue-Sat 1100-1730).

Starry Starry Night, 19 Dowanside La, T 337 1837 *1000-1730 Mon-Sat. Map 3, F3, p254* Featuring the work of Bethsy Gray, a jewellery designer with a shop and workshop here. She specializes in working with silver (see also p200).

Markets

The Barras, The Barras Centre, London Rd. *Sat, Sun 0900-1700. Map 4, E2/3, p256* This is Glasgow's famous East End market with over 1000 traders flogging their wares. Worth coming if only to hear their patter. See also p45. Also worth a good rummage around is Paddy's Market, which is held around the Briggait during the same hours.

Music

Avalanche Records, 34 Dundas St, **T** 0141-332 2099. *Mon-Sat 0930-1800, Sun 1200-1800.* Map 4, E2/3, p256 Lots of obscure labels and vintage vinyl.

Fopp Records, 358 Byres Rd, **T** 0141-357 0774. *Mon-Sat 0930-1900, Sun 1100-1800. Map 3, D4, p254* Part of a chain offering bargain prices on all CDs from pop to jazz. Features a great range of CDs from well-known artists starting at £5.

Outdoor gear

Graham Tiso, 129 Buchanan St, T 0141-248 4877. *Mon-Tue, Thu-Sat 0930-1730, Wed 1000-1730, Sun 1200-1700. Map 2, D7, p253* An outdoor shop, which has 5 floors of boots, waterproofs, maps and everything else you'll need for exploring the hills.

Shopping malls

Buchanan Galleries, 220 Buchanan St, **T** 0141-333 9898 *Mon-Wed, Fri, Sat 0900-1800, Thu 0900-2000, Sun 1100-1700. Map 2, C7/8, p253* Has a large branch of the John Lewis department store, and clothes shops like Mango, Morgan, Gap and H&M.

Princes Square, Buchanan St, **T** 0141-221 0324 *Mon-Wed and Fri 0930-1800, Thu 0930-2000, Sat 0900-1800, Sun 1200-1700. Map 2, E/F7, p253* Classy shopping centre with a Rennie Mackintosh theme. Clothes and shoe shops here include: French Connection, Whistles, Calvin Klein, Reiss, Monsoon and Jo Malone for women and Ted Baker, Hugo and Lacoste for men. For unusual gifts there's Illuminati and for cosmetics and perfumes there's Space NK and Penhaligons. There's also a branch of Bo Concept for all sorts of cool homewares.

St Enoch Centre, Argyle St, **T** 0141-204 3900 *Mon-Sat 0900-1800 (Thu till 2000), Sun 1100-1730. Map 2, G7, p253* Huge mall crammed with all the usual high street suspects and places to re-fuel.

Tattoo you
The Glasgow tattoo is not the kitsch tourist extravaganza of its city rival, but means going under the needle, probably at Terry's, the oldest parlour in town.

Tattoos and body piercing

The Glasgow Piercing Studio, 24 Parnie St, **T** 0141-552 6655. *Map 2, H9, p253* Offers everything from the tame to the eye watering.

Terry's Tattoo Studio, 23 Chisholm St, **T** 0141-5525740. *Map 2, G/H10, p253* If you fancy a bit of body adornment while you're here, look no further than Terry's, which has been around since 1965.

Sports

People often forget that this great industrial city is within half an hour's drive of some of Scotland's most stunning scenery. Loveliest of all is Loch Lomond, heart of Scotland's first National Park, and easily reached from Glasgow. Once here you can simply stroll by the water, go canoeing or hire a bike. The city's also an excellent base for walkers, whether you want to get out and about on the hills or just do some gentle rambling. The West Highland Way long distance path starts from the leafy Glasgow suburb of Milngavie and runs for 92 miles, all the way to Fort William. A classic section runs beside Loch Lomond. For those who prefer their walks punctuated by the thwack of a golf ball, there are several golf courses around, including the swish ones of Turnberry and Royal Troon. If you're a footie fan, it's well worth catching an Old Firm game between arch rivals Celtic and Rangers, the teams that dominate the Scottish league. There is more spectator sport at the Kelvin Hall Sports Arena which hosts an array of sporting events including athletics, boxing and gymnastics.

American football

Scottish Claymores, Hampden Park, **T** 0141-222 3800, ticket hotline T 0500 353535, www.claymores.co.uk. Scottish Claymores play in the NFL League and are Scotland's only professional American football team.

Cycling and mountain biking

There are numerous paths and cycle routes through the centre of Glasgow out into the surrounding countryside. One of these starts from Bell's Bridge (by the SECC) and runs to Erskine Bridge and back to the city centre via Paisley. It's a total distance of 31 miles and OS Landranger sheet 64 covers the entire route. The **Clyde Coast Cycle Route** runs from Bell's Bridge, through some of the city's parks, and closely follows the old Paisley-Ardrossan Canal to Greenock, Gourock and on to Ardrossan, for ferries to the Isle of Arran. It's 28 miles one-way as far as Gourock and the route is covered by the Glasgow and Clyde Coast Cycle Routes leaflets, Glasgow to Paisley and Paisley to Greenock sections.

The **Glasgow Loch Lomond Cycle Way** is for both walkers and cyclists. It runs from the centre of Glasgow, following a disused railway track to Clydebank, the Forth and Clyde Canal towpath to Bowling, then a disused railway to Dumbarton, finally reaching Loch Lomond by way of the River Leven. The route continues all the way to Killin, in the heart of the Perthshire Highlands, via Balloch, Aberfoyle and Callander. An alternative route turns back at Clydebank and follows the Forth and Clyde Canal towpath all the way to the Firhill Basin and from there back to the city centre. OS Landranger sheet 64 covers the route. There's also a new Glasgow-Edinburgh route, which incorporates part of the Clyde Walkway (see p82).

For the most up-to-date information on the expanding network of cycle routes in the area, and throughout the country, contact **Sustrans** (53 Cochrane St, **T** 0141-5720234, www.sustrans.org.uk). A useful book is *25 Cycle Routes In and Around Glasgow*, by EB Wilkie, HMSO, price £8.99. **The Cyclists' Touring Club** (CTC) (Cotterell House, 69 Meadrow, Godalming, Surrey, GU7 3HS, **T** 01483-417217, www.ctc.org.uk), the largest cycling organization in the UK, providing a wide range of services and information on transport, cycle hire and routes, from day rides to longer tours.

Bikes can be taken free on most local rail services on a first-come-first-served basis (call ScotRail bookings, **T** 08457-550033). On long-distance routes you'll have to make a reservation and pay a small charge (£3.50). Space is limited on trains so it's a good idea to book as far in advance as possible. Bus and coach companies will not carry bikes, unless they are dismantled and boxed. Ferries transport bikes for a small fee and airlines will often accept them as part of your baggage allowance. Check with the ferry company or airline about any restrictions. There's also the option of a cycling holiday package, which includes transport of your luggage, pre-booked accommodation, route instructions and food and backup support.

The Scottish Tourist Board (STB) publishes a free booklet, Cycling in Scotland, which is useful and suggests routes in various parts of the country, as well as accommodation and repair shops. Many area tourist boards also provide cycling guides for their own areas.

Bremner's, 17 Cardiff St, **T** 01475-530707. Bike hire.

Can You Experience, **T** 01389-602576, www.canyouexperience.com. Mountain bike hire by Loch Lomond, 2 hours £7 adults, £5 kids; 4 hours £10 adults, £8 kids; 8 hours £15 adults, £10 kids. Also guided mountain bike tours lasting 3 hours – £18. See also under powerkiting, walking and watersports.

Lomond Activities, 64 Main St, Drymen, **T** 01360-660066. Bike hire.

Mapes & Son, 3-5 Guildford St, Millport, Great Cumbrae **T** 01475-530444. Bike hire.

Robb Cycles, 19E East Princes St, Rothesay, Bute, **T** 01700-502333. Bike hire, April to October daily 0900-1800, cost from £12 per day.

West End Cycles, 16 Chancellor St, off Byres Rd**T** 0141-357 1344. Hire out mountain bike for £12 per day, or £50 per week. ID and £50 deposit required.

Football

The two main Glasgow teams are **Rangers** and **Celtic**, who regularly attract crowds of over 50,000 and are two of the wealthiest clubs in Britain. They completely dominate the Scottish football scene. The domestic season runs from August to mid-May. Most matches are played on Saturday and there are also games during the week on Tuesday and Wednesday evenings. Ticket prices are around £20. Celtic FC are based at Celtic Park (Parkhead, **T** 0141- 556 2611, www.celticfc.net) while Rangers FC are based at Ibrox Stadium (**T** 0870-600 1972, www.rangers.co.uk). The national team plays at Hampden Park, which boasts UEFA five-star facilities. It's the location of the Football Museum and stadium tours are available.

Golf

There are many municipal courses in and around Glasgow, as well as several top-class championship courses within easy reach of the city. Green fees will often cost from £40 upwards.

Football crazy

The late Bill Shankly, former manager of Liverpool FC, once said that "football's not a matter of life and death – it's more important than that". This may seem fatuous to some, but to the supporters of Glasgow's two big clubs, **Celtic** and **Rangers**, collectively known as the 'Old Firm', he was talking their language. There is no greater rivalry in world football than the one which exists between Glasgow's two main teams.

Yet neither Celtic not Rangers were the first football team to be formed in the city. That was Queens Park, formed in 1867, in the South Side suburbs by members of the Glasgow YMCA. Six years later, Queens Park, along with eight other clubs (Clydesdale, Dumbreck, Vale of Leven, Eastern, Third Lanark Rifle Volunteers, Rovers and Granville) set up the Scottish Football Association.

In 1872, a team was formed on Glasgow Green calling themselves Rangers then, in 1888, a Roman Catholic priest formed a team called Celtic in an effort to alleviate poverty in the East End. The next development was the setting up of a Scottish League in 1890-91, in which both clubs played an important part, followed by the introduction of professionalism into the game in 1893, a move opposed by Queens Park who still remain an amateur club.

Celtic and Rangers both took full advantage of the creation of a professional league and adopted a businesslike approach to their development. By the end of the 19th century, they were becoming the biggest names in the city and beyond. Their first meeting was in 1894 when Rangers defeated Celtic 3-1. They worked together to ensure they could get the most lucrative fixtures, and as a large percentage of their revenue came from playing each other, both realised there was money to be made from exploiting their religious and ethnic differences, with Rangers in blue representing the Protestant community, and Celtic in green the Catholic Irish.

Throughout the 20th century, football has stirred powerful emotions amongst the supporters of both clubs. George Blake, in his 1935 novel *The Shipbuilders*, called the Old Firm players "peerless and fearless warriors, saints of the Blue and Green". Though sectarianism grew in the 1920s and 30s and went on to scar the image of the Old Firm, football at least provided an escape for both sets of supporters from the insecurities of the depression.

During the inter-war years, Rangers dominated the Scottish League, winning the old first division 14 times, but, under the brilliant guidance of Jock Stein from 1965, Celtic went on, not only to dominate the domestic game, but also to conquer Europe by becoming the first ever British club to win the European Cup, in 1967, defeating the highly-fancied Inter Milan 2-1. The famous Lisbon Lions – as the Celtic side became known – were all the more remarkable as the entire squad were born and lived within a 35 mile radius of the city centre, a quite inconceivable notion today.

Big changes took place in Scottish Football in the 1970s, which raised the stakes for both clubs. Rangers brought Graeme Souness from Liverpool and he revolutionized the club by making big-name international signings and raising their profile considerably. But, at the same time, Rangers realised they had to lose their sectarian image in order to attract the best players and to this end they broke their policy of never employing a Roman Catholic player in 1989 and signed Maurice Johnston. This shook the foundations of football in the city but paved the way for a long period of total domination by Rangers, broken only recently by a rejuvenated Celtic under the shrewd guidance of Martin O'Neill.

Haggs Castle, 70 Dumbreck Rd. An 18 hole course. Visitors welcome Mon-Fri.

Knightswood golf course, Lincoln Av, **T** 0141-959 6358. Nine holes.

Lethamhill golf course, 1240 Cumbernauld Rd, **T** 0141-7706220, www.glasgow.gov.uk. 18 holes.

Loch Lomond, Luss, **T** 01436-860223, www.lochlomond.com. This members-only course is currently ranked 44 in the top 100 courses in the world.

Prestwick, T 01292 477404, www.prestwickgc.co.uk. Visitors welcome.

Royal Troon, Craigend Rd, Troon, **T** 01292-311555, www.royaltroon.co.uk. Features the Old Course – reputedly one of the best in Scotland.

Turnberry, Ayrshire, **T** 01655-331000, www.turnberry.co.uk. A lovely course amidst some stunning scenery.

World of Golf centre, 2700 Great Western Rd, Clydebank **T** 944 4141, www.worldofgolf-uk.co.uk. There is a large driving range and a teaching academy here.

Health and fitness

Bellahouston Leisure Centre, Bellahouston Dr, **T** 0141-427 9090. Glasgow's oldest sports centre with a leisure pool, fitness centre, squash, sports hall and health suite.

Kelvin Hall International Sports Arena, Argyle St, **T** 0141 337 1806. Hosts all sorts of major events such as athletics, gymnastics and boxing. In January 2004, it hosted the Norwich Union International, a springboard to the Olympics in Athens.

Power kiting

Can You Experience, T 01389-602576, www.canyouexperience.com. Adrenalin junkies needing a fix might want to try power kiting on the hills around Loch Lomond – a bit like kite surfing on land. A taster session of 2 hours is available for £18.

Skiing

Bearsden Ski Club, Stockiemuir Rd, Bearsden, **T** 0141-943 1500. *Mon-Fri 0930-2200, Sat 1330-2100, Sun 1000-2100.* Floodlit artificial ski slope, offering skiing and snowboarding out in posh Bearsden. Private lessons £32 per hour adults, £28 per hour for kids. General use, juniors 1 hour £6.50, 2 hours £8; adults 1 hour £7, 2 hours £10.

Glasgow Ski and Snowboard Centre, Bellahouson Park, **T** 0141-427 4991. *Mon-Fri 0930-2300, Sat, Sun 0930-2100.* Floodlit artificial ski slope for urban ski bunnies. Private lessons available from £25. There is also a wide range of group lessons (booking required). For general use, juniors pay from £8 and adults from £10 for an unlimited time.

Walking

Can You Experience, T 01389-602576, www.canyouexperience.com. Offer guided walks around Loch Lomond, £18 for 3 hours.

Walk Wild Loch Lomond, T 01360-870476, www.walkwild lochlomond.co.uk. Offer 1-day guided walks in the National Park, pick-ups from Balloch or Drymen. £29 per person including lunch and possible boat trip.

Watersports

Can You Experience, T 01389-602576, www.canyouexperience.com. Operate on and around Loch Lomond. Canoe, kayak and pedalo hire £10 for 30 minutes, £15 for 1 hour, and also offer guided canoe trips on the loch, 2 hours £18, 4 hours £30, full day walking and canoeing £43. Telephone for details or ask at Lomond Shores.

Lomond Adventure, Balmaha House, Balmaha, **T** 01360-870218. Canoe/kayak hire from £20 per day, sailing in dinghys or catamarans from £35 a day, watersking from £45 for 1 hour.

Lomond Shores National Park Gateway, Balloch, **T** 08707 200631. This centre is open daily for all activities on Loch Lomond. See p115.

Sportscotland National Centre, Great Cumbrae, **T** 01475-530757, www.nationalcentrecumbrae.org.uk. Huge watersports centre with facilities and courses for dinghy sailing, windsurfing, kayaking and power boating. Accommodation available. See p103.

Gay and lesbian

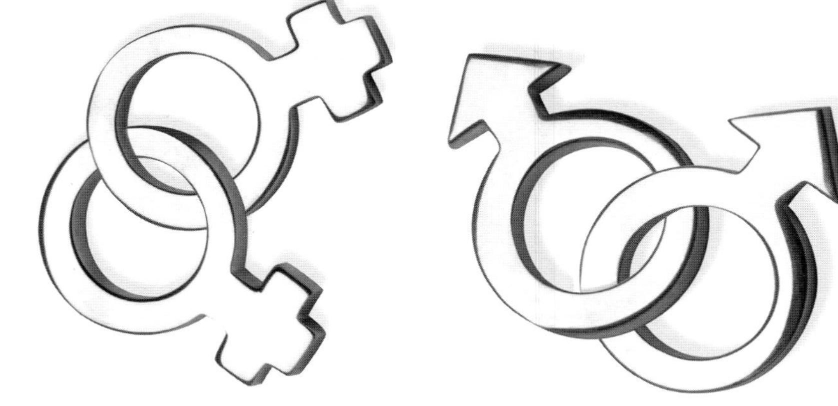

In the past, Glasgow had a reputation for being violent (where the 'hard man' originated from), yet its inhabitants are known for being friendly, unpretentious and extremely talkative. Gay Glasgow is fun, thriving, visible and full of diversity. There are plenty of pubs, clubs and cafés to choose from – many of them downtown at the 'gay village' in the Merchant City. You can dip into them briefly, until you find out which one you like. And with them being open all hours, there is something for everyone.

Glasgow is easy to get round, either by the orange subway, by bus or on foot, so it is worth venturing beyond the gay village. The city is beautiful with a gay presence all over. Byres Road in the West End has plenty of coffee shops and in the summer Kelvingrove Park and Queens Park are ideal for gay sunbathing. Culturally, there's plenty happening in terms of great theatre, stimulating movies, live music, and impressive art galleries (most of them free).

Each year **Glasgay**, the lesbian and gay arts festival, running from late October to November, becomes stronger.

Gay contacts

There's a UK gay-scene index at www.queenscene.com, which has information on clubs, gay groups, accommodation, events, HIV/AIDS and cultural and ethical issues. Other good sites include: www.gaybritain.co.uk; www.gaytravel.co.uk. www.rainbownetwork.com and www.gaypride.co.uk.

Bi-G-Les, c/o LGBT, 11 Dixon St, **T** 0141-221 7203. Weekly youth group for bisexuals, lesbians and gay men.

Body Positive, 3 Park Quadrant, **T** 0141-332 5010. HIV/AIDS support and advice.

Centre for Women's Health, 2 Sandyford Pl, **T** 0141-211 6700. Centre providing information and services to women. Specific services for lesbians.

Gay Scotland, **T** 0141-557 2625. This magazine is a good source of information, and **The List**, the Edinburgh and Glasgow listings magazine, is also useful.

Glasgow Women's Library, 109 Trongate, **T** 0141-552 8345. *Tue-Fri 1300-1800; Sat 1400-1700.* Lesbian archive and information centre.

Lesbian Line, PO Box 686, G3 7TL, **T** 0141-552 3355. Lesbian support line.

PHACE West, 49 Bath St, **T** 0141-332 3838. Information and support for those affected by HIV or AIDS.

Steve Retson Project, 2 Sandyford Pl, **T** 0141-221 8601. *Tue and Thu 1730-2030.* Sexual health clinic for gay men.

Stonewall Scotland, LGBT Centre,11 Dixon St, **T** 0141-204 0022. Campaigning equality group for lesbians and gay men.

Strathclyde Lesbian & Gay Switchboard, PO Box 38, G2 2QE, **T** 0141-332 8372. *Open 1900-2200 daily.*
Helpline for gay men and lesbians.

Sleeping

Glasgow Guest House, 56 Dumbreck Rd, **T** 0141-427 0129. 6 twin bedrooms, gay-friendly guest house, 5 mins from the city centre by bus.

Eating and drinking

easyInternet Café, 57-61 St Vincent St, **T** 0141-222 2365. Open 24 hours. After the clubs, this centrally-located café gets filled with gay punters surfing on the internet.

Bars

Café Delmonica's, 68 Virginia St, **T** 0141-552 4803. *Daily 1200-2400.* Attracting both gay men and women, Delmonica's is a fun bar. Particularly busy with the young office crowds and late on in the evening when it becomes drunken and deafening. Activities include DJs on Mondays, Tuesdays, Fridays and Saturday, a games night on Wednesdays and quiz night on Thursdays.

Candle Bar, 20 Candleriggs, **T** 0141-564 1285. *Mon-Sat 1200-2400, Sun 12302400. Free.* Relatively new to the Merchant City's gay scene, this lively bar has yet to assert its identity. Live music, DJs and karaoke throughout the week.

Court Bar, 69 Hutcheson St, **T** 0141-552 2463. *Mon-Sat 0900-2400, Sun 1230-2400.* Old-fashioned city centre bar, straighter during the day and becoming increasingly more gay as the day develops. Small and chatty, attracting an older clientele.

LGBT Centre, 11 Dixon St, **T** 0141-400 1008. *Daily, 1200-2400.* The GLC bar/cafe in the back of the LGBT Centre serves cheap food and drink. Waiters are fast and helpful, and the whole place has a community feel to it. Needs a stronger extractor fan to get rid of frying smells though. Karaoke from Fri to Sun.

Polo Lounge, 84 Wilson St, **T** 0141-553 1221. *Mon-Thu 1700-0100, Fri-Sun 1700-0300. Free before 2300 Thu-Sun.* Beautiful, sumptuous city centre venue, and the only gay bar which is full of antiques and chaise-longues. Appeals to young, attractive, professionals and their admirers. The sound system can be a bit too loud. Check out the live singing of Marj Hogarth on Tue nights. Extremely busy at weekends.

Revolver, 6a John St, **T** 0141-553 2456. *Mon-Sat 1100-2400, Sun 1230-2400.* Sexy brand new bar opposite the Italian Centre, run by cheerful gay manager Brendan Nash. Has an amazing free jukebox with over 5,000 top tunes. Attracts men of all ages looking for action! Check out their interesting theme nights.

Sadie Frosts, 8-10 West George St, **T** 0141-332 8005. *Mon-Sat 1200-2400, Sun 1400-2400. Underneath Queen St Station.* This is an extremely popular, busy and noisy bar. Cheap food and a whole range of activity throughout the week, including quizzes (Tue and Wed), karaoke (Thu and Sun) and DJs (Fri, Sat and Mon). Sun is women-only in the Blue Room.

Waterloo, 306 Argyle St, **T** 0141-229 5891. *Mon-Sat 1200-2400, Sun 1230-2300.* Glasgow's oldest gay bar with a friendly, unpretentious, working-class, older clientele. Attitude-free, it becomes incredibly busy and lots of fun late at night.

Clubs

Bennets, 90 Glassford St, **T** 0141-552 5761. *Daily 2300-0330. £3-6 (£2-5).* Bennets is the longest-running gay club in Glasgow. Attracting a young crowd, ready to whip off their shirts at a moment's notice, it has a new top floor for when it gets busy. At weekends it's packed. With attentive staff, Bennets is open 5 nights a week (Wed to Sun) with student night on Thu. Women-only night is the first Fri of each month on the top floor.

Cube, 34 Queen St, **T** 0141-226 8990. *Daily 2300-0300. £3 (£2 with flyer).* Previously known as Planet Peach, Cube holds gay nights on Mon and Tue only, playing chart music and house.

Polo Lounge, 84 Wilson St, **T** 0141-553 1221. *Fri-Sun 2200-0300. £5. Free before 2300.* Downstairs at the Polo Lounge, there's a choice of the main club for harder dance sounds or trashy retro in the wee, intimate Trophy Room. Promos, theme nights, shag-tags a-plenty. Club anthems and chart hits.

Entertainment

The Citizens Theatre, 119 Gorbals St, **T** 0141-429 0022. World-class, visually stunning theatre in the heart of the Gorbals, often imbued with a gay sensibility and a certain campness. See p188.

GFT,12 Rose St, **T** 0141-332 8128. Glasgow's friendly arts cinema always has a wide selection of movies, often with a gay or lesbian slant. Check their free monthly brochure. Meet in the café before the film. See p181.

The Stand Comedy Club, 333 Woodlands Rd, **T** 0870-6006055. 'OOT in Glasgow' is a gay comedy night, on the second Sunday of every month. Hosted by the endearing Craig Hill with surprise guests. See p182.

The Tron Theatre, 63 Trongate, **T** 0141-552 8578. An eclectic programme of theatre and live music, along with three diverse bars makes this an attractive venue for discerning folk. See p190.

Festivals

Glasgay, **T** 0141-334 7129 *Late Oct-early Nov.* Britain's largest lesbian and gay arts festival, runs at various venues throughout the city. A great outreach programme makes Glasgay felt all over (see also p194).

Shopping

Clone Zone, 11 Dixon St, **T** 0141-248 4485. In the foyer of the LGBT centre, a small shop crammed full of gay goodies.

Saunas

Centurion Sauna, 19 Dixon St, **T** 0141-248 4485. *Daily 1200-2200.* Ring the buzzer, then ascend the steps to this sauna on the first floor, above Somerfield supermarket. It used to be an office complex, and the sticky floor still hints at its past. It has sauna cabins, a steam room, rest areas, and attracts a mixed age range.

The Lane, 60 Robertson St La, **T** 0141-221 1802. *Daily 1200-2200. £10/8.* Small out-of-the-way sauna with lockers and private cabins.

Kids

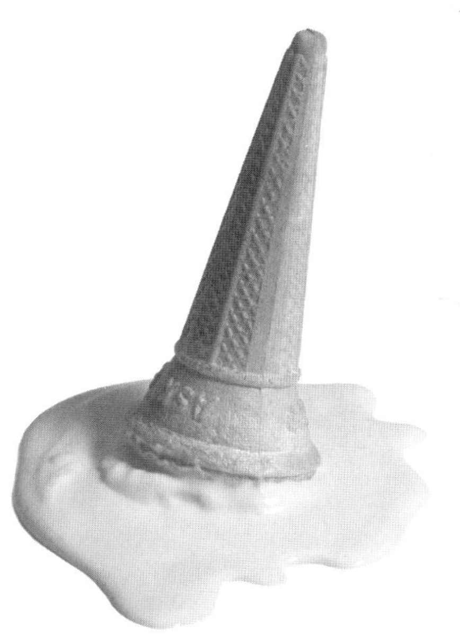

Glasgow's a great city if you've got kids in tow. Not only has it got a whole range of attractions to suit children – be it tiny tots or sulky teenagers – but it's also got plenty of green spaces and is close to some stunning unspoilt countryside so you can easily take them somewhere to let off steam. As well as the sights listed in this section, there are also places like the partly educational Tall Ship at Glasgow Harbour and the child-oriented aspects of the displays at The Lighthouse, Scotland's Centre for Architecture and Design. Then there are also Ghost Tours that would suit older children and trips along the Clyde in the grand old paddle steamer Waverley – great for the whole family.

As Glaswegians are generally friendly and helpful, eating out with children is generally less hassle than it can be in more po-faced UK cities – and the strong Italian influence means that there are plenty of fairly child-friendly places to eat. However, as in the rest of the UK, the attitude towards breast-feeding in public is still some way behind that in other parts of Europe.

Sights

Glasgow Science Centre, 50 Pacific Quay, **T** 0141-420 5000, www.gsc.org.uk. *Science Mall daily 1000-1800. IMAX Theatre Sun-Wed 1100-1700, Thu-Sat 1000-2030 (hours subject to change). Science Mall £6.95, £4.95 concession. IMAX or Glasgow Tower £5.95, £4.45 concession. Discounts available if purchasing tickets to more than 1 attraction. Arriva buses 23 and 24 go to the Science Centre from Jamaica St, or simply walk across the footbridge from the SECC and Armadillo.* This shiny new centre on the Clyde is sure to please surly teenagers and smaller children – and it's interesting for adults too. It has lots of interactive exhibits and looks as all aspects of science, from the workings of human body (cue fart jokes), to genetic modification and the internet. There's even a lab where kids can examine specimens under microscopes. If the tower is open you'll get great views of Glasgow too.

New Lanark World Heritage Site, New Lanark Mills, **T**01555-661345, www.newlarnark.org. *Visitor centre open daily 1100-1700. Passport tickets to all attractions £5.95, £3.95, concession, children. Access to the village at all times. Hourly trains from Glasgow Central station. Hourly bus service from Lanark train station to New Lanark, but the 20-min walk is recommended for the wonderful views. The last bus back uphill from the village leaves at 1700.*
If you've got a car it's worth making the journey out here as there's enough to keep a family occupied for a whole day. This industrial village was planned and built in the 18th-century and is full of atmosphere. You can go round the old mills, see how people once lived, get sweets from the sweet shop and then go for a walk up to the waterfall.

The People's Palace, Glasgow Green, **T** 0141- 554 0223, www.glasgowmuseums.com. *Mon-Thu and Sat 1000-1700, Fri and Sun 1100-1700. Free. Bus 16, 18, 43, 64, 203, 263.* This place really does manage to please the whole family – so if you've got granny in tow as well then it's your best bet. It tells the story of life in Glasgow and has exhibits like an old 'cludgie' or outside toilet which pleases young children, and funny old bathing suits worn on holidays 'doon the watter' at resorts on the Clyde (look out for the knitted bikini). Very popular too is the original 'steamie' steam laundry, that once stood on Ingram St. It's got old clothes and a washboard and kids are encouraged to play.

Scotland Street School Museum, 225 Scotland St, **T** 0141-287 0500, www.glasgowmuseums.com. *Mon-Thu & Sat 1000-1700, Fri & Sun 1100-1700. Free. Take the Underground to Shields Rd. Bus 89, 90, 96, 97 from city centre.* A real taste of nostalgia here – you can almost smell the floor polish. This preserved school was designed by Rennie Mackintosh and only closed in 1979. It has reconstructed classrooms from the Victorian era, the 1940s and even 1960s. Kids are fascinated at the idea of those rigid rows of desks, inkwells and strict rules. There are computer activities too.

Strathclyde Country Park, Hamilton Rd, Motherwell, **T** 01698-266155. Over 1000 acres of parkland and lots of recreation opportunites such as watersports on Strathclyde Loch and woodland trails.

The Time Capsule, 100 Buchanan St, Coatbridge, **T** 01236-449572. Lots of watery fun for the kiddies with flumes, waves, and even some swimming. There's also an ice rink.

Transport Museum, 1 Bunhouse Rd, Kelvin Hall, **T** 0141-287 2720, clyde-valley.com/glasgow/index.htm *Mon-Thu and Sat 1000-1700, Fri and Sun 1100-1700. Free. Buses 9, 16, 18, 42, 62 and 63. Near Kelvinhall underground station.* Kids just aren't politically correct – there's no doubt that boys prefer this place to girls. They love the old trams, trains, cars and motor bikes – as do their Dads. There's also a reconstruction of a 1938 cobbled street, an old Underground station and a cinema showing old films of Glaswegians heading "doon the watter".

Eating

£££ Brooklyn Café, 21 Minard Rd, **T** 0141-632 3427. *Mon-Wed 0900-2200, Thu-Sat 0900-2300, Sun 1000-2200.* A venerable Southside café that deals in old fashioned jars of sweets, hearty pizzas and pastas – and lusciously sticky ice cream confections served in tall glasses. Children's menu and welcoming staff.

£££ The Canal, 300 Bearsden Rd, **T** 0141-954 5333. *Daily 1200-2200.* This out of town American style bar/restaurant has a separate children's menu and offers 'emergency distraction' with colouring books and activities such as face painting. There's also a garden so you can sit outside on fine days.

£££ Di Maggio's, 21 Royal Exchange Sq, **T** 0141-248 2111. *Mon-Sat 1200-2400, Sun 1230-2230.* Good-value favourite with Glasgow parents, with a menu that offers burgers and pizzas and staff who are friendly to those with kids. Also branches at 18 Gibson St, 61 Ruthven Lane and 1038 Pollokshaws Rd.

£££ Harry Ramsden's, 251 Paisley Rd, **T** 0141-429 3700. *Sun-Thu 0700-1000, 1200-2200, Fri, Sat 0800-1000, 1200-2300.* The Harry Ramsden fish and chip chain is geared up for kids and does a tasty line in fish, chips and mushy peas.

££ TGI Fridays, 113 Buchanan St, **T** 0141-221 6996. *Mon-Sat 1200-2330, Sun 1200-2300.* Old favourite child friendly chain in the city centre.

Directory

Banks and ATMs

Bank opening hours are Monday-Friday from 0930 to between 1600 and 1700. Some larger branches may also be open later on Thursdays and on Saturday mornings. Banks are usually the best places to change money and cheques. Outside banking hours you'll have to use a bureau de change, which can be found in the city centre and also at the airport and train stations.

Car hire

Arnold Clark, 10-24 Vinicombe St, **T** 0141-334 9501 (also at the airport, **T** 0141-848 0202), www.arnoldclark.co.uk. **Avis**, 161 North St, **T** 0141-221 2877 (also at the airport, **T** 0141-887 2261). **Budget**, 101 Waterloo St, **T** 0141-2264141 (also at the airport, **T** 0141-887 0501). **easyCar**, www.easycar.com. **EuroDollar**, **T** 01895-233300. **Europcar**, **T** 08457-222525. **First European**, **T** 0141-886 1072. **Hertz**, 106 Waterloo St, **T** 0141-248 7736 (also at the airport, **T** 0141-887 7845). **Holiday Autos**, **T** 8705-300400, www.holidayautos.co.uk. **Discount Car Hire Scotland**, **T** 0870-2430733, www.discount-car-hire-scotland.co.uk. **National Car Rental**, **T** 08705-365365. **Thrifty**, **T** 0141-445 4440.

Currency exchange

American Express, 115 Hope St, **T** 0141-221 4366. *Mon-Fri 0830-1730, Sat 0900-1200.* **Thomas Cook**, Central station, **T** 0141-204 4496. *Mon-Wed ,Sat 0800-1900, Thu, Fri 0800-2000, Sun 1000-1800.*

Dentists

Glasgow Dental Hospital, 378 Sauchiehall St, **T** 0141- 211 9600. For dental emergencies.

Disabled

The Ultimate Guide to Disability Access & Transport Within Glasgow provides access transport information and includes eating out, shopping, places of interest, entertainment, places of worship and accommodation. For more information contact **The Glasgow Access Panel**, c/o GCVS, 11 Queens Cres, Glasgow, G4 9AS, T 0141-332 2444, gcvs@cqm.co.uk.

Emergency numbers

Police, fire brigade and **ambulance, T** 999

Hospitals

Glasgow Royal Infirmary, 84 Castle St, **T** 0141-211 4000, near the cathedral. **Southern General Hospital**, Govan Rd, **T** 0141-201 1100. Th is the main South Side hospital.

Internet/email

There are too many internet cafes in Glasgow to list here. A few of the more central ones include: **easyEverything**, 57 St Vincent St, a huge facility and the cheapest service in town; **The Internet Café**, 569 Sauchiehall St, **T** 0141-564 1052, charges £2-2.50 per ½ hour on-line. **Internet Exchange**, 136 Sauchiehall St, **T** 0141-353 0535. **Café Internet**, 153-157 Sauchiehall St, **T** 0141-3532484.

Left luggage

At **Buchanan bus station**, open daily 0630-2230. Also lockers at **Central** and **Queen Street** train stations (£2 per day).

Pharmacies (late night)

Superdrug, Central Station, **T** 0141-221 8197; open Mon-Fri till 2130, Sat, Sun till 1700. **Munroes'**, 693 Great Western Rd, **T** 0141-3390012, open daily till 2100.

Police

If you are robbed or assaulted and need to report the crime, phone the police on **T** 999. **Strathclyde Police Headquarters** are at 173 Pitt St, **T** 0141-204 2626, 24 hours; lost property open 0900-1700.

Post offices

The main post office is at 47 St Vincent St, **T** 0345-222344. Services include poste restante, currency exchange and cash withdrawal at the German Savings Bank. *Mon-Fri 0830-1745, Sat 0900-1900*. Also at 85-89 Bothwell St, 216 Hope St and 533 Sauchiehall St.

Public holidays

New Year's Day and **2 January**, **Good Friday** and **Easter Monday**, **May Day** (the first Monday in May), **Victoria Day** (the last Monday in May), **Christmas Day**, **Boxing Day** (25 and 26 December) are the main bank holidays. There are also local public holidays in spring and autumn. Dates vary.

Telephone

Most public payphones are operated by **British Telecom** (BT) and take either coins or phonecards, available at newsagents and post offices displaying the BT logo. These cards come in denominations of £2, £3, £5 and £10. Some payphones also accept credit cards.

Transport enquiries

Strathclyde Travel Centre, in front of the St Enoch Centre, **T** 0141-226 4826. *Mon-Sat 0830-1730*. They can provide maps, leaflets and timetables. Their free *Visitor's Transport Guide* includes a particularly useful map of the city. There are other travel information centres at: **Buchanan bus station**, **T** 0141-332 7133. *Mon-Sat 0630-2230, Sun 0700-2230*; **Hillhead Underground station**, on Byres Rd, **T** 0141-333 3673. *Mon 0800-1730, Tue-Sat 0830-1730*; and at **Glasgow airport** (see p20). Travel information is also available from **Traveline Scotland T** 08706-082608, www.travelinescotland.com, or **First Glasgow T** 0141-423 6600.

Travel agents

STA Travel, 184 Byres Rd, **T** 0141-338 6000; 112 George St, **T** 0141-552 6505. **Flight Centre UK**, 280 Sauchiehall St, **T** 0141-353 1351.

Background

A sprint through history

1st-2nd centuries AD	The Romans build the Antonine Wall between the Firths of Clyde and Forth in order to stem the flow of nasty northern tribes southwards.
5th century	Christian missionary St Ninian and his sidekick St Kentigern, or Mungo, arrive.
6th century	Mungo establishes an episcopal church somewhere near the site of the present city, though its precise location is unknown.
1114	The establishment of a bishopric in 1114 under papal authority, leads to the construction of the cathedral.
1136	The cathedral is dedicated by King David I of Scotland.
1175-90	Glasgow is granted burgh status. This gives the city certain trading privileges, such as the right to hold a weekly market. The original cathedral is destroyed by fire but is quickly rebuilt on a much grander scale, making it the second largest Gothic church in Scotland after St Andrews.
1451	Glasgow gains significant academic kudos with the founding of the university.
1490	The granting of a royal charter secures the right to export goods, namely cured salmon and herring to European ports.
1450 - 1550	The population more than doubles and the town grows along the present route of the High Street, from the cathedral south to Glasgow Cross.
1600	Glasgow continues to thrive and its population rises to around 7,000 making it the most important trading market in the west of Scotland.

1603	The Union of Crowns leads to an increase in trade with England.
1611	Glasgow becomes a royal burgh.
1647	A Glasgow ship brings a cargo of tobacco from the French Caribbean island of Martinique, setting a trend which will eventually change the face of the city.
1630-1650s	The university, or college, is rebuilt near the cathedral in the High Street, followed by Hutcheson's Hospital in Trongate and the Merchant's House in Bridgegate.
1660	The Town Council builds a large harbour nearly 20 miles down the river and calls it Port Glasgow.
Late 17th century	Tobacco and sugar become profitable commodities for merchants, despite the constraints of English navigation laws.
1707	Union of Parliaments with England allows Glasgow's merchants access to English colonial markets and paves the way for the tobacco trade, which transforms the city into a truly international trading centre.
1771	Glasgow has risen to become the most important tobacco port of the United Kingdom and Scotland's second most important town behind Edinburgh.
1775	American colonists rebel against British rule and the ensuing War of Independence has a devastating effect on the tobacco trade.
Late 18th-early 19th century	James Watt, a Glasgow man, educated at the city's university, invents the steam engine – which drives forward the Industrial Revolution.

Late 18th - early 19th century	The Industrial Revolution leads to a cotton boo,m but by the 1830s, Glasgow loses out to the more productive Lancashire mills.
Mid 1830s	Transport is revolutionized by the coming of the railway and the demand for Scottish pig-iron grows.
1840s	Work begins on the Glasgow-Edinburgh railway.
1844	Scotland's first formal stock exchange opens .
Mid 19th century	Glasgow's population reaches nearly 400,000, usurping Edinburgh as Scotland's largest city.
1850s and 1860s	Clyde shipbuilders produce 70% of all iron-built ships launched in Britain.
Early 20th century	Glasgow can justifiably call itself the 'Second City of the Empire'. By 1912 the population has risen to over a million.
1920s and 1930s	Glasgow's economic fortunes go down as demand for shipping falls drastically after the war.
After 1945	Glasgow's population falls to less than 700,000 as people are decanted from slum tenements into 'new towns' outside the city.
1983	The city launches the 'Glasgow's Miles Better' campaign in an attempt to reverse its fortunes.
1990	The city's proudest moment comes when it is chosen as European City of Culture.
1999	Glasgow is chosen as the European City of Architecture and Design.
2003	Glasgow hosts the European Champions League final.

Art and architecture

16th century	Glasgow consists of little more than a single street running from the cathedral south to Glasgow Cross.
Pre 18th century	The city has only extended east along the Gallowgate and west along Trongate.
1770	The Tobacco Lords build streets of Palladian mansions. It is around this time that unique Glasgow squares and distinctive street plans start to appear.
Late 18th century	Glasgow's New Town is built around George Square. Many of the public buildings here, notably the Trades Hall and the Assembly Rooms, are designed by the Adam brothers, two of Scotland's greatest architects.
1817	Alexander Thomson is born in Balfron, Stirlingshire. He will go on to become the greatest architect of Victorian Glasgow.
Mid 19th century	The city begins to spread west and the grid-like street network extends across Blythswood Hill.
1857	Thomson designs Holmwood House (see p94), an example of his Classical style, which earned him the nickname 'Greek' Thomson.
1859	Thomson designs the St Vincent Street Free Church (see p59).
1868	Mackintosh is born in Glasgow. He will become one of Scotland's most celebrated architects.
1870s-1880s	The revolutionary 'Glasgow Boys' shake the foundations of the art establishment with new techniques and methods learned from Paris, Japan and London.

1875	Thomson dies.
Late 19th century	Charles Rennie Mackintosh pursues his studies at the Glasgow School of Art where his experimental style brings him into contact with kindred spirits. Their work becomes known as the 'Glasgow Style'. Glasgow can now boast some of the most exciting architecture in Europe. While Gilbert Scott's Glasgow University is inspired by Flemish cloth halls.
1890s	The city embraces Beaux Arts rationalism when John Burnet returns from New York to design tall, narrow-fronted buildings with steel frames.
1896	Mackintosh designs the Glasgow School of Art (see p62), which is completed in 1907.
1914-1928	Mackintosh is forced to leave Glasgow, where his designs are criticised for being too modern. He becomes depressed and alcoholic, and tragically dies.
1945-1970s	Many historic buildings are demolished in an effort to find solutions to urban overpopulation and decay.
1980s	The 'new Glasgow Boys' – Peter Howson, Adrian Wiszniewski, Ken Currie and Steven Campbell – appear on the scene.
1999	Glasgow is chosen as the UK's City of Architecture and Design. The Lighthouse (see p54) becomes Scotland's Centre for Architecture, Design and the City. The city pays tribute to Alexander Greek Thomson, with a major exhibition about his work.

Books

Fiction

Blake, G, *Shipbuilders*. (1935), Faber and Faber. The definitive portrayal of Glasgow during the Depression.

Brookmyre, C, *Quite Ugly One Morning*. (1996), Little, Brown. First novel of one of Glasgow's most successful literary sons has received brickbats and blandishments in equal measure.

Friel, G, *Grace and Mrs Partridge*. (1969), Calder and Boyars. One of the best novels to come out of the 1960s by one of the city's greatest writers. A humorous portrayal of tenement life, and a lot more besides.

Galloway, J, *The Trick is to Keep Breathing*. (1990), Vintage. Debut novel which was on the shortlist for Whitbread First Novel.

Gray, A, *Lanark*. (1981), Canongate. Totally original debut novel which changed everything. It single-handedly raised the profile of Glasgow fiction.

Hanley, C, *A Taste of Too Much*. (1960), Hutchinson. An unprecedented perspective of life through the eyes of an adolescent boy on a council housing estate.

Jenkins, R, *A Very Scotch Affair*. (1968), Gollancz. Hailed as the Scottish Hardy, Jenkins put the city firmly on the literary map. This is still regarded as a highpoint in pre-1970s Glasgow fiction.

Kelman, J, *How Late It Was, How Late*. (1994), Secker and Warburg. Brilliant, Booker Prize-winning fourth novel of a literary giant who revolutionized Scottish fiction by writing not just dialogue but his entire novels in his own accent.

Kennedy, AL, *Night Geometry and the Garscadden Trains*. (1991), Edinburgh: Polygon. Another brilliant collection of mostly Glasgow short stories.

Mcilvanney, WM, *Laidlaw*. (1977), Hodder and Stoughton. McIlvanney explores Glasgow's seedy, criminal underbelly through the eyes of the eponymous police Detective-Inspector, who became as much a part of the city as Ian Rankin's Rebus has become a part of Edinburgh.

McArthur, A, *No Mean City*. (1935), Longmans, Green. Highlighted the violence and alienation of life in the Gorbals, the city's most notorious slum. This novel has, more than any other before or since, (dis)coloured most people's perceptions of the city.

McCrone, G, *Wax Fruit*. (1947), Constable. The matriarchal Bel Moorhouse is something of a prototype of the strong Glasgow women who would come to characterize many Glasgow novels.

Mills, G, *The Beggar's Benison*. (1866), Cassell, Petter and Galpin. One of the few novels which focussed on the problem of the city's notorious slums which mushroomed during the rapid industrial expansion of the late 19th century.

Spence, A, *Its Colours They are Fine*. (1977), Collins. Follows the path of a Glasgow hard man from adolescent delinquency to macho 'maturity'.

Torrington, J, *Swing Hammer Swing*. (1992), Secker and Warburg. The Linwood car-plant shop steward won the Whitbread Prize for his debut novel, which is set in the Gorbals of the late 1960s.

Glasgow on screen

"Glasgow's citizens are larger than life. They live life as though it was a movie..." So said one commentator on the city and he certainly had a point. Glasgow's gritty history, and the strong character and sense of humour of its people, has provided plenty of potential for film-makers in recent years – and the city has recently witnessed something of a renaissance in film-making. Although it must be said that films tend to focus on the darker side of Glasgow life – even comedies, such as Bill Forsyth's 1984 film, *Comfort and Joy*, which dealt with the city's famously violent ice-cream wars. Films set in Glasgow are inclined to have a hard edge, as if film makers cannot, or do not want to, forget the city's old 'razors and rivets' image.

It was the shooting of *Shallow Grave* in 1993 that really put Glasgow on the movie map. This film, in which a group of flatmates try to dispose of a dead body, was not only filmed on location in Glasgow but also launched the career of Ewan McGregor. It was a commercial and critical success and encouraged investment in more films set in the city. Since then there have been several films made in Glasgow including *Small Faces* (1996), *The Slab Boys* (1996) which was filmed entirely in a disused warehouse in the heart of the city, *Ratcatcher* (1999), *My Name is Joe* (1998) and *Sweet Sixteen* (2002), both directed by Ken Loach, and David Mackenzie's *Young Adam* (2003), based on the novel by Alexander Trocchi and starring Ewan Mcgregor, Tilda Swinton and Peter Mullan, who also starred in *My Name is Joe*. Other Glasgow films have included *The Acid House* (1998), the film adaptation of Irvine Welsh's novel, and *Carla's Song* (1996). One of the latest films to be set in the city is Peter Capaldi's *Strictly Sinatra* (2001), which stars Ian Hart, Kelly Macdonald and Brian Cox.

On the small screen Glasgow is probably most famous for the long-running TV detective series *Taggart*, in which the police deal with a seemingly inexhaustible number of grisly murders and brutal crimes. It has done nothing to dent the city's tough image.

The city's distinctive mix of flamboyant Victorian buildings, rundown high-rise flats, derelict industrial sites and acres of green parks and gardens, means that Glasgow is not only a suitable subject for a film, it also has plenty of suitable locations for film-makers. *Regeneration*, the First World War film based on the novel by Pat Barker, was filmed in Glasgow, and the Glasgow to Dumfries railway line featured – unlikely as it may seem – in the Hollywood blockbuster *Mission Impossible*. The city also doubled as Moscow in the 1983 film *Gorky Park*, while film crews on *The House of Mirth* (2000) used several places in Glasgow: Kelvingrove art gallery and museum was used as a train station, and the City Chambers became an apartment foyer. The City Chambers also featured in *Heavenly Pursuits* (1985); doubling as, of all things, the Vatican – which can't have pleased the 'blue-nosed' elements of the population, who still detest all things Catholic.

Glasgow and the Clyde towns have also produced an extraordinary number of famous actors. As well as Ewan Macgregor, there are people like Tom Conti, Kelly Macdonald, Alan Cumming, Daniella Nardini, and Billy Connolly – the comedian whose first big screen role was as Queen Victoria's devoted servant in Mrs Brown. Then of course there's Robert Carlyle, who has a string of big-screen successes like *Trainspotting* and *The Full Monty*, and Robbie Coltrane – who played Hagrid in *Harry Potter and the Philosopher's Stone*. With major stars like these, and any number of talented directors, designers and technicians based in the city, it looks likely that Glasgow will feature in plenty more films in the years to come.

Index

A

accommodation 119
  see also sleeping
airlines 20
airports 19
Alexander Thomson Society 60
Anderston Quay 83
antique shops 197
architecture 237
Ardencraig Gardens 109
Ardgarten 105
Ardlui 116
Argyle Arcade 52
Argyle Street 52
Argyll Forest Park 104
'Armadillo' 80
Arrochar Alps 104
art 237
art shops 197
arts 179
Athenaeum 59
ATMs 230
Auchineden Hill 118

B

Baird Hall 62
Balloch 115
bank holidays 232
banks 230
Barras, the 45
Barrowlands 46
bars 163
Buchanan Street to Charing Cross 168
gay and lesbian 218
George Square and the Merchant City 165
South of the Clyde 178
Trongate to the East End 167
West End 175
Bell, Henry 102
Bellahouston Park 90
Ben Arthur 105
Ben Lomond 117
bicycle hire 207
Blythswood Square 60
boat tours 28
Bonnie Prince Charlie 46
Bonnington Linn 113
bookshops 197
books 239
Botanic Gardens 73, 76
Bothwell Castle 85, 111
Braehead 81
Bridgegate 44
Briggait 44
Britannia Music Hall 42
Broomielaw Quay 83
Buchanan Galleries 60
Buchanan Street 52, 55
Burrell Collection, the 91, 97
bus 21, 25
bus tours 29
Bute 103, 106, 108
Byres Road 72

C

Ca d'Oro 53
Cadzow Castle 112
cafés 137
  Buchanan Street to Charing Cross 151
  George Sauare and the Merchant City 144
  South of the Clyde 161
  Trongate to the East End 147
  West End 158
Cambuslang Bridge 85
Campsies, the 114, 117
Candleriggs 41
car 22, 26
car hire 230
Cathedral 49
Cathedral of the Isles 103
Celtic Connections 193
Centre for Contemporary Arts (CCA) 62, 97
Charing Cross 52
Chatelherault 111
children 223
cinema 181
City Chambers 36
City Hall 41
Royal Scottish National Orchestra Proms 193
clothes shops 198
clubs 163
  Along the Clyde 178
  Buchanan Street to Charing Cross 171
  folk 184
  gay and lesbian 220
  George Square and the
Merchant City 166
  jazz 184
  pop 184
  rock 184
  West End 177
Clyde Auditorium 80
Clyde Valley, the 109
Clyde Walkway 82
Clydebuilt 81 97
coach 21
comedy 182
  International comedy
festival 193
Conic Hill 117
Connolly, Billy 48
Corinthian 39
Corra Castle 113
Corra Linn 113
Cowal 105
Cowal Peninsula 103, 104
Craigend Castle 77
Craignethan Castle 114

Cranston, Kate 61
Crianlarich 116
Crossford 114
Cunninghame Mansion 37
currency exchange 230
Customs House Quay 83
cycling 207

D

Dalí, Salvador 51
David Livingstone Centre 110
dentists 230
department stores 200
directory 229
disabled 230
Doge's Palace 47
drinking 137
Drumkinnon Tower 115
Drymen 117
Dumbarton 101
Dumbarton Castle 101
Dumbarton Road 74
Dumgoyne Hill 118
Dunoon 103

E

Earl's Seat 118
East End 42
eating 137
  Around Glasgow 161
  Buchanan Street to Charing Cross 147
  George Square and the Merchant City 140
  South of the Clyde 160
  Trongate to the East End 145
  West End 152
Egyptian Halls 53
email 231
emergency contacts 231
entertainment 179
events 191

F

Falls of Clyde Nature Reserve 113
ferry 22 26
festivals 191
Finnieston Crane 83
Fintry 117
Fletcher's Haugh 84
food shops 201
football 209, 210
Forth and Clyde Canal 75, 78
Fossil Grove 74

G

galleries 32
Gallery of Modern Art 37, 97
Gardner's Warehouse 53
gay and lesbian 215
George Square 36
ghost tours 31
Glaidstone, the 104
Glasgay 194, 221
Glasgow Art Fair 193
Glasgow Boys 37, 237
Glasgow Celtic Football Club 210
Glasgow Cross 42
Glasgow Fair 46, 47
Glasgow Green 46
Glasgow Harbour 80
Glasgow Rangers Football Club 209, 210
Glasgow School of Art 62
Glasgow Style 39, 54
Glasgow Tower 79
Glasgow University 69
Glencallum Bay 108
Glengoyne Distillery 118
golf 209
Gorbals 88
Gourock 103
Govan Old Parish Church 89
Great Cumbrae Island 103
guesthouses 119

H

Hamilton 111
Hamilton Mausoleum 112
Hamilton, David 39
Hatrack, the 59
health and fitness 212
Heatherbank Museum of Social Work 97
Helensburgh 102
Hill House 102
history 234
Hogmanay 194
Holmwood House 94
Holy Loch 104
homeware shops 201
hospitals 231
hostels 119
hotels 119
House for an Art Lover 90
Hunterian Art Gallery 71, 97
Hunterian Museum 69, 97
Hutcheson's Hall 39

I

IMAX 80
Inchmarnock 109
International Comedy Festival 193
internet 231
Inverbeg 116
Italian Centre 39
Italians 38
itineraries 10

J

Jamaica Street 53
Jazz Festival 193
jewellery shops 202
John, Logie Baird 102

K

Kelvin Walkway 75
Kelvingrove Museum and Art Gallery 61, 68
Kibble Palace 73
kids 223
Kilchattan Bay 108
Knightswood 74

L

Lanark 112
Lanarkshire House 39
left luggage 231
lesbian 215
Lighthouse, the 54, 97
Linn Park 95
Loch Fad 109
Loch Fyne 104
Loch Lomond 104, 114, 115
Loch Lomond Shores 115
Loch Long 104
Luss 116

M

Mackintosh House 72
Mackintosh, Charles Rennie 51, 63, 74, 88, 90, 102, 237
maps 32
Marine Life Museum 97, 103
markets 202
Mary, Queen of Scots 93
McLean, Jack 58
McLellan Galleries 61, 97
Merchant Square 42
Merchants' House 37
Merchants' Steeple 44
Millport 103
Milngavie 75
Mitchell Library 67
money 24
monuments 32
Mount Stuart 107
mountain biking 207
Mugdock Castle 77
Mugdock Country Park 77
Museum of Scottish Country Life 97, 110
museums 32
music 182
classical 183
country 184
folk 184
jazz 184
opera 183
pop 184
rock 184
shops 202

N

National Park Gateway Centre 115
Nelson Mandela Place 59
New Lanark World Heritage Site 41, 112, 226

O

outdoor gear shops 203

P

Paddy's Market 44
Park Conservation Area 67
People's Palace 48, 97
pharmacies 231
Piping Centre, the 65
police 231
Pollok Country Park 91, 92
Pollok House 92, 97
post offices 232
Princes Square 55
Provand's Lorship 51
PS Waverley Terminal 83
public holidays 232
pubs
see also bars

Q

Queen Elizabeth Forest Park 118
Queen's Cross Church 74
Queen's Park 93
Queen's View 118

R

restaurants 137
River Clyde 78
River Kelvin 73, 75
River Nethan 114
Rothesay 103, 107
Rothesay Castle 107
Rotten Calder 85
Rotunda 83
Rowardennan 116
Royal Exchange Square 37
Royal Highland Fusiliers Military Museum 98
Royal Highland Fusiliers Mueum 62
Ruchill Church 75

S

safety 24
Saltmarket 44
Sauchiehall Street 60
saunas 222
Scalpsie Bay 108
Science Centre 98
Scotland Street School Museum 88, 98, 225
Scottish Football Museum 93, 98
Scottish Maritime Museum 98, 102
Scottish Wildlife Trust 113
SECC 80
Sharmanka Kinetic Gallery and Theatre 43, 98
shoe shops 198
shopping 195
malls 203
skiing 213

sleeping 119
Around Glasgow 135
Buchanan Street to Charing Cross 124
George Square and the Merchant City 122
South of the Clyde 135
Trongate to the East End 124
West End 129
Snuff Mill Bridge 95
sports 205
American football 207
cycling 207
football 209
golf 209
health and fitness 212
kiting 213
mountain biking 207
skiing 213
walking 213
watersports 214
SPT Travel Centre 52
SS Glenlee 80
St Andrew's Church 45
St Andrew's Hall 67
St Andrew's Square 44
St Andrew's-by-the-Green 45
St Blane's Chapel 108
St David's (Ramshorn) Church 41
St Enoch Centre 52
St Enoch Square 52
St George's Tron Church 59
St Mungo Museum of Religious Life and Art 50, 98
St Vincent Street 59
St Vincent Street Church 59
Stock Exchange 59
Strathclyde Country Park 227
SWT Wildlife Centre 113

T

Tall Ship 80
Tarbet 116
taxi 27
taxi tours 30
telephone 24, 232
Templeton's Carpet Factory 47
Tenement House, the 64
The People's Palace 226
theatre 188
Thomson, Alexander 'Greek' 59, 94, 237
Tighnabruaich 105
time 24
tipping 24
Tobacco Merchants' House 41
Tolbooth Steeple 43
tourist information 31
tours 28
Trades Hall 40
train 22, 27
transport
air 19
bus 21, 25
car 22, 26
coach 21
ferry 22, 26
taxi 27
train 22, 27
Underground 27
transport enquiries 232
Transport Museum 68, 98, 225
travel agents 232
Tron Steeple 43
Trongate 42

U

Uddingston 85
Underground 27
Union Street 53

V

Victoria Bridge 83
Victoria Park 74
Virginia Galleries 40

W

walking 213
walking tours 30
watersports 214
Watt, James 235
Wemyss Bay 103
West End 66
West End Festival 193
West Highland Way 78, 117
Western Baths Club 72
Whangie, the 118
White Cart 95
Willow tea rooms 55, 61
Windy Hill 109
Winter Gardens 49, 107

Z

Zoology Museum 71

Credits

Footprint credits
Text editor: Davina Rungasamy
Map editor: Sarah Sorensen

Publisher: Patrick Dawson
Series created by Rachel Fielding
Cartography: Claire Benison, Kevin Feeney, Robert Lunn
Design: Mytton Williams
Maps: Footprint Handbooks Ltd

Photography credits
Front cover: Epic (detail from House for an art lover)
Inside: Brian Sweeney (p1 lamp-post outside School of Art, p5 Science Centre, p33, The Lighthouse)
Caledonian MacBrayne (ferry image, p99)
Generic images: John Matchett
Back cover: Brian Sweeney (bar front)

Print
Manufactured in Italy by LegoPrint.
Pulp from sustainable forests.

Footprint Feedback
We try as hard as we can to make each Footprint guide as up to date as possible but, of course, things always change. If you want to let us know about your experiences – good, bad or ugly – then don't delay, go to www.footprintbooks.com and send in your comments.

Publishing information
Footprint Glasgow
2nd edition

ISBN 1 904777 01 5
CIP DATA: a catalogue record for this book is available from the British Library

Published by Footprint Handbooks
6 Riverside Court
Lower Bristol Road
Bath, BA2 3DZ, UK
T +44 (0)1225 469141
F +44 (0)1225 469461
discover@footprintbooks.com
www.footprintbooks.com

Distributed in the USA by
Publishers Group West

Complete title list

Latin America & Caribbean

Argentina
Barbados (P)
Bolivia
Brazil
Caribbean Islands
Central America & Mexico
Chile
Colombia
Costa Rica
Cuba
Cusco & the Inca Trail
Dominican Republic
Ecuador & Galápagos
Guatemala
Havana (P)
Mexico
Nicaragua
Peru
Rio de Janeiro
South American Handbook
Venezuela

North America

New York (P)
Vancouver (P)
Western Canada

Middle East

Israel
Jordan
Syria & Lebanon

Africa

Cape Town (P)
East Africa
Egypt
Libya
Marrakech (P)
Marrakech & the High Atlas
Morocco
Namibia
South Africa
Tunisia
Uganda

Asia

Bali
Bangkok & the Beaches
Cambodia
Goa
Hong Kong (P)
India
Indian Himalaya
Indonesia
Laos
Malaysia
Myanmar (Burma)
Nepal
Pakistan
Rajasthan & Gujarat
Singapore
South India
Sri Lanka
Sumatra
Thailand
Tibet
Vietnam

Australasia

Australia
New Zealand
Sydney (P)
West Coast Australia

Europe

Andalucía
Barcelona
Barcelona (P)
Berlin (P)
Bilbao (P)
Bologna (P)
Cardiff (P)
Copenhagen (P)
Croatia
Dublin (P)
Edinburgh (P)
England
Glasgow (P)
Ireland
London
London (P)
Madrid (P)
Naples (P)
Northern Spain
Paris (P)
Reykjavik (P)
Scotland
Scotland Highlands & Islands
Seville (P)
Spain
Tallinn (P)
Turin (P)
Turkey
Valencia (P)
Verona (P)

(P) denotes pocket Handbook

For a different view…
choose a Footprint

Over 100 Footprint travel guides

Covering more than 150 of the world's most exciting countries and cities in Latin America, the Caribbean, Africa, Indian sub-continent, Australasia, North America, Southeast Asia, the Middle East and Europe.

Discover so much more…

The finest writers. In-depth knowledge. Entertaining and accessible. Critical restaurant and hotels reviews. Lively descriptions of all the attractions. Get away from the crowds.

Map 1 Glasgow
MILNGAVIE
BEARSDEN
DRUMCHAPEL
KNIGHTSWOOD
ANNIESLAND
KELVINSIDE
MARYHILL
BRAEHEAD
PARTICK
GOVAN
PORT DUNDAS
GORBALS
Craighdu Rd
Glasgow Rd
Milngavie Rd
Auchenhowie Rd
Allander Water
Bardowie Loch
River Kelvin
Drymen Rd
Roman Rd
Boclair Rd
Balmore Rd
Wilderness Plantation
Great Western Rd
Switchback Rd
Maryhill Park
Possil Loch
Dawsholm Park
Dumbarton Rd
Ferry Rd
Kelvindale Rd
Maryhill Rd
Bilisland Dr
Hawthorn St
Ruchill Park
Botanic Gardens
Hunterian Art Gallery
Byres Rd
Victoria Park
Clydebuilt
High St
Glasgow Rd
Renfrew Rd
Craighall Rd
University
Clyde Tunnel
Govan Old Parish Church
Southern General
Clydeside Expressway
Argyle St
George Square
Shieldhall Rd
Ibrox
Glasgow Science Centre
Finnieston Crane
Waverley
Edmiston Dr
Glasgow Green
House for an Art Lover
Paisley Rd W
Scotland Street School Museum
Citizens' Theatre
People's Palace
Gorbals St
Eglinton St
Bellahouston Park
Dumbreck Rd
Tramway Theatre
Cathcart Rd
Cookston Rd
Titwood Rd
Pollokshaws Rd
Pollok Country Park
Pollok House
Burrell Collection
Haggs Rd
Queen's Park
Aikenhead Rd
White Cart Water
Hurlet Rd
Barrhead Rd
Levern Water
Kilmarnock Rd
Thornliebank Rd
Hampden Park & Scottish Football Museum
King's Park
Parkhouse Rd
Nitshill Rd
Holmwood House
A807
A879
A81
A809
A814
A82
A741
A877
A739
A808
A804
A736
A8
M8
A77
A728
M77

Map symbols
Airport
Train station
Bus station
Underground station
Hospital
Post office
Market
Cathedral, church
Museum
Police
Tourist information
Parking
Related map
Detail map
KIRKINTILLOCH
UDDINGSTON
Forth & Clyde Canal
Balmore Rd
Glasgow Rd
A803
A8006
Lenzie Rd
Waterside Rd
Kirkintilloch Rd
Crosshill Rd
Gadloch
Auchinairn Rd
Springburn Rd
Standburn Rd
Robroyston Rd
M80
Cumbernauld Rd
Hogganfield Loch
Gartlock Rd
Stepps Rd
A80
M8
Alexandra Pde
Cathedral
Edinburgh Rd
A8
M73
Gallowgate
Shettleston Rd
A89
Ballieston Rd
Glasgow Rd
Celtic Park
Tollcross Park
London Rd
A74
Dalmarnock Rd
Belvedere
Tollcross Burn
Hamilton Rd
A749
M74
Cambuslang Rd
River Clyde
A763
Cambuslang Bridge
Bridge St
A724
Newton Av
Newton Burn
Westburn Rd
Blantyre Rd
Rotten Calder
Stonelaw Rd
Mill St
A730
East Kilbr
Hamilton Rd
Coatbridge Rd
Bothwell
0 km 1
0 miles 1
ERGLEN
Av

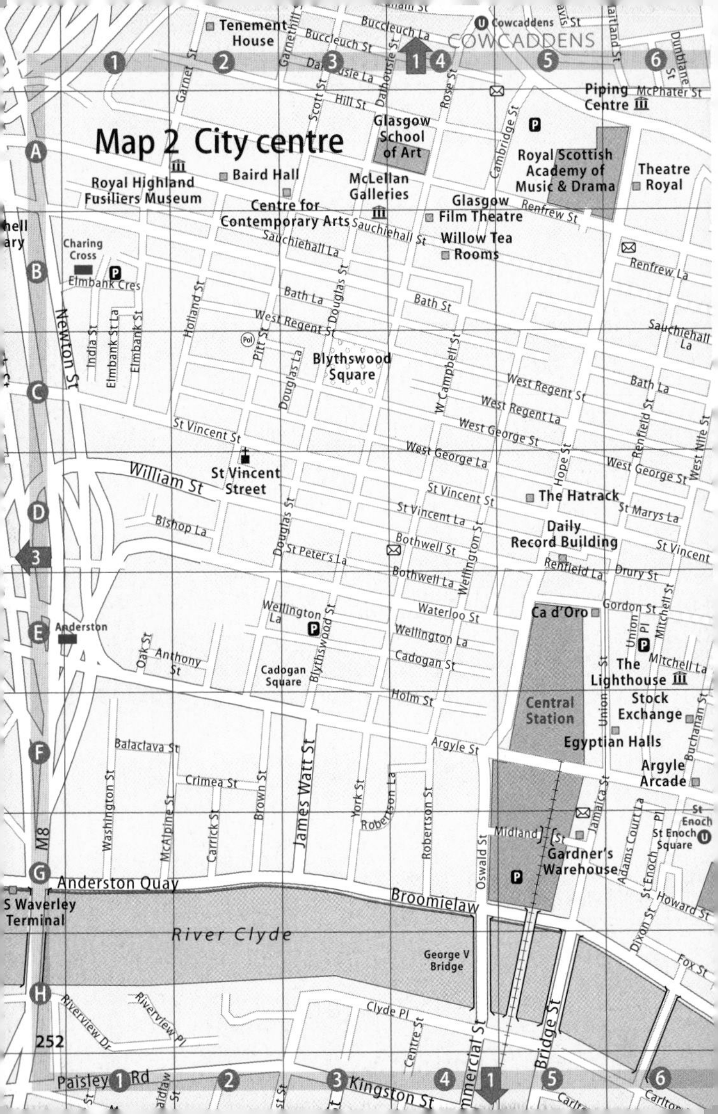

Map 2 City centre
Tenement House
Cowcaddens
COWCADDENS
Buccleuch St
Buccleuch La
Dalhousie La
Hill St
Garnethill St
Garnet St
Scott St
Dalhousie St
Rose St
Dunblane St
Piping Centre
McPhater St
Glasgow School of Art
Cambridge St
Royal Scottish Academy of Music & Drama
Theatre Royal
Royal Highland Fusiliers Museum
Baird Hall
McLellan Galleries
Centre for Contemporary Arts
Glasgow Film Theatre
Renfrew St
Sauchiehall St
Sauchiehall La
Willow Tea Rooms
Renfrew La
Charing Cross
Elmbank Cres
Bath La
Bath St
Douglas St
Holland St
West Regent St
Newton St
India St
Elmbank St La
Elmbank St
Pitt St
Blythswood Square
Douglas La
W Campbell St
West Regent La
West George St
St Vincent St
West George La
Hope St
Renfield St
West Nile St
William St
St Vincent Street
The Hatrack
St Marys La
St Vincent La
Bishop La
Daily Record Building
Bothwell St
St Peter's La
Bothwell La
Wellington St
Renfield La
Drury St
Waterloo St
Wellington La
Ca d'Oro
Gordon St
Blythswood St
Union Pl
Mitchell St
Anderston
Oak St
Anthony St
Cadogan Square
Cadogan St
Mitchell La
The Lighthouse
Holm St
Central Station
Union St
Stock Exchange
Buchanan St
Balaclava St
Argyle St
Egyptian Halls
Argyle Arcade
Crimea St
Washington St
McAlpine St
Carrick St
Brown St
James Watt St
York St
Robertson La
Robertson St
Jamaica St
Adams Court La
St Enoch Pl
St Enoch
St Enoch Square
Oswald St
Midland St
Gardner's Warehouse
M8
Anderston Quay
Broomielaw
Howard St
S Waverley Terminal
River Clyde
George V Bridge
Dixon St
Fox St
Riverview Dr
Riverview Pl
Clyde Pl
Centre St
Bridge St
Paisley Rd
Kingston St
Carlton

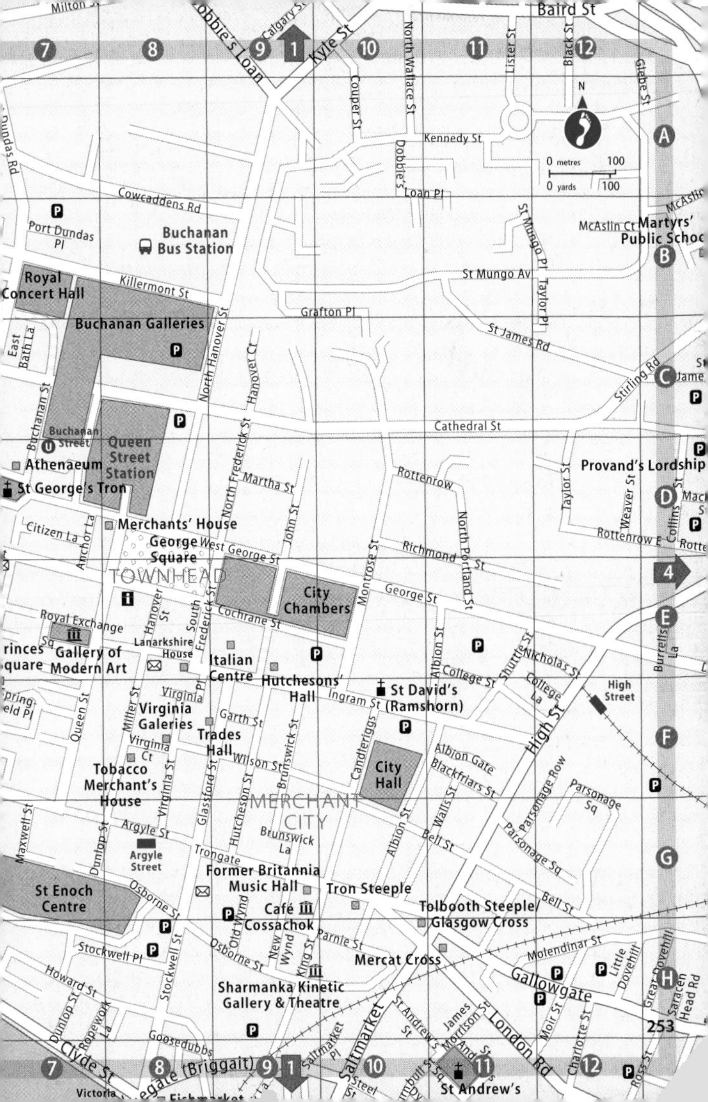
Milton St
Dobbie's Loan
Calgary St
Kyle St
Baird St
North Wallace St
Couper St
Lister St
Black St
Glebe St
N
0 metres 100
0 yards 100
Kennedy St
Dobbie's Loan Pl
Dundas Rd
Cowcaddens Rd
Port Dundas Pl
Buchanan Bus Station
McAslin Ct
McAslin
Martyrs' Public Schoo
St Mungo Pl
St Mungo Av
Taylor Pl
Royal Concert Hall
Killermont St
Buchanan Galleries
Grafton Pl
St James Rd
East Bath La
North Hanover St
Hanover Ct
Stirling Rd
St James
Buchanan St
Buchanan Street
Queen Street Station
North Frederick St
Cathedral St
Athenaeum
St George's Tron
Martha St
Rottenrow
Taylor St
Provand's Lordship
Weaver St
Collins St
Mac
Citizen La
Anchor La
Merchants' House
George Square
West George St
John St
Montrose St
Richmond St
North Portland St
Rottenrow E
Rotte
TOWNHEAD
City Chambers
George St
Cochrane St
Royal Exchange Sq
Hanover St
South Frederick St
Lanarkshire House
Albion St
Shuttle St
Nicholas St
Burrell's La
rinces quare
Gallery of Modern Art
Italian Centre
Hutchesons' Hall
St David's (Ramshorn)
College St
College La
High Street
pring eld Pl
Queen St
Miller St
Virginia Pl
Virginia Galeries
Ingram St
Garth St
Virginia Ct
Trades Hall
Wilson St
Brunswick St
Candleriggs
City Hall
Albion Gate
Blackfriars St
High St
Parsonage Row
Parsonage Sq
Tobacco Merchant's House
Virginia St
Glassford St
Hutcheson St
MERCHANT CITY
Walls St
Maxwell St
Dunlop St
Argyle St
Argyle Street
Brunswick La
Albion St
Bell St
Parsonage Sq
Trongate
Former Britannia Music Hall
Tron Steeple
St Enoch Centre
Osborne St
Tolbooth Steeple/ Glasgow Cross
Bell St
Café Cossachok
Old Wynd
Parnie St
Stockwell Pl
Stockwell St
Osborne St
New Wynd
King St
Mercat Cross
Molendinar St
Gallowgate
Little Dovehill
Great Dovehill
Saracen Head Rd
Howard St
Sharmanka Kinetic Gallery & Theatre
Dunlop St
Ropework La
Goosedubbs
Saltmarket
Saltmarket Pl
St Andrew's St
James Morrison St
London Rd
Moir St
Charlotte St
Clyde St
Briggait
Steel St
St Andrew's Sq
St Andrew's
Victoria
Fishmarket
Ross St
A
B
C
D
E
F
G
H
4
7
8
9
1
10
11
12

Map 3 West End

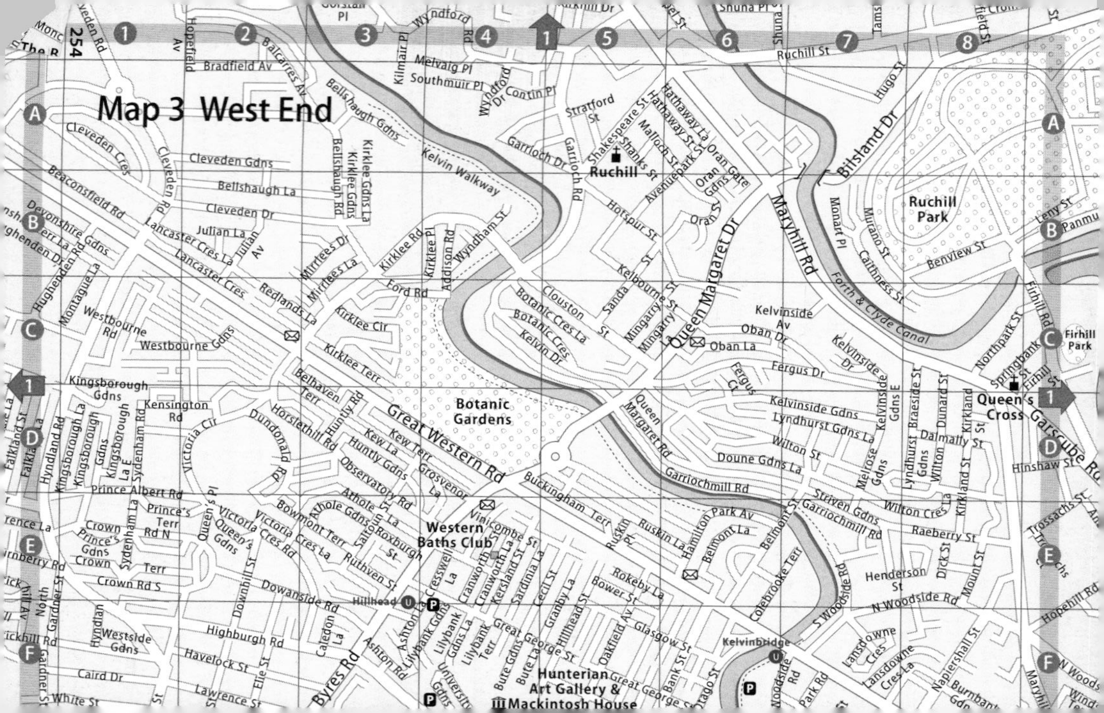